GPST STAGE 2
PROFESSIONAL DILEMMAS

100

DILEMMAS

FOR GPST/GPVTS ENTRY

Olivier Picard

Gail Alls

D1438457

4th edition

Published by ISC Medical
97 Judd Street, London WC1H 9JG
www.iscmedical.co.uk - Tel: 0845 226 9487

4th edition: ISBN13: 978-1-905812-22-6
A catalogue record for this book is available from the British Library.

1st Edition: December 2006
2nd Edition: October 2007
3rd Edition: June 2008
This Edition: November 2011

Printed in the United Kingdom by:
Purbrooks Ltd, Gresham Way, Wimbledon Park, London SW19 8ED

The authors have, as far as possible, taken care to ensure that the information given in this text is accurate and up to date. However, readers are strongly advised to confirm that the information with regards to specific patient management complies with current legislation, guidelines and local protocols.

The information within this text is intended as a study aid for the purpose of the GPST/GPVTS selection examinations. It is not intended, nor should it be used as a medical reference for the direct management of patients or their conditions.

CONTENTS

| A | Introduction | 6 |

| B | Worked Examples | 9 |

| C | Practice Scenarios | 13 |

D   Suggested Answers   115

Introduction

Purpose of the Professional Dilemma paper

The Professional Dilemma paper (also sometimes called Situational Judgement Test or SJT) forms part of Stage 2 of the GPST recruitment process. It is used to assess your ability to use your judgement in resolving problems in a work-related situation. It is designed to test generic competencies as opposed to clinical or technical skills and therefore a good dose of common sense is required instead of strong clinical knowledge (which is tested in the first Stage 2 paper: Clinical Problem Solving, through MCQs and EMQs).

The competencies tested are all those listed in the National Person Specification for the GP selection process, but with a specific emphasis on the following:

- **Empathy & Sensitivity**
  Your ability to take on board other people's perspectives and to handle other people, whether patients or colleagues, with care, attention and understanding.

- **Coping with Pressure**
  Your ability to recognise your own limitations and deal with pressure and stress by developing appropriate coping mechanisms.

- **Professional Integrity**
  Your willingness to take responsibility for your own actions and to respect others.

The full National Person Specification can be found on the national GP recruitment website at http://www.gprecruitment.org.uk.

Two styles of Professional Dilemma / SJT questions

Professional Dilemma questions usually come in two distinct formats, both of which are used in the GPST selection paper.

- *Type 1: Ranking possible actions*
  You are given a scenario which highlights a particular problem or dilemma. The question sets out five or more possible actions that you may envisage taking. Your task is to rank these options from the most suitable to the least suitable.

- *Type 2: Selecting multiple appropriate actions*
  You are given a scenario which highlights a particular problem or dilemma. The question sets out a large number of options (typically seven). Out of the list, you must pick the one, two or three actions that you deem most suitable. There is no need to rank them in any particular order.

See Section B for worked examples of each type of SJT question.

Answering the questions

All questions must be answered from the perspective of a junior trainee doctor. Typically the professional dilemma paper will contain 50 to 60 questions that you will need to answer in 110 minutes. This makes it an average of 2 minutes per question. Although this seems a lot at first glance, in reality many people run out of time, not least because the scenarios and possible options take some time to read, but also because each question requires a degree of analysis which may take you well beyond the average allocated time. In many ways, Professional Dilemma / SJT questions are testing your instinctive reactions and therefore favour those candidates who naturally match the desired criteria for entry into General Practice – after all, this is the primary aim the examiners are seeking to reach. Nevertheless, with a little practice, everyone can gain an understanding of how the questions are structured and the level of answer required.

Marking Scheme

Unlike MCQs or EMQs, where there is a clear correct answer that you must find in order to score, the marking of professional dilemma questions is done in relation to the distance between your answer and the "benchmark" answer specified by the examiners through consensus.

In simple terms, all exam questions are attempted by several GPs/examiners, their answers (which may vary from one examiner to the next) are carefully recorded and a consensus agreed between them on what constitutes the "correct" answer for each of the questions. For each question, your answer is then compared to the "consensus" answer. If it matches, then you score the maximum possible mark. If it doesn't match, then you either score "nil" or partial marks if your answer is close enough to the consensus answer or not. So, for example, the ideal answer may be ABCDE, but the panel may have concluded that an answer such as ACBDE could also work, but would attract a slightly lower score.

This marking system reflects the fact that, although there is an ideal answer, in many cases it would not be totally wrong to take a slightly different approach. It therefore offers more flexibility and helps distinguish between the candidates who got it totally wrong and those who are not far away from the desired final answer. In any case, your aim should be to match the benchmark answer exactly in order to maximise your personal score.

Such marking scheme means that, in some cases, you may feel that you have given an appropriate answer (and indeed it would also be considered appropriate by many doctors) but could end up scoring low simply because your answer does not quite match what most other doctors would do in the situation set out in the question. For that reason, it is important that you understand exactly the principles which are underlying each answer, and not just treat the exercise as a true or false question and answer session.

To assist you in this task, in this book you will find:

- 2 worked examples (one for each type of scenario)
- Over 100 practice scenarios dealing with a wide range of dilemmas
- Fully explained answers for all scenarios.

Good luck with your preparation.

Olivier Picard & Gail Allsopp

B Worked Examples

Worked Example 1

You have just finished a long 12-hour medical take and you are feeling washed out. You need to send an application form for your next post by tomorrow and you realise far too late that it will take you a good 5 hours to complete it. It is already midnight and you have a busy shift tomorrow which starts at 8 am. What do you do?

Rank in order the following actions in response to this situation
(1= Most appropriate; 5= Least appropriate):

A. Forget the application form. There is nothing that you can do about it.

B. Call your registrar first thing in the morning to see if you can get some time off to finish the form. You can then go to work in the afternoon.

C. Complete the form until 5am and then go to work at 8am.

D. Copy the answers from a form that your friend did last year and which got him through.

E. Call in sick the next morning and do the form properly.

Suggested answer: 1:B – 2:A – 3:E – 4:C – 5:D

How to approach this question
Option A seems a sensible approach but then you will lose out (admittedly by your own fault, but there may be a way around it).

Option B seems sensible too. You are involving your senior. You are taking a gamble because he might refuse but if he does then you will be no worse off than under option A anyway. At least you will have tried to find a solution by using the appropriate channels. This shows good insight and also a good approach to team work.

Option C would only give you 3 hours' sleep and would be unsafe.
Option D is plagiarism.
Option E would be lying and is therefore dishonest.

From this you can deduce the following:

- A and B are the two most sensible options with B being better than A because it may achieve the desired result in the most acceptable manner. A is just giving up when there may be an alternative which would satisfy most people.

- There is a grey area with C and E. Staying up late when you are already tired and then going in with little sleep could be potentially dangerous for patients. On the other hand, lying is also unacceptable. Faced with two bad options you must think about the consequences of both. Going to work whilst tired may be fatal for a patient. In addition, your team will be relying on you to be fully performing when you may not be. On the other hand, lying may look bad but at least you are not compromising patient safety. Also, if you call in sick, you are giving your team an opportunity to organise itself around your absence and to optimise patient care. In conclusion, neither C nor E are really acceptable but E must be better than C purely on the grounds of patient safety. You might be forgiven for lying to your team but you risk being struck off for placing a patient in danger.

We have now identified that B and A are the top two options in that order and that E and C are two of the bottom options in that order. This gives us the sequence B – A – E – C. The only outstanding issue is where D should fit.

Option D is a grave offence which would potentially be punished by being struck off the Register. No excuse that you could give would justify your behaviour. Option C as discussed earlier is potentially unsafe, with the emphasis being on the word "potentially": provided you remain alert and recognise a situation when you have become unsafe, then it may just about be acceptable (and you still retain the option to go home later if you are too tired). Therefore D must be worse than C.

Worked Example 2

During a very busy shift, the relatives of a recently deceased patient want to see you to discuss "things". What do you do?

Choose the THREE most appropriate actions to take in this situation:

A. Ask the nurse to talk to the relatives to get an understanding of the type of "things" that they want to discuss so that you can be fully prepared when you see them.

B. Tell the nurse to let the relatives know that you are aware they are waiting, that you are busy right now but that if they go home you will call them as soon as you are free.

C. Ask one of your juniors to talk to the relatives, to let them know that you cannot see them because you are busy, and to deal with any queries.

D. Tell the nurse that you will only grant the relatives 5 minutes and no more as you are busy.

E. Inform your registrar that you need to see the relatives and ask him whether he can cover for you.

F. Tell the nurse to send the relatives to PALS as your involvement with the patient is over.

G. Tell the nurse to find an excuse to send the relatives home as the patient is dead and the matter is therefore less important than the patients that you are currently dealing with.

Suggested answer and approach
Here are some issues that should cross your mind when reading this scenario:

A – You are using another team member appropriately; the nurse is already with the relatives and it makes sense that you may want to know more about the relatives' request in order to ensure that you can have the relevant information ready when you do meet with them eventually.

B – This may be a little inconvenient for the relatives as they would obviously prefer to get answers straight away. But you are being honest with them and there is a feeling that you want to get their queries resolved even if it is only on the phone.

C – This is potentially placing your junior in a difficult situation and it also looks a little like you are trying to pass the buck. But this is a possibility.

D – This places the nurse in a difficult position. It is also a fairly aggressive stance.

E – Talking to your registrar may help you identify a good way around the problem. Also, if you need to go and see the relatives, then this option will make the registrar aware of the situation and the team will be able to deal with your temporary absence.

F – PALS won't be able to deal with the relatives' queries. They will only encourage the relatives to contact you so it will defer the problem. It may sound like a good tactic in the short term but it is really unhelpful. In any case, you should consider it part of your duty to deal with the relatives, particularly if you have been dealing with the patient before his death.

G – This is rude both to the relatives and to the nurse, whom you will place in a difficult position.

There are therefore four possible candidates for the most appropriate actions: A, B, C and E. We need to eliminate one: it will be C because of the potential difficulty to which you will be exposing your junior colleague.

The answer is therefore A, B and E. (Note that these do not need to be ranked.)

C Practice Scenarios

Scenario 1

A patient has complained to you that a small amount of cash has disappeared from his bedside table.

What do you do?

Rank in order the following actions in response to this situation (1= Most appropriate; 5= Least appropriate):

A. Organise a team meeting and ask the culprit to replace the money as soon as possible.

B. Call the police. Theft is a criminal offence.

C. Ask the patient for details about the alleged theft, reassure him that you will do what you can to deal with the issue, and notify a senior nurse of the problem.

D. Send an email to all your colleagues notifying them of the incident and asking them to warn their patients to be careful about personal possessions.

E. Remind the patient that he should have been more careful about his possessions and tell him that you will see what you can do.

Scenario 2

You are working on a busy ward, having to deal with many admissions every morning.

You share the workload with another junior colleague who has been constantly late by 20 minutes for the past week.

What do you do?

Choose the THREE most appropriate actions to take in this situation:

A. You call your colleague's wife to see whether your colleague has personal problems which may explain his delay.

B. You arrange a discussion with your colleague, express your discontent and tell him to make sure that he comes on time as his delay is slowing you down.

C. You arrange a discussion with your colleague to enquire about the reasons behind the delay.

D. You work harder to compensate for his absence, in the knowledge that his delay is likely to be short term.

E. You discuss your concerns with a group of nurses from your ward to gain insight into his behaviour at work.

F. You mention the delay to your registrar and ask him whether he can deal with it.

G. In order to avoid confrontation with the colleague you do nothing for the time being, knowing senior colleagues will soon notice his behaviour.

Scenario 3

After a long day, the SHO who was meant to take over from you has called in sick 10 minutes before the end of your shift, just as you were supposed to hand over to him.

You had arranged to go out with friends that evening and they are expecting you in 2 hours' time.

What do you do?

Rank in order the following actions in response to this situation (1= Most appropriate; 5= Least appropriate):

A. Do your colleague's shift for him. He can then take on one of your shifts when he gets back.

B. Stay for two hours and hand over to the registrar on call afterwards.

C. Contact the registrar on call to hand over to him and go home to prepare for your evening.

D. Contact the registrar on call to hand over to him, offer to stay behind for a couple of hours and join your friends later.

E. Explain to your colleague that this places you in a difficult position, offer to stay for an hour and ask him to come in an hour's time to take over as you cannot stay any longer.

Scenario 4

During a ward round, your consultant prescribes penicillin on a drug chart whose allergy box has been left blank by the admitting doctor. The patient's hospital notes clearly state a penicillin allergy.

Having spotted the discrepancy, the nurse brings you the chart a short while later to cross off the penicillin and prescribe an alternative.

What would you do subsequently?

Choose the THREE most appropriate actions to take in this situation:

A. You contact a senior nurse and express concerns at the fact that the allergy was not mentioned on the drug chart.

B. You discuss the incident with your consultant and complete a critical incident form.

C. You inform the patient that you have correctly identified he is allergic and that you will get back to the consultant to discuss how the misunderstanding took place.

D. You organise a meeting with your consultant to discuss the reasons behind his decision to prescribe penicillin when the notes clearly showed that the patient was allergic.

E. You organise a team meeting to discuss the problem and to give the person responsible a chance to explain why the incident happened.

F. You bring the issue up at the next junior doctors' meeting without mentioning the name of the offending doctor.

G. You report the admitting doctor to a senior pharmacist for possible escalation of the matter and retraining.

Scenario 5

After a 13-hour day, you are waiting for the arrival of your colleague so that you can hand over to him. You are exhausted because you have just switched over from a week of nights and you are starting to feel sleepy.

Your colleague is already 15 minutes late and has not called to say that he is ill.

What do you do?

Rank in order the following actions in response to this situation (1= Most appropriate; 5= Least appropriate):

A. Inform your registrar that you are too tired to stay and that you need to leave immediately because you cannot function effectively.

B. Go and see your consultant and let him know that, because you are in breach of the 13-hour limit imposed by the European Working Time Directive, you will hand over to him before leaving.

C. Patiently wait for your colleague and cover his shift until he arrives.

D. Hand over to a nurse and leave the hospital.

E. Contact your colleague to see what the matter is and how long the delay is likely to last.

Scenario 6

One of your patients, a taxi driver, has recently been diagnosed with epilepsy. Before discharge, you made him aware of his duty to inform the DVLA. You have also made it clear to him that he should not be driving at this current time.

On a shopping trip to town, you see him at the wheel picking up a passenger.

What do you do?

Rank in order the following actions in response to this situation (1= Most appropriate; 5= Least appropriate):

A. Report the matter to his boss

B. Call the patient to express your concerns and organise a meeting with him to discuss the incident.

C. Call the patient's wife to express your concerns and enlist her help to stop the patient from driving.

D. Report the matter to the DVLA.

E. Send a letter to the patient warning him that you will report him to the DVLA next time you see him pick up a customer.

Scenario 7

You have arranged to go out for dinner with your partner tonight.

Just before leaving your shift you have been informed that a junior doctors' teaching session that was meant to take place tomorrow morning has now been brought forward and starts in 10 minutes.

What do you do?

Rank in order the following actions in response to this situation (1= Most appropriate; 5= Least appropriate):

A. Tell another junior doctor to apologise to the group for your absence.

B. Find out what the meeting is about and discuss with the person running the meeting whether your attendance is strictly necessary as you have organised a dinner with your partner.

C. Slip away unnoticed.

D. Tell a nurse to let the organiser know that you cannot make it.

E. Call your partner and inform him/her that you cannot make the dinner as you must attend an important teaching session.

Scenario 8

During a discussion with a fellow junior doctor in the mess, you notice that a bag of marijuana has fallen out of his bag.

What do you do?

Choose the THREE most appropriate <u>immediate</u> actions to take in this situation:

A. Inform the GMC as it is not appropriate for any doctor to take drugs since it can endanger patients.

B. Call the police as marijuana is an illegal substance.

C. Recommend that your colleague considers professional help.

D. Have a discussion with your colleague about the incident to understand what the situation is.

E. Seek his reassurance that he is not using the drug, and tell him that you will keep quiet about the incident if he flushes it down the toilet.

F. Discuss the incident with your registrar.

G. Report the incident to the Clinical Director.

Scenario 9

One of your consultants came in this morning obviously drunk.

You have advised him to go home but he has dismissed you and is about to start his regular clinic.

What do you do?

Choose the THREE most appropriate actions to take in this situation:

A. Call the GMC to warn them of the problem.

B. Discuss cancelling the clinic session with the outpatients administrator / clinic manager.

C. See another consultant to discuss the situation.

D. Let the consultant run the clinic and ask him to contact you if at any point he feels unable to continue running the clinic so that someone else can take over.

E. Insist that the consultant should only see patients with a chaperone.

F. Sit in the clinic with the consultant yourself to ensure that patients are safe.

G. Complete a critical incident form.

Scenario 10

One of your friends, who is asthmatic and works as an engineer, is going on holiday to Europe tomorrow. He has forgotten to order a repeat prescription for his inhaler.

He is asking you whether you can help in any way.

What do you do?

Rank in order the following actions in response to this situation (1= Most appropriate; 5= Least appropriate):

A. Tell him to go to his nearest A&E.

B. Get an inhaler from A&E yourself.

C. Get an inhaler from the ward.

D. Ask him to contact his GP.

E. Write a prescription for him.

Scenario 11

One of your colleagues arrives consistently late for his shifts.

What do you do?

**Rank in order the following actions in response to this situation
(1= Most appropriate; 5= Least appropriate):**

A. Tell their senior about the delays.

B. Discuss the problem with other junior doctors.

C. Approach your late colleague, tell him that his lateness is causing problems and that he must be on time.

D. Ask your colleague if there is a reason for being late and whether there is anything you can do to help.

E. Make a record of the lateness and watch and wait.

Scenario 12

A colleague asks you to review one of his patients as he is busy on the ward.

This means that you will have to stay late but it is already 5pm and you are about to go out with your family, who have come to collect you.

What do you do?

Rank in order the following actions in response to this situation (1= Most appropriate; 5= Least appropriate):

A. Agree to see the patient and tell your family to go home.

B. See the patient quickly and ask your family to stay in the waiting room.

C. Ask your colleague to hand over the job to the SHO on call.

D. Contact the SHO on call yourself and hand over the job

E. Tell your consultant to see the patient.

Scenario 13

You are about to give a case presentation to your department when a nurse bleeps you for an emergency on the ward.

What do you do?

Rank in order the following actions in response to this situation
(1= Most appropriate; 5= Least appropriate):

A. Go straight away without telling anybody.

B. Tell the nurse that you cannot attend the patient but that you will go after the meeting.

C. Ask a colleague to attend the ward.

D. Cancel the teaching session and attend the emergency.

E. Apologise to the team at the meeting and ask a colleague to fill in while you find out more information and see if you need to attend at once.

Scenario 14

One of your colleagues confides in you that he has a cocaine addiction problem.

He is asking you to keep the information to yourself as he needs your support and no aggravation.

What do you do?

Rank in order the following actions in response to this situation (1= Most appropriate; 5= Least appropriate):

A. Tell your colleague that you have no option but to report the matter to a senior straight away.

B. Reassure your colleague that you will support him but tell him that he needs to address the matter with his seniors, otherwise you will have no option but to tell them yourself.

C. Report the matter to a consultant without telling your colleague that you have done so.

D. Agree with your colleague and keep quiet about it.

E. Investigate whether your colleague has performance problems and report the matter to the consultant if he has any.

Scenario 15

A patient has revealed to you that they have a history of taking illegal substances.

They are begging you to delete any mention of drug-taking from the notes as it could compromise their medical insurance if the information ever came to light.

What do you do?

Choose the THREE most appropriate actions to take in this situation:

A. Reassure the patient that you are bound by a duty of confidentiality and you simply cannot divulge any information about them to a third party without their consent.

B. Tell the patient that you cannot guarantee his confidentiality but that you will inform him first if you need to breach it.

C. Tell the patient that you simply cannot delete any information from the notes.

D. Delete the information from the notes.

E. Delete the information from the notes if it has no relevance to the patient's current health problems.

F. Tell the patient that you will have to reveal the information if asked by the insurance company.

G. Contact the insurance company naming the patient, inform them of the issue and ask for advice.

Scenario 16

A young patient, whom you have been treating on your ward for the first time, offers you a £100 book voucher to thank you for your help in their recovery on your ward.

During their short admission your only contact with the patient was with the team during ward rounds. You do not expect the patient to come back for another stay on your ward.

What do you do?

Rank in order the following actions in response to this situation (1= Most appropriate; 5= Least appropriate):

A. Tell the patient that you cannot accept the gift because it would not be ethical.

B. Accept the gift and give it to your wife/husband/partner.

C. Accept the gift and put it towards ward funds.

D. Politely refuse the gift because their recovery is the best recompense for you.

E. Accept the gift but tell the patient not to let any of the team know as you do not want any trouble.

Scenario 17

You are dealing with a ward patient whose wife's best friend works on your ward as a nurse.

The patient has asked you specifically to ensure that no information about his health should be given to the nurse in question so that his wife cannot gain information about his health.

What do you do?

Rank in order the following actions in response to this situation (1= Most appropriate; 5= Least appropriate):

A. Inform the patient that there is nothing that you can do about it and that they will need to put up with the situation as it stands.

B. Have a word with the rest of the team to ensure that the patient's confidentiality is maintained.

C. Tell the nurse that she must take some time off whilst the patient is in the ward so as not to compromise his right to confidentiality.

D. Have a word with the patient to understand the reasons behind his request and see if there is a possible compromise that can be reached.

E. Transfer the patient to another part of the ward where the nurse does not work.

Scenario 18

During a clinic run by your consultant, you walk into the room and find the consultant with his arms around the patient's shoulder.

What do you do?

Rank in order the following actions in response to this situation (1= Most appropriate; 5= Least appropriate):

A. Assume that there must be a reasonable explanation for the situation and ignore the issue.

B. Ask the patient to leave the room so that you can have a word with the consultant.

C. Report the matter to the Clinical Director.

D. Have a word with the consultant after the patient has left and ask him about the circumstances.

E. Seek advice from the registrar who is running the clinic next door.

Scenario 19

During a late-running clinic, one of your colleagues is reduced to tears after receiving racist remarks from one of the patients in anger at the delay he is experiencing.

Your colleague is distressed and has told you that she does not want to see that patient.

What do you do?

Rank in order the following actions in response to this situation
(1= Most appropriate; 5= Least appropriate):

A. Tell the patient to go home and to book another appointment with another doctor once he has calmed down.

B. Agree to see the patient and explain to the patient at the start of the consultation that what he did was unacceptable.

C. Tell the patient that he will be seen but by a different doctor and that he will need to wait until one of them is free. If he does not like this, he has the opportunity to rebook another appointment.

D. See him yourself and make sure that his appointments are scheduled early on the list in future.

E. Tell your colleague to see the patient, as she should learn to handle such situations by herself.

Scenario 20

You work in a GP practice and you require an ECG urgently for a patient who is experiencing chest pains.

There is one ECG machine in the practice but it is new and you simply have not had time to learn how to use it. Only one of the nurses knows how to operate the machine and she appears to be busy with a patient at present.

What do you do?

Rank in order the following actions in response to this situation
(1= Most appropriate; 5= Least appropriate):

A. Search for the instructions in the supply cupboard.

B. Interrupt the nurse and ask if she is able to carry out the ECG straight away.

C. Using your experience of previous models, perform the ECG yourself.

D. Call an ambulance and send the patient to A&E.

E. Send the patient home and ask him to call you if the pain gets worse.

Scenario 21

You work in a GP practice and you require an ECG urgently for a patient. There is one ECG machine in the practice but it is new and you simply have not had time to learn how to use it. Only one of the nurses knows how to operate the machine.

When you asked the nurse to carry out the ECG, she replied in an angry tone that she was too busy when, in reality, she was simply doing some filing. With no other alternative, you sent the patient to A&E.

What do you do next?

Choose the THREE most appropriate actions to take in this situation:

A. Inform the nurse that she compromised the safety of the patient, ask for an explanation and explain that you will need to inform the head of the practice next time such an incident takes place.

B. Bring this up at the next management meeting to see if anyone else has experienced that problem and whether any personnel matters should be attended to.

C. Organise for training for yourself and the rest of the team on the ECG machine.

D. Organise a discussion with the nurse to understand the basis of her behaviour.

E. Report the incident to the head of the PCT.

F. Write to the patient informing him that he can make a complaint if he wants to.

G. Send an email to all your colleagues asking them to watch out for that nurse as she may cause problems.

Scenario 22

A 25-year-old pregnant Indian woman who cannot speak English presents to your GP surgery accompanied by her father.

The father tells you that his daughter would like to have a termination of pregnancy.

What do you do?

Rank in order the following actions in response to this situation
(1= Most appropriate; 5= Least appropriate):

A. Ask the father to interpret for his daughter.

B. Obtain an interpreter and discuss the situation with the patient and her father.

C. Obtain an interpreter and ask the father to leave the room so that you can talk to the patient alone.

D. Ask the father if someone else from the family could interpret for the daughter.

E. Attempt to talk to the daughter through the use of diagrams and other non-verbal means.

Scenario 23

Mrs Smith is a 70-year-old lady who has been your patient for over 30 years and whom you see regularly throughout the year.

She gives you a standard bottle of your favourite drink for your birthday.

What do you do?

Rank in order the following actions in response to this situation (1= Most appropriate; 5= Least appropriate):

A. Refuse the gift because it is against regulations.

B. Graciously accept the gift, telling the patient that it is kind of her.

C. Accept the gift but make sure that the practice manager is aware of it.

D. Accept the gift but tell the patient that it has to be the last time.

E. Refuse the gift but double-check with your defence union afterwards.

Scenario 24

In a clinic, a female patient mentions that, during her previous consultation, one of your colleagues examined her breasts. This seems odd to you as there is nothing mentioned in the notes.

What do you do?

**Rank in order the following actions in response to this situation
(1= Most appropriate; 5= Least appropriate):**

A. Ask the patient about the circumstances surrounding the examination and, after the consultation, ask your colleague for further details on the issue.

B. Tell the patient that this might constitute an assault and explain the complaint procedure to her.

C. Say nothing to the patient and report the incident to the Clinical Director.

D. Seek advice from a trusted senior colleague.

E. Contact the GMC.

Scenario 25

Another junior doctor on your team confides in you that he has contracted Hepatitis C during his previous job and needs your advice. He would appreciate that you keep the matter confidential.

What do you do?

Choose the THREE most appropriate actions to take in this situation:

A. Inform the Personnel/Medical Staffing department.

B. Refer your colleague to Occupational Health to be vaccinated.

C. Discuss the matter with a senior colleague.

D. Discuss the situation with a senior colleague if you see that your colleague performs risky procedures.

E. Ask a senior sister to alert you if he is doing any exposure-prone procedure.

F. Recommend to your colleague that he should get advice from his defence union.

G. Recommend to your colleague that he should discuss the matter with his seniors.

Scenario 26

You have noticed that one of the consultants on your team is often making remarks of a sexual nature to one of the secretaries. On the surface she does not seem to be affected by this.

What do you do?

Choose the THREE most appropriate actions to take in this situation:

A. Encourage the secretary to check the staff manual to determine what action she should take.

B. Let the secretary know that you have observed the consultant harass her and that she should raise the issue with her seniors.

C. Arrange a discussion with the consultant in question to let him know that such behaviour must stop.

D. Approach a senior colleague that you can trust to discuss the matter.

E. Contact the GMC, who will handle the situation from then on.

F. Inform the HR or personnel department.

G. Wait until the next incident to mention something to the consultant about how inappropriate his remark was.

Scenario 27

In the past few minutes, you have flushed an intravenous cannula with lidocaine instead of saline. The patient does not seem to be experiencing any adverse reaction.

What do you do?

Choose the THREE most appropriate actions to take in this situation:

A. Tell the patient that you have made a mistake, apologise and offer the means to make a complaint if he so wishes.

B. Bleep your registrar for information and further advice.

C. Wait 5 more minutes and if the patient is fine then do not take any further action.

D. Write the mistake in the notes but do not notify the patient as there was no adverse reaction.

E. Tell the patient that you have injected a bit of local anaesthetic (which is a procedure that is sometimes carried out) so as to be open but not to worry him.

F. Explain to the patient that you have made a mistake caused by wrong labelling, which is the nurse's responsibility. Give the patient the means to make a complaint against the nurse if he so wishes.

G. Complete a critical incident form.

Scenario 28

Your registrar looks permanently tired. You know that he has been working very hard over the past few months.

He seems to be burning himself out and makes simple mistakes every day, though none have actually had any adverse effect on patients so far.

What do you do?

Choose the THREE most appropriate actions to take in this situation:

A. Approach the registrar and express your concerns about his health and the simple mistakes that he has been making.

B. Inform the registrar that all mistakes, even small, are a danger to patients and that you will have no choice but to talk to the consultant if the situation does not improve.

C. Discuss with your registrar the possibility to take on some of his work.

D. Encourage the registrar to raise the issue with his consultant to find a workable solution to the situation.

E. Contact Medical Staffing to see if they can get a locum to relieve the pressure on the registrar.

F. Inform Occupational Health and encourage them to contact the registrar before it is too late.

G. Complete a critical incident form the next time a mistake occurs.

Scenario 29

You are a GP and you are seeing a newly registered patient, a 30-year-old heroin addict who is asking for methadone. The patient's notes have not arrived from his previous practice.

What do you do?

Rank in order the following actions in response to this situation
(1= Most appropriate; 5= Least appropriate):

A. Ask the patient which dose he normally takes and prescribe one dose only.

B. Send the patient to A&E.

C. Tell the patient that you cannot prescribe any controlled drugs until his notes have arrived.

D. Call his previous GP, check the normal dose previously prescribed and prescribe one dose to the patient.

E. Prescribe the patient one week's worth of an average dose of methadone and call his GP to ensure that his notes reach you within one week.

Scenario 30

One Friday morning, one of your colleagues calls the ward from his home and says that he will not be coming in as he is feeling unwell. Subsequently, you find out that in fact he spent a long weekend abroad with his family and was never ill in the first place.

What do you do?

Rank in order the following actions in response to this situation (1= Most appropriate; 5= Least appropriate):

A. Do nothing.

B. Tell your consultant as soon as you find out about the lie.

C. Ask the colleague in question about the situation and warn him that you will have no option but to mention something to the consultant if this reoccurs.

D. Discuss the matter with your fellow junior doctors.

E. Ask the colleague about the situation at the next team meeting.

Scenario 31

You walk into the doctors' mess and see one of your registrars watching child pornography on his laptop.

What do you do?

Rank in order the following actions in response to this situation (1= Most appropriate; 5= Least appropriate):

A. Nothing. He is watching the images on his private computer and therefore it is his own business.

B. Call the police. Child pornography is illegal.

C. Send an anonymous note to your colleague saying that you spotted him watching the images and that the consultant will be warned next time it happens.

D. Approach a senior colleague that you can trust and let them handle the matter.

E. Notify the HR department.

Scenario 32

You walk into the doctors' mess and see one of your registrars watching standard adult pornography on a hospital computer.

What do you do?

Choose the THREE most appropriate actions to take in this situation:

A. Notify Personnel as this is clearly an abuse of NHS property.

B. Tell your colleague that it is not really appropriate to watch these kinds of images on hospital property and that he should be careful as some people may find it offensive.

C. Discuss the situation with other junior colleagues and confront him as a group so as to have maximum impact and make him stop.

D. Have a word with your consultant if this occurs too often.

E. Have a word with your consultant if the registrar's performance is affected by his activities.

F. Contact the IT department so that they can monitor the computer's activities.

G. Notify the police.

Scenario 33

One of the nurses you used to work with on another ward tells you that one her colleagues was very drunk during the Christmas party and was heavily flirting with one of the paramedics. Her seniors were not present at the party.

What do you do?

Rank in order the following actions in response to this situation (1= Most appropriate; 5= Least appropriate):

A. Do nothing.

B. Approach the nurse and tell her that by making a fool of herself, she acted unprofessionally.

C. Have a word with one of her seniors.

D. Ask your consultant to have a word with one of her seniors.

E. Contact the Director of Nursing about the issue.

Scenario 34

You see a nurse pick antibiotics out of a drug trolley and place them in her handbag for personal use.

What do you do?

**Rank in order the following actions in response to this situation
(1= Most appropriate; 5= Least appropriate):**

A. Approach the nurse in question and explain that it is not best practice.

B. Report the matter to your consultant.

C. Report the matter to a senior nurse.

D. Report the matter to the Director of Nursing.

E. Write a critical incident form.

Scenario 35

You work with only one other junior colleague on the ward. It is 3pm and all ward jobs have been completed.

The shift normally ends at 5pm but your colleague says that he is going out for a birthday meal and would like to leave straight away so that he has time to go home, get ready and drive to the restaurant.

What do you do?

Choose the THREE most appropriate actions to take in this situation:

A. Make sure that he has agreed it with the registrar before he leaves.

B. Let him slip away without a word so that no fuss is made.

C. Take his bleep from him.

D. Insist that he stays.

E. Tell him to clear it with Medical Staffing.

F. Make him double-check that there is nothing left to be done before he leaves.

G. Ask him to redirect his bleep to the doctor on call for the evening.

Scenario 36

You leave the hospital and see a tramp on a bus stop bench just outside A&E. He is holding an empty bottle of wine and is vomiting on the pavement.

What do you do?

Rank in order the following actions in response to this situation (1= Most appropriate; 5= Least appropriate):

A. Walk past him and ignore him.

B. Go up to the tramp and see if he is okay.

C. Take him to A&E.

D. Go to A&E yourself and ask a member of the team to take charge of the tramp.

E. Call 999.

Scenario 37

During a ward round with your consultant (your registrar is away today), a patient goes into cardiac arrest. The arrest call has been put out and the team has yet to arrive.

Having completed your ALS course a month ago and led several arrests since, you are best placed to assume the role of team leader. Your consultant has not recertified his ALS for many years but is now giving orders that you know are inappropriate.

What do you do?

Rank in order the following actions in response to this situation (1= Most appropriate; 5= Least appropriate):

A. Ensure that only basic life support is being given while you are waiting for the arrest team to arrive.

B. Let the consultant take over the handling of the arrest and discuss with him later how it may be better to let colleagues more experienced with cardiac arrest lead such situations in future.

C. Let the consultant give orders but signal to the nurses to do differently when you feel his orders are not appropriate.

D. Reassure the consultant that you are the most experienced and up-to-date person on the team. Then take over the leadership of the team.

E. Ask a nurse to call another consultant with cardiac arrest experience from the adjacent ward. Let your consultant lead the arrest while waiting for the other consultant to arrive.

Scenario 38

During a bedside teaching session, your consultant asks you a range of questions, some of which you struggle to answer.

Towards the end of the session, you are left with the feeling that the consultant is rude and has embarrassed you in front of the patient.

What do you do?

Choose the THREE most appropriate actions to take in this situation:

A. Contact the Human Resources department to complain about the incident.

B. Complain about the incident to a senior nurse.

C. Take some time out to think about the incident and how you might want to react to it.

D. Argue with the consultant at the bedside so that he knows straight away that he is being harsh on you.

E. Once the session is over, apologise to the patient about the consultant's behaviour.

F. Arrange a meeting with the consultant to discuss the incident.

G. Complete a critical incident form.

H. Discuss the incident with your educational supervisor.

Scenario 39

You walk into the mess and find one of your colleagues taking a sip at a bottle of whisky, whilst you know that his shift does not end for another 3 hours.

What do you do?

Rank in order the following actions in response to this situation (1= Most appropriate; 5= Least appropriate):

A. Let your colleague know that his behaviour makes him unsafe towards patients and that, as a result, you will need to inform his educational supervisor.

B. As your colleague does not appear drunk, let the matter drop without addressing the issue with him in case he becomes embarrassed.

C. As your colleague does not appear drunk, let the matter drop but let him know that you will need to talk to senior colleagues if you catch him again.

D. Discuss the situation with your colleague to determine the reasons for his drinking and offer to help him out. Encourage your colleague to discuss the situation with his seniors.

E. At the end of your colleague's shift, organise a meeting with other junior doctors to discuss how you can best proceed.

Scenario 40

You are bleeped to attend a crash call for Mr Smith who is arresting. On reading the notes, you do not find any DNR order and proceed with CPR, unsuccessfully.

A little while later, whilst reading another patient's notes, you notice a DNR order for Mr Smith, which had evidently been misfiled. The relatives have witnessed the arrest. They are upset and are still with the patient.

What do you do?

Choose the THREE most appropriate actions to take in this situation:

A. Contact your consultant and complete a critical incident form.

B. Contact your consultant but complete a critical incident form only later on when/if such misfiling happens again.

C. Let the resuscitation team know about the recently discovered DNR form.

D. Nothing, since the patient has died.

E. Talk to the relatives in a separate room.

F. Wait until your consultant comes back to talk to the relatives.

G. Inform senior managers at Trust level.

Scenario 41

A 17-year-old female patient presents to your surgery covered with severe bruises. She explains that she lives with a criminal who sometimes beats her up when he is high on drugs.

When you offer to help her out, she refuses to allow you to tell anyone about it.

What do you do?

Rank in order the following actions in response to this situation (1= Most appropriate; 5= Least appropriate):

A. Maintain your patient's confidentiality and do nothing.

B. Tell the patient that, unless she cooperates, you will have no alternative but to contact social services or the police.

C. Seek advice from one of your senior colleagues about how you should proceed.

D. Ask the girl if she would be prepared to discuss the issue with someone from social services. If she refuses, do it anyway but without her knowledge.

E. Contact her partner to discuss the situation with him.

Scenario 42

During your on calls you work with a registrar who is often unobtainable. For the fifth time in a week, you bleeped him to review a very sick patient urgently and he has failed to turn up.

Whenever you ask him where he has been, his only excuse is that his bleep functions erratically and that he wasn't aware that you had bleeped him.

What do you do?

Choose the THREE most appropriate actions to take in this situation:

A. Contact your consultant to inform him about the problem.

B. Ignore the problem but make sure that whenever you require help on a patient-related matter you seek advice from another suitable registrar.

C. Ignore the problem but make sure that whenever you require help on a patient-related matter you seek advice from another junior doctor at your level.

D. Initiate a meeting with your registrar to get to the bottom of the problem.

E. Ask some of the nurses whether they have heard the registrar's bleep go off so as to check whether he is telling the truth.

F. Complete a critical incident form.

G. Complain to a senior nurse about the problem.

Scenario 43

A patient presents to A&E. He is very impatient and insists on the best possible care. You diagnose folliculitis and recommend salt water bathing and a no-shave period.

The patient does not want to take your advice and demands to be referred to a dermatologist for a second opinion.

What do you do?

Rank in order the following actions in response to this situation
(1= Most appropriate; 5= Least appropriate):

A. Tell the patient that he will need to go back to his GP in order to be referred to a dermatologist.

B. Reassure the patient that you are confident about the diagnosis and that he should trust you.

C. Ask another doctor from A&E to review the patient to confirm the diagnosis as a second opinion.

D. Tell the patient that you can refer him privately if he wants a referral to a dermatologist.

E. Ask the patient to come back on another day to see a different A&E doctor.

Scenario 44

Your hospital has recently been in the news because of an adverse event and a phone call from a journalist is being transferred to you in the very busy A&E department where you work.

What do you do?

**Rank in order the following actions in response to this situation
(1= Most appropriate; 5= Least appropriate):**

A. Tell the journalist that you are confident that the hospital is doing a very good job and that you know that everything is being done to remedy difficult situations quickly and efficiently.

B. Tell the journalist that you cannot speak with him and put the phone down.

C. Tell the journalist that, if he gives you his contact details, you will pass them on to the relevant person.

D. Tell the journalist to contact the Trust's Press Officer.

E. Tell the journalist that you will call them back at the end of your shift when you have more time to speak.

Scenario 45

You are doing an audit for your practice. It is Friday lunchtime and you must present your preliminary results on Monday morning to your supervisor. To finish the current phase of the audit you still need to enter data from the notes of 20 patients into a database that resides on your own laptop.

In view of your workload, you may not be able to collect all the remaining data before the end of the day. The practice will be closed during the weekend and you do not have the keys.

What do you do?

Rank in order the following actions in response to this situation
(1= Most appropriate; 5= Least appropriate):

A. Take the patients' notes home with you to continue the data input at home over the weekend.

B. Make photocopies of the relevant pages of the patient notes, removing any patient-identifiable information, and take these photocopies back home with you to work on over the weekend.

C. Draw a quick plan of the data required on a piece of paper and quickly collect the data needed before the practice shuts for the day.

D. Look at the average profile of the patients that you have already entered into your database and create new patient data matching the average profile in order to reach the number of patients discussed with your supervisor.

E. Ask your supervisor to defer the meeting to another day, once you have had time to complete your input.

Scenario 46

One of the nurses on your ward is complaining about the bad body odour of one of your colleagues and is asking you if you could have a word with him.

What do you do?

Choose the THREE most appropriate actions to take in this situation:

A. Tell the nurse that this is really an issue for the consultant to deal with and that she should go and talk to him.

B. Go and talk to the consultant about it yourself.

C. Ask a few other colleagues whether they agree with the nurse's view before going to see the consultant yourself.

D. Raise the issue at a team meeting when the colleague in question is present.

E. Raise the issue at a team meeting in the absence of the colleague in question.

F. Raise the issue in confidence with the colleague in question.

G. Send the colleague an anonymous note asking him to sort the issue out.

Scenario 47

You overhear a receptionist talking to one of the regular patients in front of other patients. She is making fun of an ugly patient who came in earlier.

What do you do?

Rank in order the following actions in response to this situation (1= Most appropriate; 5= Least appropriate):

A. Firmly tell the receptionist to stop the discussion there and then.

B. Do nothing for the time being but raise the problem with the clinic manager at the next occurrence.

C. Contact the clinic manager immediately, alerting them to the situation.

D. Have a private word with the receptionist once the patient has left.

E. Apologise to the other patients present and reassure them that it will not happen again.

Scenario 48

You have written a case report for publication and your consultant has recently reviewed your final draft. When he gives you his comments back, you notice that he has added two names to the list of authors.

On enquiring, he tells you that they are his wife and his ex-registrar who are both currently unemployed and need publications on their CV to enhance their chances of employment. Neither were involved with the case discussed in your paper.

What do you do?

Choose the THREE most appropriate actions to take in this situation:

A. Tell the consultant that you cannot publish the case reports with their names on and that you will submit it with your name only.

B. Discuss the situation in confidence with the Clinical Director and envisage contacting the GMC about the two other doctors.

C. Agree to add the two names to the publication as it is only a case report and not a research paper.

D. Check with other colleagues whether something similar has happened to them and contact the GMC about your consultant if it has.

E. Discuss the matter with the consultant in a private meeting.

F. Report your consultant to the GMC.

G. Contact the paper where the case report is due to be published to tell them about the situation.

Scenario 49

Your consultant asks you to make a backdated alteration to the notes in order to cover up for a past mistake made by the team.

What do you do?

Choose the THREE most appropriate actions to take in this situation:

A. Make the change requested by the consultant as you are worried that he may give you a bad reference.

B. Refuse to make the entry.

C. Make a note of the conversation that you have had with the consultant and contact your defence union.

D. Report the matter to the Clinical Director at the earliest opportunity.

E. Inform the patient of the consultant's request and of the mistake made.

F. Inform the GMC.

G. Inform the police as there are potentially legal implications.

Scenario 50

You work as the SHO on a general surgical ward. A 20-year-old girl was brought in earlier to A&E by her father after collapsing in the street.

She subsequently developed abdominal pains and has been accepted by your team. She is now clinically stable and preliminary tests are unremarkable.

Her father is on the phone to you, asking for information about his daughter's admission. What do you do?

Rank in order the following actions in response to this situation
(1= Most appropriate; 5= Least appropriate):

A. Tell the father that you simply cannot communicate with him on any matter relating to his daughter as this would be breaching her confidentiality.

B. Reassure the father that his daughter is fine but that you cannot give any further details without talking to his daughter first.

C. Explain to the father that his daughter has developed abdominal pains but that you cannot give any further details without talking to his daughter first.

D. Explain to the father that you will need to determine whether his daughter is competent before deciding whether you are able to release any further details to him.

E. Hand the phone over to the registrar and ask him to handle the call.

Scenario 51

A woman presents to your surgery and explains that she has caught a sexually-transmitted infection (STI). The infection must have come from her husband since she is "faithful".

The patient thinks that her husband came to see you recently and she suspects that it was about an STI. In fact, he came to see you last week and told you that he was "100% faithful" and that he might have caught an infection from his wife.

What do you do?

Rank in order the following actions in response to this situation (1= Most appropriate; 5= Least appropriate):

A. Tell her that you got a completely different story from her husband as he felt that he had caught his infection from her.

B. Seek advice from a colleague about how to handle the matter.

C. Tell her that the husband indeed came to see you but that you are not at liberty to divulge the matters discussed during the consultation.

D. Tell her that you cannot discuss any issues relating to other patients, including whether or not they have attended your surgery recently.

E. Tell her that you are facing a potential conflict of interest and that she should register with another GP.

Scenario 52

You have been charged with providing a series of lectures to final year medical students on a range of topics with which you are very familiar.

One of the students whom you know well has somehow managed to get hold of a photocopy of the forthcoming exam papers and asks you to make sure that you address all the relevant issues at your teaching sessions.

What do you do?

Rank in order the following actions in response to this situation
(1= Most appropriate; 5= Least appropriate):

A. Confiscate the papers and report the matter straight away to the deanery, naming the student involved.

B. Confiscate the papers and report the matter straight away to the deanery, withholding the student's name.

C. Advise him to throw away the papers without looking at them.

D. Ignore the matter.

E. Inform the student that in order to maintain a fair process he will need to make sure that all other students also have a copy of the exam papers.

Scenario 53

You are an F1 doctor on call covering the general medical wards.

You already have a list of things to do and receive a further call from CCU regarding a conscious hypotensive patient. The nurses insist that you attend immediately.

What do you do?

Rank in order the following actions in response to this situation (1= Most appropriate; 5= Least appropriate):

A.   Drop everything and run to CCU to assess the patient.

B.   Tell the nurses they will have to wait as you have a list of things to do.

C.   Ask the nurses to call someone else as you are busy, giving them the bleep number of the doctor who will help them.

D.   Ask for more information about the patient including their diagnosis and other vital signs.

E.   Put out a crash call as you are unable to attend immediately.

Scenario 54

Judy, one of your patients in General Practice, is 35 years old and has recently been diagnosed with an underactive thyroid (hypothyroidism). The endocrine team have commenced her on Thyroxine.

She comes to see you and tells you that she is not taking the Thyroxine as she uses homeopathic remedies for her hypothyroidism and is feeling much better as a result.

What do you do?

Rank in order the following actions in response to this situation (1= Most appropriate; 5= Least appropriate):

A. Ask her what she understands about her illness and if she will come back to see you for a blood test in 3 months' time.

B. Tell her she should take the thyroxine and refer her back to the endocrinologists.

C. Tell her that she is being unreasonable, that homeopathy doesn't work and that she should take the thyroxine.

D. Do nothing now but offer her the option of coming back to see you. After all it's her choice.

E. Ask her if there were any problems with the thyroxine, if she understands why she should take it and what will happen if she doesn't take it. Explain anything she doesn't understand but offer her the choice of what to do, with a follow up appointment.

Scenario 55

You are an F2 doctor in General Practice. An elderly Turkish patient, who cannot speak or understand English, comes to see you. A 6-year old girl is present; the girl tells you that she will interpret for her grandmother.

What do you do?

Rank in order the following actions in response to this situation (1= Most appropriate; 5= Least appropriate):

A. Refuse to see the patient at all. Tell the receptionist to get them to rebook their appointment.

B. See the patient but refuse to use the 6 year old as an interpreter. It's inappropriate.

C. See the patient; ask what the problem is and if it is something simple that you feel a 6 year old could explain to her grandmother then continue with the consultation, ensuring at the end of the consultation that the grandmother knows she should try not to use the child again.

D. See the patient but explain through the 6 year old that it is not advisable to use a child as an interpreter asking if there is anyone else with her to help.

E. See the patient and explain to them via the child that you will call language line (telephone interpreting service) and use that instead of the child

Scenario 56

You are an F2 doctor in A&E and have just been present at an arrest situation where the patient did not survive.

You were team leader at the arrest and need to inform the relatives of the patient's death. Your shift ends in 10 minutes.

What do you do?

Rank in order the following actions in response to this situation (1= Most appropriate; 5= Least appropriate):

A. Ask the A&E sister to get the family a cup of tea.

B. Go to tell the family immediately of the outcome. It is not fair to make them wait.

C. Finish writing the notes from the arrest, compose yourself and arrange to meet the relatives in the relative room.

D. Hand over the job to your F1. They need the experience.

E. Hand over the job to the doctor who is taking over from you. After all the family don't know it was you who ran the arrest and your shift is ending.

Scenario 57

You are an F2 doctor in elderly care and have been called to write a death certificate for one of your patients, who was admitted 2 weeks ago and died overnight.

You saw him yesterday before going off shift and confirmed with the nurses that it was an expected death. Overnight, a locum doctor confirmed death. You have not seen the dead patient's body since he died.

What do you do?

Rank in order the following actions in response to this situation (1= Most appropriate; 5= Least appropriate):

A. Go and write the death certificate as soon as is possible.

B. Agree to do the death certificate and then add it to your list of jobs for the day.

C. Tell the bereavement officer to call the doctor who saw the patient after death last night.

D. Go and see the body to confirm death yourself and then go and write the death certificate.

E. Go and write the death certificate as soon as is possible and offer to take your F1 with you to show them what they should do.

Scenario 58

You are an F2 doctor working in General Practice.

Another doctor's patient attends your surgery, requesting a repeat prescription of sleeping tablets.

What do you do?

Rank in order the following actions in response to this situation (1= Most appropriate; 5= Least appropriate):

A. Check that the patient is not overusing their medication, issue the script telling them that they do not need to waste the GP's time for repeat prescriptions.

B. Review the notes fully and ask the patient why they need the sleeping tablets advising them of their potential addictiveness and offer alternative help.

C. Review the notes fully looking for the commencement date of the medication and the amount they are using per month. If they are using them appropriately, then issue a script.

D. Issue the script automatically without review of the notes.

E. Tell the patient they cannot have the prescription and that they need to see the GP who started them.

Scenario 59

You are an F2 doctor working in General Practice. A patient whom you know very well attends and informs you that her ex-boyfriend is about to be released from prison and has called her, threatening to kill her. She is too scared to go to the police.

What do you do?

Rank in order the following actions in response to this situation (1= Most appropriate; 5= Least appropriate):

A. Call the police and tell them about the threats.

B. Give her support, listen to her fears and then tell her that you will call the police to inform them of the threats made.

C. Give her support, listen to her fears and ask her if she will let you inform the police of the threats made.

D. Tell her there is nothing you can do as this does not fall within your remit.

E. Give her support, listen to her fears and wish her luck.

Scenario 60

You are an F2 doctor in General Practice and whilst on a home visit, your 92 year old patient tells you that they no longer want to take their medication for hyperlipidaemia (high cholesterol) as they are ready to die.

What do you do?

Rank in order the following actions in response to this situation
(1= Most appropriate; 5= Least appropriate):

A. Refer them to a psychiatrist to assess their capacity.

B. Ask them to explain why they feel they want to die, offering support explaining that stopping their medication for high cholesterol is unlikely to hasten their death.

C. Offer to help them die.

D. Tell them it's ok, that it's their choice and if they want to stop they can.

E. Assess their capacity and only if they are competent then tell them it's ok, that it's their choice and if they want to stop they can.

Scenario 61

You are an F2 doctor working in General Practice. A 13-year-old girl attends on her own asking for the combined oral contraceptive pill (COCP).

What do you do?

Rank in order the following actions in response to this situation (1= Most appropriate; 5= Least appropriate):

A. Assess her to ensure that she understands the nature, purpose and consequences of both taking the oral contraceptive pill and of not taking the oral contraceptive pill and if she does, then prescribe it.

B. Refuse to prescribe it. It's illegal for a 13 year old to have sex.

C. Tell her she must return with an adult before you will prescribe it.

D. Insist she has a contraceptive implant instead once you have ensured she is not "at risk" and is competent.

E. Prescribe the pill.

Scenario 62

You are an F2 doctor working in general surgery. As part of your role, you run the pre-assessment clinic for patients who are to be admitted major surgery.

One of the patients you saw in clinic last week has just arrived on the ward, ready for surgery today and on review of the notes you realise that you forgot to listen to their heart in clinic. You do this immediately and hear a murmur.

What do you do?

Rank in order the following actions in response to this situation
(1= Most appropriate; 5= Least appropriate):

A. Ignore the murmur; you don't want to get into trouble with your consultant.

B. Tell the anaesthetist that he may want to listen to the patient's heart before proceeding.

C. Document the murmur, inform the patient of what you've found and then inform your consultant that the patient will need further investigations that are likely to delay the surgery.

D. Document the murmur and inform your consultant that the patient will need further investigations that are likely to delay the surgery.

E. Document the murmur and run to the echo lab to beg for an urgent echo in the next 15 minutes before theatre calls the patient for surgery.

Scenario 63

You have been asked by your consultant to consent the next patient for theatre. When you look at the list it is for a Whipple's procedure (complicated surgery usually performed for pancreatic cancer) and you do not know what it is.

What do you do?

Rank in order the following actions in response to this situation (1= Most appropriate; 5= Least appropriate):

A. Consent the patient anyway.

B. Go onto the internet and find out what a Whipples procedure is and then return to your consultant to ask if they can help you.

C. Contact your registrar (ST3-5) and ask them to come and help you.

D. Go onto the internet and find out what a Whipples procedure is and proceed with the consent.

E. Go back to your consultant and tell them you cannot proceed with the consent.

Scenario 64

You are an F2 doctor in General Practice. Whilst on a home visit, your 86-year-old patient, who is wheelchair bound following a bilateral below knee amputation, asks you to help them die.

What do you do?

Rank in order the following actions in response to this situation (1= Most appropriate; 5= Least appropriate):

A. Offer to help them die.

B. Refer them to a psychiatrist. They must be depressed.

C. Explain that you cannot help them die but give them information about assisted suicide in Switzerland.

D. Assess their capacity and if competent, explain that you cannot help them die but give them information about assisted suicide in Switzerland.

E. Assess their capacity and if competent assess them for depression.

Scenario 65

You are an F2 doctor working in General Practice. A fit and healthy 37-year old woman attends with a cold. Her examination is normal and so you decide that it is likely to be a viral infection and explain that antibiotics will not help her.

She insists that you give her a prescription as her colds "always turn into chest infections" and it is really difficult to get an appointment to see you.

What do you do?

Rank in order the following actions in response to this situation (1= Most appropriate; 5= Least appropriate):

A. Refuse to give her the antibiotics with no further explanation.

B. Advise her to go and see another GP who may prescribe them for her insisting that you won't.

C. Explain the reason for you not giving antibiotics and offer her an appointment to return in 48 hours if she is no better.

D. Give her a prescription of antibiotics as she asks.

E. Give her a delayed prescription for antibiotics asking her not to take them for 48 hours to see if she improves without them.

Scenario 66

You are an F2 doctor working in A&E. A 65 year old smoker attends with a cough that has been present for 6 weeks and he has had 2 episodes of haemoptysis.

He is otherwise well. He tells you that his GP has refused to give him antibiotics.

What do you do?

Rank in order the following actions in response to this situation (1= Most appropriate; 5= Least appropriate):

A. Immediately admit the man, he's obviously got lung cancer.

B. Call the GP and complain that this man has been mistreated.

C. Organise immediate investigations including a chest X-ray and blood tests.

D. Prescribe antibiotics and refer him back to his GP.

E. Refer him to oncology, he's obviously got lung cancer.

Scenario 67

You are an F2 doctor on call for General Medicine. The nurses on ward H have called you as they want you to review an ECG that the nurse practitioner ordered for a patient with chest pain. The patient is stable.

What do you do?

Rank in order the following actions in response to this situation (1= Most appropriate; 5= Least appropriate):

A. Advise them to call the nurse practitioner to review the ECG and if she needs help to ask her to call you and you will attend immediately.

B. Attend immediately; this may be a myocardial infarction (heart attack).

C. Ask for more information regarding the patient to assess how urgent this task is.

D. Add it to your list of things to do and attend when it reaches the top of the list.

E. Advise them to review their own ECG. After all they should not request investigations that they cannot interpret.

Scenario 68

You are an F2 doctor in General Practice and are staying late on your own in the practice to complete some paperwork. The practice is closed and all other members of staff have left.

As you are about to leave at 21:00, the fax machine starts to whirl and a fax arrives. It is from the local haematologist with URGENT written at the top of the paper. The fax states that one of the practice's patients has a haemoglobin of 5 and is profoundly anaemic.

What do you do?

Rank in order the following actions in response to this situation (1= Most appropriate; 5= Least appropriate):

A. Call the haematologist at the hospital and advise them there is no one at the practice and they need to contact the patient and arrange admission.

B. Ignore it. It is only by chance that you are in the building. Usually no one would be there to respond to a fax at such a late hour.

C. Place the fax on your desk to ensure that you remember to act on it first thing in the morning.

D. Read the fax and act on it by calling the patient and arranging an admission to the local hospital.

E. Read the fax and act on it by calling the patient and advising them to go to A&E.

Scenario 69

You are an F2 doctor working in General Practice. At 9am, one of your patients, a 25-year-old Eastern European, states that they have severe toothache and a temperature.

What do you do?

Rank in order the following actions in response to this situation (1= Most appropriate; 5= Least appropriate):

A. Assess the patient for a dental abscess and treat it with antibiotics if required.

B. Tell them to go and see a dentist.

C. Advise the patient that you are not trained in dental treatment and advise them to seek help from a dentist.

D. Give them pain killers and advise them to see a dentist.

E. Assess the patient fully to determine why they have a temperature and if it is a dental cause, refer them to a dentist the same day.

Scenario 70

You are an F2 doctor in General Practice. At the end of each surgery, you are supposed to meet with your trainer to go over any problems that you may have encountered during the session.

Your trainer always leaves the practice before you have finished and is never available for your debrief.

What should you do?

Rank in order the following actions in response to this situation (1= Most appropriate; 5= Least appropriate):

A. Nothing.

B. Ask another GP partner in the practice to meet with you at the end of each surgery.

C. Report your trainer to the deanery.

D. Arrange a meeting with your trainer and tell them you need to see them at the end of each surgery.

E. Arrange a meeting with your trainer and ask them whether you could arrange a daily meeting to discuss problems.

Scenario 71

You are an F2 in General Practice. An emergency patient comes in with signs that are consistent with anaphylaxis following a bee sting.

What do you do?

Rank in order the following actions in response to this situation (1= Most appropriate; 5= Least appropriate):

A. Call an ambulance.

B. Assess the patient's airway, breathing and circulation and give the appropriate dose of adrenaline.

C. Assess the patient's airway, breathing and circulation and give the appropriate dose of atropine.

D. Start basic life support.

E. Assess the patient's airway, breathing and circulation and call an ambulance if you are concerned.

Scenario 72

You are an F2 doctor in A&E. An otherwise well patient presents with lower back pain. Following a detailed examination, you notice he has foot drop and saddle anaesthesia.

What do you do?

Rank in order the following actions in response to this situation (1= Most appropriate; 5= Least appropriate):

A. Refer him immediately to a neurosurgeon.

B. Organise a back X-ray.

C. Organise an urgent MRI.

D. Discharge home.

E. Admit to a medical ward.

Scenario 73

You are an F2 doctor working in general surgery. In an outpatient clinic, you see an 85 year old gentleman with an abdominal aortic aneurysm that has expanded over the last 3 months and now measures 8cm on ultrasound.

Your consultant has reviewed the patient, fully explained the procedure and advised him he needs to come into hospital for an abdominal aortic aneurysm repair. When the consultant has left the room, the man tells you he will not have the surgery.

What do you do?

Rank in order the following actions in response to this situation (1= Most appropriate; 5= Least appropriate):

A.   Offer to talk to the man to re-explain the advantages and disadvantages of surgery before talking to your consultant.

B.   Advise the man that he must have surgery.

C.   Tell him it is his choice if he does not want surgery.

D.   Tell your consultant.

E.   Assess his capacity and if he is competent then inform him that it is his choice if he does not want surgery.

Scenario 74

You are an F2 doctor working in Obstetrics and Gynaecology. In the middle of winter, whilst reviewing a lady who is 36 weeks pregnant in antenatal clinic, you notice that her 3-year-old little girl who is in attendance with her is wearing severely soiled clothes and has no shoes on.

You are concerned that the child may be being neglected.

What do you do?

Rank in order the following actions in response to this situation (1= Most appropriate; 5= Least appropriate):

A. Nothing, the child is not your patient.

B. Immediately admit the child to paediatrics.

C. Confront the mother and ask why the child looks so dirty.

D. Ask the patient to wait outside and then call her GP to ask if there are any concerns regarding the welfare of the child.

E. Ensure you add a comment at the end of your clinic letter to the GP asking them to review the child.

Scenario 75

You are an F2 doctor in General Practice. You receive a hospital letter regarding one of your patients whom you have been seeing regularly for antenatal checks stating that her baby was born 5 weeks ago and has been unexpectedly diagnosed with Down's Syndrome.

What do you do?

Rank in order the following actions in response to this situation (1= Most appropriate; 5= Least appropriate):

A. Code the diagnosis in the baby's notes and wait for the 6-week check.

B. Discuss the case with the health visitor and then contact the patient offering a home visit or a surgery visit if they wish.

C. Arrange to go on a home visit to see the family and talk to your patient face to face.

D. Contact the patient to express your sympathy offering support if she needs it.

E. Write to the patient offering support if she needs it.

Scenario 76

You are an F2 working in respiratory medicine. After being trained to perform pleural aspirations, your consultant asks you to perform your first aspiration without supervision. You agree, feeling confident.

Everything goes well until you try to aspirate the fluid and get a dry tap. On review of the large pleural effusion on X-ray, you realise that you have tried to aspirate the wrong side of the chest.

What do you do?

Rank in order the following actions in response to this situation (1= Most appropriate; 5= Least appropriate):

A. Ensure the patient is stable, seek help from your consultant and then explain what has happened and apologise to the patient.

B. Tell your consultant that it was a dry tap and organise for an ultrasound guided aspiration for another day

C. Ensure the patient is stable and immediately inform your consultant

D. Ensure the patient is stable and then proceed to aspirate the correct side

E. Ensure the patient is stable, explain what has happened, apologise to the patient and then seek help from your consultant

Scenario 77

You are an F2 doctor in General Practice. A patient comes to see you and tells you that they will be out of the country travelling for a year and want you to prescribe 12 months of medication for them.

Their medication includes antidepressants, sleeping pills, thyroxine and anti-hypertensives.

What do you do?

Rank in order the following actions in response to this situation (1= Most appropriate; 5= Least appropriate):

A. Refuse and ask the patient to submit their NHS card to the primary care trust (PCT).

B. Prescribe 3 months of medication as this is the maximum your practice protocol allows.

C. Prescribe a year's worth of medication.

D. Review the patient's notes to assess how stable their hypertension and thyroid hormone levels are and if they are ok then prescribe a years worth of medication.

E. Advise the patient that the medication they are on requires regular review and give them the standard supply.

Scenario 78

You are an F2 doctor in General Practice and are the allocated "on call" doctor for the morning. At the beginning of a busy surgery the receptionist puts a call through to you from a 70-year old man with central crushing chest pain that has lasted for 45 minutes and was not relieved by sublingual GTN. He had a heart attack 6 months earlier.

You tell him that you will dial 999 on his behalf from your mobile while he stays on the practice phone line, but he refuses. He states that he does not want an ambulance; he wants you to visit him at home and is willing to wait until the end of morning surgery.

What do you do?

Choose the THREE most appropriate answers to this scenario

A. Agree to go and see him at the end of surgery

B. Call 999 anyway

C. Tell him you will visit him straight away

D. Advise him you will refer him to the medical team at the local hospital and arrange for an ambulance to take him

E. Advise him he may be having another heart attack and that it is important he is treated as soon as possible

F. Tell him to take more sublingual GTN and you will call back in 30 minutes to see if he is any better

G. Advise him you will visit him as soon as possible depending on how busy your morning clinic is

Scenario 79

You are an F2 doctor in General Practice and your trainer has asked you to go through his blood results to help you learn how to use the practice computerised system.

On reviewing his results you uncover a problem. A blood test from one month ago which your trainer has filled as "normal, no action" is grossly abnormal. The CRP (C-reactive protein) and ESR (Erythrocyte sedimentation rate) are both elevated and there is a positive rheumatoid factor. On review of the notes, you discover that the patient is a 36-year old man with new onset multiple joint pain.

You are concerned that this is a missed diagnosis of early onset rheumatoid arthritis. What do you do?

Choose the THREE most appropriate answers to this scenario

A.   Nothing, you don't want to embarrass your trainer.

B.   Show your trainer the results and ask them to teach you on it.

C.   Fill in an incident form

D.   Inform the practice manager of your trainer's mistake

E.   Inform a senior partner of your trainer's mistake

F.   Report your trainer to the GMC

G.   Arrange for the patient to be referred immediately to a rheumatologist

Scenario 80

You are an F2 doctor working in general medicine. You are just finishing your shift and leaving the hospital when you see a woman collapse in the car park. Her friend shouts out for help stating that she is not breathing.

What do you do?

Choose the THREE most appropriate answers to this scenario

A. Call 999 from your mobile phone

B. Carry on walking to your car, you're off duty

C. Immediately go to the collapsed person and assess their airway

D. Immediately go to the collapsed person and give 2 rescue breaths

E. Immediately go to the collapsed person and start ALS (advanced life support)

F. Tell the "friend to call 999" from their mobile phone

Scenario 81

You are an F2 doctor working in paediatrics. On the paediatric assessment unit you review an 8-year-old child with a mild chest infection. Whilst mum leaves the ward to go to the toilet, the child tells you that his father keeps hitting him.

What do you do?

Choose the THREE most appropriate answers to this scenario

A. Admit the child immediately and inform the registrar on call for child protection.

B. Tell the child they must not lie about such things and then ask them to tell you the truth about what happened

C. Listen to them and document everything they say

D. Listen to them and document it if the child repeats the same allegation

E. Wait until mum returns, then ask the child to explain and examine the child fully.

F. Call the nurse on the admission unit to sit in with you while you listen to the child and allow them to talk to you

G. Ask the child if this has ever happened before

Scenario 82

You are an F2 doctor working in General Practice. You are on your way into work and bump into a patient who was newly diagnosed with type-1 diabetes one week ago and whom you had sent to hospital to be commenced on insulin. He is eating a bar of chocolate and drinking a can of sugary fizzy drink whilst chatting to his friends.

What do you do?

Choose the THREE most appropriate answers to this scenario

A. Nothing, you are not on duty

B. Confront the patient and ask them why they are eating chocolate

C. Say hello, smile and make a mental note to ask them about it when you see them next

D. Say hello, smile and make a mental note to call them later to ask them to come in for a review

E. Say hello, smile and ask how they are.

F. Ensure the patient does not see you, you don't want to embarrass them but make a mental note to call them later to ask them to come in for a review.

Scenario 83

You are an F2 doctor working in Obstetrics and Gynaecology. You are doing the preadmission clinic and see a 21-year-old lady who is attending the day unit for her 4th termination of pregnancy (TOP).

What do you do?

Choose the THREE most appropriate answers to this scenario

A. Offer her the contraceptive implant.

B. Advise her that you can insert a coil at the time of TOP if she consents to it.

C. Give her a supply of the combined oral contraceptive pill.

D. Give her a supply of condoms.

E. Advise her that surgical TOP is dangerous and is not a form of contraception.

F. Offer her counselling.

Scenario 84

You are an F2 doctor working in General Practice. Your patient has not attended for their appointment and when you look in their notes to annotate them you notice that this is the 5th consecutive appointment that they have not attended. They have never tried to cancel an appointment.

What do you do?

Choose the THREE most appropriate answers to this scenario

A. Annotate the notes but do nothing else.

B. Inform your practice manager of the non-attendance asking them to make contact with the patient.

C. Call the patient and ask if they are ok and where they are.

D. Call the patient and demand to know why they have not attended the last 5 appointments.

E. Flag the notes so that when the patient next books an appointment the receptionists can advise the patient to telephone if they cannot make the appointment.

F. Write to the patient asking if they are ok and explain the practice policy on missed appointments.

G. Write to the patient and ask them to find another GP practice.

Scenario 85

You are an F2 doctor working in General Practice. You see a patient whose blood pressure measures 190/100. She is otherwise well.

The patient tells you that it is always normal when the nurses measure it and that she is scared of seeing the doctor.

What do you do?

Choose the THREE most appropriate answers to this scenario

A. Believe the patient and ask her to always attend her blood pressure assessments with the practice nurse.

B. Review the notes and her medication.

C. Advise her she needs to be admitted to the local hospital.

D. Ask her to use a blood pressure monitor at home and record the results.

E. Arrange for a 24-hour blood pressure monitor assessment at the local hospital.

F. Advise her she needs more medication to control her hypertension.

Scenario 86

You are an F2 doctor working in orthopaedics. You discharged an elderly lady yesterday following a total hip replacement that was complicated by a deep vein thrombosis (DVT) and she was therefore sent home on warfarin. As you write her discharge summary, you notice that her INR on leaving hospital yesterday was 8 (therapeutic range 2-3).

What do you do?

Choose the THREE most appropriate answers to this scenario

A.   Contact the anticoagulant clinic and advise them of the problem.

B.   Call the patient and tell them to stop their warfarin.

C.   Call the patient and tell them to stop their warfarin and to go to A&E.

D.   Arrange for the patient to attend for a repeat INR tomorrow.

E.   Arrange for the patient to attend for a repeat INR today.

F.   Call the patients GP and advise them of the problem.

G.   Immediately contact the patient and ask them to return to the hospital so you can review them.

Scenario 87

You are an F2 doctor working in general surgery. Your consultant has asked you to discharge a post operative patient back to her care home immediately as he urgently requires the bed for another patient who is due to come in for major surgery later that day.

On reviewing the notes of the patient you are due to discharge, you notice that the occupational therapist (OT) has stated that she needs to do a "home visit" prior to discharge.

What do you do?

Choose the THREE most appropriate answers to this scenario

A. Inform the ward manager of the problem.

B. Return to your consultant with the patients notes and ask them what to do in view of the OT's entry

C. Return to your consultant and explain that you are unable to discharge the patient

D. Call the OT and tell them the patient is being discharged

E. Call the OT and ask them when they are able to do the home visit

F. Call the OT and ask them to do the home visit today as the patient is going home

G. Discharge the patient as your consultant requested

Scenario 88

You are an F2 doctor working in General Practice. A patient has attended the practice with acute onset headache and you are convinced this is a subarachnoid haemorrhage and requires urgent admission.

You call the medical registrar on call who states that since the patient has no neurological signs she will not accept the referral.

What do you do?

Choose the THREE most appropriate answers to this scenario

A. Send the patient to A&E

B. Telephone the consultant on call and request the admission

C. Accept the medical registrars refusal to admit the patient

D. Try another local hospital to see if they will review the patient for you

E. Call the on call hospital manager and make a complaint about the on call registrar

F. Call the ST1-2 (SHO level) on call and make the referral to them

G. Call the medical registrar back after 5 minutes and tell them that their patient has neurological signs, even though it is not true.

Scenario 89

You are an F2 doctor in General Practice and have looked after a complicated elderly epileptic patient on multiple medications for months. You finally get her stabilised on her drugs after 6 months, when unfortunately she falls and fractures her wrist.

After a 3-day stay in hospital she is discharged back into your care and you notice from the discharge summary that 3 out of 4 of her antiepileptic medications have been changed by the hospital doctors.

What do you do?

Choose the TWO most appropriate answers to this scenario

A. Make no changes

B. Immediately change the medication back to what it was preadmission

C. Slowly change the medication back to what it was before admission over a couple of weeks

D. Call the team who admitted her and ask for clarification of the changes

E. Call the hospital / ward pharmacist and ask for clarification of the drug changes

F. Write a letter of complaint to the consultant in charge of her care in hospital

Scenario 90

You are an F2 doctor in General Practice. A 50-year-old gentleman tells you that he wants to be screened for prostatic cancer and he knows there is a PSA (prostatic specific antigen) blood test.

What do you do?

Choose the TWO most appropriate answers to this scenario

A. Refuse the test explaining that there is no screening programme for prostatic cancer

B. Arrange the test

C. Counsel the gentleman with regard to the possible false positive result of the PSA test

D. Perform a digital rectal examination

E. Counsel the gentleman about the possible false negative result of the test

Scenario 91

You are an F2 doctor working in A&E. A woman with a history of breast cancer attends with severe jaundice and on examination you feel a large mass in the right upper quadrant consistent with a hard craggy liver.

What do you do?

Choose the THREE most appropriate answers to this scenario

A. Tell her that the cancer has spread and arrange admission

B. Refer her to the palliative care team

C. Arrange immediate admission

D. Organise urgent tests to include liver function tests, liver MRI and mammogram

E. Organise urgent blood tests to include liver function tests

F. Tell the patient that there is something wrong with her liver and she needs more tests. If she asks, tell her that it may be related to the breast cancer.

G. Arrange the community palliative care team to review the patient at home

Scenario 92

You are an F2 doctor working in General Practice. You have serious concerns regarding the welfare of a 2-year-old child whose parents have just joined the practice and are both drug addicts.

You have seen the child on 3 occasions and have witnessed verbal abuse from both the parents. You ring social services to make a formal referral requesting a family assessment and are told by the duty social worker that, since there is no physical abuse, there are no grounds for an assessment.

What do you do?

Choose the THREE most appropriate answers to this scenario

A. Ask to speak to the senior social worker on-call as you are not happy with the decision that the duty social worker made

B. Insist that the duty social worker take the case on as you have concerns

C. Accept the duty social workers decision

D. Call back the following day as you know there will be a different social worker on duty

E. Put your concerns in writing and post them to the social work department

F. Put your concerns in writing and send an urgent fax to the social work department

G. Call the named doctor for child protection

Scenario 93

You are an F2 doctor working in general surgery. One morning at an X-ray meeting, the consultants are discussing the CT results of one of your patients, a 62-year old woman admitted with abdominal pain.

The radiologist comments on the size of your patient's uterus suggesting they need an MRI scan, but you know she had a hysterectomy 12 years ago.

What do you do?

Choose the TWO most appropriate answers to this scenario

A. Nothing

B. Go back to the patient later that day and ask them about their hysterectomy

C. Tell your consultant after the meeting about the hysterectomy

D. Speak up during the meeting stating what the patient has told you about the hysterectomy

E. Review the patient's notes later that day to check whether she had a hysterectomy 12 years ago

F. Quietly approach your consultant as the scan is being reviewed to explain about the hysterectomy

Scenario 94

You are an F2 doctor working in A&E. It is coming to the end of a busy shift when an 86-year old gentleman is brought in by ambulance. The paramedics say he called them stating he had central crushing chest pain.

This is the 8th time this week that the man has called the paramedics with the same story, his investigations are always normal and he told you last time that he was lonely and liked seeing everyone in the A&E department.

What do you do?

Choose the THREE most appropriate answers to this scenario

A. Refuse to see the patient.

B. Advise the paramedics that he is a non-urgent case and will have to wait.

C. Tell the gentleman that he is wasting NHS time and resources.

D. Tell the paramedics to take him back home.

E. See him as an urgent case.

F. Repeat the same investigations that have been performed every time he presents to A&E.

G. Ask the gentleman about his family.

Scenario 95

You are an F2 doctor working in paediatrics. You are on call and receive a telephone call from a local GP asking you to review a 4-year-old girl.

The GP says that the child's examination is normal and that he does not think there is anything wrong with her, but her mother is insistent on being referred "just in case" she has meningitis since her temperature was high that morning.

What do you do?

Choose the ONE most appropriate answer to this scenario

A. Tell the GP to review the child later the same day and if the mother still wants a referral to send her in then.

B. Advise the GP to refer her as a non-urgent outpatient.

C. Tell the GP to review the child the following day and if the mother still wants a referral to send her in then.

D. Ask to speak to the mother on the telephone so you can tell her that it is inappropriate to refer the child to hospital.

E. Tell the GP that, if they are happy that there is nothing wrong with the child, then they should tell the mother no.

F. Refuse the referral.

G. Accept the referral.

Scenario 96

You are an F2 doctor working in General Practice and are on call for the practice. A 21-year old calls you and requests a home visit as her 3-year-old daughter has a temperature and a sore throat.

You ask her to come to the practice and she refuses stating that she has no way of getting to the practice.

What do you do?

Choose the THREE most appropriate answers to this scenario

A.   Suggest ways of attending the practice such as walking, the bus, a taxi or a neighbour driving her there.

B.   Offer the patient money to get a taxi

C.   Accept the home visit and go and see the child

D.   Insist that the child be brought to the practice

E.   Advise her to go to A&E

F.   Ask for more details regarding the child's illness

G.   Advise her to call an ambulance

Scenario 97

You are an F2 doctor working in general medicine and have accepted a referral from a GP.

Before you see the patient, you read the GP referral letter. In capital letters at the top of the letter is written "VIOLENT PATIENT. HAS PREVIOUSLY ATTACKED A GP AT THE PRACTICE".

What do you do?

Choose the TWO most appropriate answers to this scenario

A. Refuse to see the patient without a chaperone

B. Refuse to see the patient

C. Request security attend whilst you see the patient

D. Call the GP who referred the patient and ask for more information regarding the attack before seeing the patient

E. Call the GP who referred the patient and tell them they should have warned you when they referred them, as you would then have been able to refuse the admission

F. See the patient without any precautions

G. Ask your F1 to see the patient

Scenario 98

You are an F2 doctor working in A&E. A 38-year-old man attends with a testicular lump. He is convinced that he has testicular cancer.

When you examine it, you are certain that it is a small, uncomplicated benign epidymal cyst that requires no treatment.

What do you do?

Choose the THREE most appropriate answers to this scenario

A. Inform the man of the benign diagnosis and send him home

B. Inform the man of his benign diagnosis but advise him to go to se his GP if he is still worried

C. Inform the man of his benign diagnosis but tell him to go to his GP and ask for an ultrasound

D. Refer him to urology

E. Organise an urgent ultrasound to confirm the diagnosis

F. Tell the man that this is not an accident, nor an emergency and he should see his GP

Scenario 99

You are an **F2 doctor working in A&E. An 18-year-old female who has been treated for a sprained ankle tells you that she wants to kill herself.**

What do you do?

Choose the THREE most appropriate answers to this scenario

A. Admit her under the psychiatrists

B. Refer her to psychiatry

C. Assess her fully from a psychiatric perspective

D. Admit her under orthopaedics to enable the nurses to monitor her for 24 hours

E. Do nothing. You have treated the sprain, which is reason she came to A&E

F. Discharge her ensuring that she has someone to stay with her for 24 hours

G. Assess her suicide risk and if you are not concerned discharge her back to her GP

Scenario 100

You are an F2 doctor working in General Practice. During a routine immunisation clinic, the mother of a 12-month old boy tells you that she does not want her child to have the MMR (measles, mumps and rubella) vaccination.

She will see a Chinese medicine doctor instead for an alternative.

What do you do?

Choose the THREE most appropriate answers to this scenario

A. Report her to the community paediatric team as this is a form of child neglect (abuse)

B. Tell her that Chinese medicine will not protect her child from Measles, Mumps and Rubella

C. Report them to social services as this is a form of child neglect (abuse)

D. Accept the mother's choice

E. Offer a follow up appointment for the vaccinations

F. Ensure that the mother has all the information about the vaccination

Scenario 101

You are an F2 doctor working in A&E. Your friend calls you saying that they have tonsillitis for the third time this year and cannot get an appointment with their own GP.

They ask you to send them some antibiotics for them to use.

What do you do?

Choose the TWO most appropriate answers to this scenario

A. Write an external (FP10) prescription to take to a local pharmacy

B. Take some antibiotics from the A&E stock

C. Write a hospital prescription for some antibiotics

D. Ask a colleague to write an outside prescription (FP10) for your friend to take to a local pharmacy

E. Refuse to organise the antibiotics

F. Call your friend's GP and try to organise an appointment for them

G. Call your friend's GP and ask for some antibiotics for them explaining that you are certain it is tonsillitis

Scenario 102

You are an F2 doctor working in General Practice. One of your patients was referred urgently to a dermatologist with a suspicious mole. You were concerned that this is malignant melanoma.

The patient returns to you 4 weeks after your initial referral, saying that the mole has grown. It is now bleeding and she has still not heard from the hospital. You are now certain that this is a malignant melanoma.

What do you do?

Choose the TWO most appropriate answers to this scenario

A. Refer the patient again, the referral must have been lost

B. Tell the patient that you will call the dermatology team and chase up the appointment later that day

C. Advise the patient to call the hospital themselves to chase up the appointment

D. Advise the patient that there is nothing you can do

E. Call the dermatology team whilst the patient is still with you to organise an urgent appointment

F. Arrange for the mole to be biopsied by your GP partner who runs an "in house "minor surgery session the following day.

D Suggested Answers

Scenario 1   ANSWER: 1:C – 2:E – 3:D – 4:A – 5:B

In many cases you will find it easier to determine the level of appropriateness in reverse order (i.e. least appropriate first), as demonstrated here:

1. B (calling the police) has to be the least appropriate. We are only talking about a small amount of cash here. The culprit could be anyone ranging from a patient, a visitor, a nurse, a doctor etc. The police will not be able to do anything about it and you will have achieved nothing by calling them. If the thefts were of controlled drugs, or if the thefts were a regular occurrence, then there would be a stronger case for doing so. However, you would need to discuss with the Clinical Director and head nurse first (i.e. someone in charge would call the police, not you. Otherwise you will alienate the whole team at the hospital).

2. C, D and E all talk about reassuring patients or warning them to be more careful. They therefore look like stronger candidates for appropriateness as they are more in line with common sense. Option A looks good at first glance but it makes the assumption that the culprit is a member of the team. This will create conflict. Do you sincerely think that the culprit will replace the money? Therefore A can be placed as the fourth least effective option.

3. Out of C, D and E, two of the options involve reassuring the victim himself (C and E). D only talks about sending an email to your colleagues to warn patients. This may well be appropriate but your first concern should be with the victim and not the potential future theft of the other patients (this comes later). Therefore, out of the three options, D is the least appropriate.

4. Out of C and E, C is a softer and more caring approach. E is slightly patronising on the patient (he probably already knows he should have been more careful) but still within acceptable limits. In this context, a softer, reassuring approach is required and C is therefore better than E.

Scenario 2 — ANSWER: C, D, F

1. There are two options that can be discounted from the outset:

   - G: doing nothing is never an option unless it is really none of your business (we will see situations like these later) or unless the other options are obviously worse than doing nothing (e.g. unsafe). In this particular option, you are prompted to do nothing because you think someone else will notice the issue. This means that you prefer to keep quiet, hoping that it will become someone else's problem. Imagine the consequences if your colleague's lateness contributed one day to the death of a patient. In a situation where patient care is potentially affected by the delay, you simply cannot afford to ignore the matter

   - E: If there is a problem to discuss, you should discuss first with other junior colleagues or a senior colleague but not with the nurses. This will only spread gossip and create a bad atmosphere.

2. Notice that B and C both talk about arranging a discussion with the colleague but differ on how the discussion should be approached.

   - B is more like a dressing-down ("express your discontent"), which could potentially result in conflict.

   - C, however, is softer, more appropriate for the occasion and hints that you keep an open mind about the reasons behind the delay. Indeed, your colleague is likely to have a good reason to be late. It could be something as common-place as train problems, or a sick child or a more serious issue such as depression. Getting your facts right and taking a sensitive approach will help you identify the best way forward.

   C is the more acceptable option of the two as it is taking a softer approach to a problem which is not yet a major issue. Although forceful, D may be acceptable too, but only if there is no better option that we can identify.

3. This leaves us with A, C, D and F. As we have seen, C is appropriate as it helps establish the situation in a soft manner. D is also appropriate because, if your colleague is not performing in line with expectations, you must make sure the patient is adequately covered at all times, even if this means working harder temporarily.

4. The final choice between A (calling his wife) and F (mentioning to the registrar) goes in favour of F because (i) if he has personal problems, the last thing you want to do is make it worse by telling his wife (it is not your place to interfere with his private life) and (ii) involving the registrar is the safest option, particularly if the problem is likely to last. The registrar will then address the problem with the colleague, which is likely to yield better results than to involve your colleague's wife.

5. This leaves us with C, D and F.

Important note
When you attempt to answer questions in this "pick three out of seven" format, you would normally start by separating the options that appear reasonable from those which are not reasonable. However, a clever question may contain a list of options which are all reasonable or all unreasonable. Your task is to find those which are the best or the "least bad" in the list. For that reason, no option can be totally excluded unless you have identified three better other options. In this particular question, B was discounted because it felt a bit forceful. But, for example, if F had been "You report your colleague to the Clinical Director" instead of "You mention the delay to the registrar" then the answer would have been B, C and D; in other words, it would have been more appropriate to be a bit forceful with your colleague than to report him straight to the top.

Scenario 3   ANSWER: 1:D – 2:C – 3:B – 4:A – 5:E

1. E makes no practical sense. If the colleague is sick (and we must take his word for it at this stage), then it would make no sense to expect him to come in an hour later. This has to be the least appropriate option.

2. A is unsafe. You simply cannot expect to do a double shift and remain safe, at least not in comparison to the other options on offer. This has to be the second least appropriate option. Also if someone is sick, then they are officially on sick leave. They should not be expected to make up for it later on.

3. B, C and D all involve contacting the registrar on call but at different times:

    ▪ B = you stay 2 hours and then involve him
    ▪ C = you involve him and leave

117

- D = you involve him, offer to stay for a while and then leave.

If an SHO is ill, the registrar will need to know at the first opportunity so that he can manage the situation appropriately. In addition, you should not take additional responsibilities without informing a senior colleague. Therefore, involving him early is best. This places B in third position.

Between C and D, option D is best because you show solidarity and willingness to help. The registrar might accept or refuse your offer to stay but that is down to him. In any case, he is also on call and therefore it will be down to him to cover for the SHO. There is no harm in showing a bit of team spirit on your part though.

Scenario 4   ANSWER: B, C, F

1. A is inappropriate because it is not a nurse's responsibility to ensure that the drug chart is accurate. Contacting the senior nurse will therefore achieve little.

2. D is inappropriate because the approach is quite confrontational ("organise a meeting"). It makes it look like the consultant is fully responsible for the mistake and it will not resolve the fundamental question, which is to know why the allergy was not written on the drug chart in the first place. Having said that, it would be true to say that the consultant should have asked for clarification about the blank allergy box and there may be value in having a word with him about the incident (hence why B is more appropriate).

3. E feels like a tribunal. If someone has made a mistake then the best approach is to go and talk to them so that they can learn from the incident. There is no need for public humiliation. In any case, the admitting doctor might not be part of your own team!

4. G is inappropriate because it is not really the pharmacist's responsibility to train doctors on how to complete drug charts or to take disciplinary action. If the error was a simple one, such action is a bit over the top. It may be a better idea to get the pharmacist to organise a training session on common drug chart errors.

5. This leaves us with B, C and F, all three of which are the most appropriate.

- C is appropriate because, if the decision was made to give him the penicillin during a ward round, then he might have heard the comment and he needs to be reassured that everything is in hand.

- B is appropriate because it is recognising that a mistake has been made and steps are being taken to discuss the nature of the mistake in a non-confrontational manner (as opposed to option D). Mentioning critical incident reporting highlights your awareness of the importance of clinical risk management and therefore makes this a particularly good option. Some may argue that completing a critical incident form might be over the top but the fact remains that the penicillin was actually written up on the drug chart by the consultant. A lack of checks further down the line could have had potentially devastating consequences.

- F is appropriate because the team benefits from your experience and you are helping to prevent future occurrences of the same type of mistake. Mentioning the name of the doctor would have little value at this stage since it is the general issue of checking that the box has been completed that really matters as far as the team is concerned.

Scenario 5   ANSWER: 1:E – 2:A – 3:B – 4:C – 5:D

1. At first glance, the following observations come to mind:

    - Quoting the EWTD as an excuse to leave (option B) seems a bit over the top, especially to a consultant. It creates a big drama when there is no need to do so. Why not simply argue patient safety since the question clearly states that you are sleepy?

    - Patiently waiting and covering (option C) when you are exhausted could be unsafe. You have already been waiting for 15 minutes. The wait could be long!
    - Handing over to a nurse could be disastrous. This may lead to miscommunication and errors, and you are assuming that she will know what to do with the information.

    - Your colleague may have been delayed for a good reason and there may not be long for you to wait. The sensible thing to do is therefore to find out more about the situation before you can take any action.

Option E therefore seems the obvious starting point. Even if you are tired, it won't take long. If you can't get hold of him or if your colleague is substantially delayed then move to the next stage.

2. Both C and D are unsafe: C is unsafe because you are tired and D is unsafe because the information may never get to the doctor or may be miscommunicated. Also, it is unfair on the nurse (and it is against team spirit) to place the responsibility onto her and it is also bad practice to simply disappear without notifying your colleagues (and in particular your registrar); therefore, D must be worse than C. Note that both D and C are bad options, but we are simply saying that D is the worst because it compounds several issues (patient safety and bad teamwork).

3. We have now established that E should come first and that C and D should come last. This leaves us with A and B to place in second and third positions. It makes no sense to hand over to your consultant if the registrar is available (and nothing in the question states that he is not available). This places A ahead of B. The fact that you used the EWTD as an excuse for handing over to your consultant also confirms that A goes ahead of B. Quoting regulations may be the right thing to do, but it does not give the impression that you are helping the team to deal with a difficult problem. Regardless of the excuse given, it is the grade that will dictate the answer here, i.e. registrar first, then consultant.

Important note:
As mentioned in the introduction, the marking scheme allows for partial marks to be awarded to answers which, although they do not match the "ideal" answer, are also acceptable. In this scenario, answering EBACD instead of EABCD would most likely grant you partial marks.

Scenario 6 — ANSWER: 1:B – 2:C – 3:D – 4:E – 5:A

1. Option A (reporting the matter to his boss) will achieve little. The boss might be reluctant to lose an employee. At worst, all he can do is sack the employee but that will not resolve the problem, which is that the patient is still driving. It is the worst option.

2. Option D (reporting the matter to the DVLA) may be what you have to do in the end but there are steps that you can take before you take such an official stance. The DVLA guidelines actually say that you must do

everything you can to resolve the matter before you contact them (which may include discussing the matter with a next of kin). So that means B and C will have to come before D.

3. The best option is to address the matter with the patient himself. However, this must be done in a manner that invites the patient to comply and therefore must be non-threatening (hence why B is the best).

4. Option E (sending a threatening letter) is a difficult one. On one hand it seems a logical thing to do before you actually report the patient to the DVLA (to warn him of the consequences of his actions), but on the other hand the wording says that you will have to catch him driving before you can report him. This will mean spying on him or relying on luck and it is highly impractical. Therefore this is a very ineffective way of dealing with the problem as it sounds like a scare tactic and a shot in the dark which you hope will have the desired effect. Still it is a little more appropriate than telling his boss.

5. Based on the above, the right approach generally would be to:
    ▪ Approach the patient to reason with him (B)
    ▪ If this does not work, involve his wife (C)
    ▪ If this still does not work, then notify the DVLA (D)

The other two options (threatening letter and notifying the boss) come last in that order as they are least effective.

Note on option E
If the letter had stated that you would report him to the DVLA "if the patient *persisted to drive* despite your warnings", then E would come between C and D. However, the current wording is too vague to place it high on the list.

Note on confidentiality
In the above answer, we mentioned DVLA guidelines. Although there is no compulsory need to be aware of these guidelines, it is of great help to be familiar with some of the guidelines that could be used for common scenarios. In any case, the same conclusions could be reached from first principles. To breach confidentiality you must be satisfied (and be able to demonstrate in court if need be) that the benefits of breaching confidentiality outweigh the disadvantages to the patient. In this particular instance, the patient represents a danger to the public and, therefore, once you have exhausted all avenues within the confidential environment (i.e. by discussing the issue with the

patient over a reasonable period of time) then you may consider that there is value in breaching confidentiality.

Once you have made the decision to breach confidentiality, you should ask yourself who would be of most help to achieve the desired result. In this case, there would be value in involving the patient's wife before going to the DVLA. In fact, the wife is most likely already aware of the patient's condition anyway so it may not constitute a breach of confidentiality after all. The only concern would be the extent to which you would be affecting your relationship of trust with the patient; but any problem will be outweighed by the benefit to the public at large.

Scenario 7 — ANSWER: 1:B – 2:A – 3:D – 4:C – 5:E

1. There are occasions when you will be required to make an effort to attend late work meetings and your seniors will expect you to make an effort to attend them, within reason. In this particular question, it is clearly stated that you have been told about the meeting just as you were about to leave your shift and therefore your seniors should be able to understand that you may not be able to make it at such short notice, particularly if you have a valid reason. After all, there may be other colleagues who will be on study leave or on annual leave and may not be able to make it either. Therefore, E will be ranked as the least appropriate. You will go to your dinner.

2. The issue now is to determine in what circumstances you will be leaving your workplace. This is testing your teamwork ability:

    - Option D (the nurse). Why involve her since she is probably not even going to the meeting. (Remember, this is a junior doctors teaching session.) This will place the responsibility on her to pass on a message that she could not care less about, on a topic that she knows nothing about.

    - Option A (the junior doctor). This is better. You are involving a relevant member of the team and you are offering your apologies.

    - Option B (the organiser). This is the most proactive option. Not only are you discussing the matter with the person who will know best, you are also finding out about the nature of the meeting. This will also help you identify ways in which you can keep up to date with what was discussed.

3. We are now left with one option to analyse: option C (slipping away). Although you might find that it saves you a lot of hassle in the short term (it saves you having to justify there and then why you have to leave), you will find that people will be wondering what has happened to you. The uncertainty surrounding your departure, particularly if one team member remembers telling you about the meeting, could develop into resentment towards you and this is bad news. In addition, the option says that you would consider lying when asked about your departure, which is really not a good idea in terms of keeping a clean image and proving your integrity. For these reasons, it has to be worse than involving the nurse. Both cause a problem relating to poor teamwork but, in the case of C, you are treating the whole team badly (as opposed to simply abusing the nurse's kindness).

Important note
Some of you may have ranked the options as BADEC rather than BADCE (i.e. you may feel that slipping away unnoticed is worse than letting your partner down). This would be also acceptable and you may get partial marks for this.

Similarly, if you felt compelled to attend the teaching session rather than going out with your partner (i.e. BEADC), you may also get partial marks. This would demonstrate a strong commitment to your career, but may be slightly misplaced in relation to your need for a good work-life balance, particularly as the scenario makes no mention of the level of importance of the meeting. If the scenario said that the meeting was crucial to your job, then you would have to give up going out in favour of attending the meeting.

This illustrates how the same scenario can be looked at in different lights, thus leading to different rankings. In this case, the ideal answer recognises that, although work is important, you must be able to put it in perspective in relation to other priorities, particularly if the issue at stake is a simple teaching session.

Scenario 8   ANSWER: C, D, F

1. Option A is not wrong but it is a little premature (it will not be immediate or in the short term). The question asks for "immediate" action. Calling the GMC may come at a much later stage if the colleague presents a real danger to patients. For the time being, all we know is that a bag of marijuana has fallen out of his bag! The road to the GMC notification is not that quick. If the GMC needs to be involved, it will not be down to you to involve them anyway but down to the Clinical Director or the Medical Director. Your role is to inform a senior.

2. B is just as bad as A. If the police need to be called, it will be by a hospital manager or someone in charge after initial investigation (also not immediate). You are hardly going to get on the phone to the police as soon as you see the bag.

3. E is a bit naïve. Of course he will give you his reassurance. He might even tell you it was planted there by a vindictive love rival! Telling him that you will keep quiet if he gets rid of the evidence is unacceptable anyway. There is a problem that needs to be looked into (and which may or may not have an impact on patient safety in the long run) so you cannot ignore it.

4. G is a bit strong, though not entirely inappropriate; however, there are other people between you and the Clinical Director and you should use them (particularly if they are in other options – like the registrar in option F or a consultant).

5. This leaves us with the three correct options, which are also the most sensible ones. Option D (discussing the issue with your colleague) should really be your starting point. Because of the possible impact on patient safety you ought to discuss the matter with a senior colleague that you can trust (option F – the registrar) and, as a friend and doctor, it would be wise to advise your colleague to seek help before his drug problem escalates (option C).

Note on option C
Some people may argue that C is not appropriate because the colleague does not necessarily have a drug problem (he might just be supplying the drug to others, or maybe just carrying it for someone else). This may indeed be the case; however, if we look at all the remaining options (excluding D and F

which are not controversial), then C is the most appropriate and the most sensible.

Make sure that you always choose the number of options asked for in the wording of the questions. The question is not "What are the appropriate options" but the "MOST APPROPRIATE". They want three, give them three.

Important note
If you have answered D, F and G, you may be eligible for partial marks. Option G (reporting to the Clinical Director) is not inappropriate per se but is less appropriate than other options. You may consider reporting to the Clinical Director in the absence of your registrar or if you have substantial worries about your colleague. The reason why G does not appear in the "benchmark" answer is that the question was designed to test not only your integrity in reporting potentially unfit colleagues to a senior, but your ability to relate to and support a colleague in difficulty. This is illustrated by C.

Scenario 9 — ANSWER: B, C, G

1. Option A: Going to the GMC will be a little premature without any kind of preliminary investigation and without giving the consultant an opportunity to change. The matter should be first handled at local level and only escalated to GMC level by your seniors if the consultant continues to present a danger to patients despite their best efforts to resolve the situation. At your level, your concern should be to ensure that someone senior to you whom you can trust is aware of the situation (hence why C is appropriate). You would only ever consider going to the GMC yourself if none of your seniors acted appropriately in relation to the matter at hand.

2. Option B: Since the consultant is "obviously" drunk there is a chance that the clinic may need to be cancelled. At the very least, some of the appointments will need to be cancelled whilst others will be seen by other doctors. The wording here is quite vague ("Discuss cancelling the clinic session"), which makes it appropriate. If the wording had been stronger (such as "Tell the manager to cancel the clinic") then it may not have been appropriate as you might have needed to consider alternatives first.

3. Option C: As mentioned above, and as mentioned in the GMC's *Good Medical Practice*, you must involve a senior colleague that you can trust. As a rule you should consider going first to your registrar, then another

consultant, then the Clinical Director. Going too high too quickly may mean that you are overreacting. It may also make your seniors feel undermined if you are not giving them the opportunity to act before going to their boss. Since the only option here is to see a consultant then it would be appropriate.

4. Options D, E and F are all unacceptable. If the consultant is "obviously" drunk, there is no way that you would allow him to see patients, whether you are with him or he is with a chaperone; and certainly not on his own. Not only is it likely to attract complaints from patients, it may also make them lose faith in the Trust. You could get sacked for letting this happen.

5. Option G is over the top for the time being, particularly as the consultant has not actually seen patients yet, but it is not a totally wrong answer (it could be considered appropriate). So far we have only identified B and C as appropriate and, out of all other possibilities, G is the only remaining appropriate option (since A is really a remote possibility and D, E and F are unsafe or pose a strong reputation risk).

Scenario 10   ANSWER: 1:D – 2:E – 3:A – 4:B – 5:C

1. Many people think that it is illegal to prescribe for friends and family. This is not entirely correct. The GMC guidance is that "Wherever possible, you should avoid providing medical care to anyone with whom you have a close personal relationship." In practice you must distinguish between a one-off event that deals with a minor issue (such as a prescription for an inhaler) and a long-term doctor-patient relationship or an involvement with a major condition. There are examples of GPs who were suspended or struck off for caring a bit too much for their friends and family but we are not talking about such things here. Therefore E is not to be totally avoided.

2. You must look at the practicality of your answers and also at how far you are prepared to go to help your friend. There is a compromise to be reached between being friendly and being helpful. As a first port of call, it is always best and safest to send anyone to their GP (unless it is a real emergency, which this is not). Therefore, D should come first.

3. Look at the practicality and look at who is inconvenienced by each option:
    - Option A inconveniences him and A&E.

- Option B inconveniences you and A&E (and why can't he go to A&E himself anyway? He has to take responsibility for his actions and play his part in resolving the issue for himself).

- Option C could cause problems on the ward, as taking an inhaler from the ward effectively means taking an inhaler that was reserved for one of your patients.

- Option E inconveniences you and is probably the quickest thing to do.

Therefore, once you have tried the GP option, it is simplest, friendliest and quickest to write him a one-off prescription for his inhaler (on the basis that it is a one-off and that the prescription is in respect of a "safe" drug in his case). It will also mean that he will have to pay for it as a private prescription and therefore it won't take advantage of the NHS.

The order of the remaining options is purely in the order of the most to least convenient.

Important note
You would also score marks for ranking the options as DAEBC (preferring to send him to A&E rather than prescribing yourself – which is probably overdoing it on the safety angle considering that he is only after an inhaler). There are times when you can be both realistic and safe at the same time. In practice, if you felt uncomfortable prescribing for a friend or a member of your family, you should seek advice and assent from a senior colleague (preferably a consultant) so that someone above you is aware of the situation. By being open about the process, you will avoid sneaky accusations.

Scenario 11	ANSWER: 1:D – 2:B – 3:A – 4:C – 5:E

The key to this question is to identify how effective each option will be in resolving the matter and how sensitive your approach is. We will look at each option in reverse order of appropriateness.

1. Option E (keeping records) might sound good if you ever have to make a case to a senior colleague later on but it really feels like you are spying on your colleague and not addressing anything. Watching and waiting (for what?!) is also counterproductive as it almost implies that you hope someone else will do your dirty work for you. It is the worst option.

2. Option C (approach your colleague) might sound good because it gives the feeling that at least you are dealing with the colleague and not going straight away to a senior colleague, but the tone is very patronising. Your colleague might have personal problems that are causing the delay and C gives no indication that you have an understanding, or are trying to gain an understanding, of what these might be. Telling your colleague off will only create conflict. If someone needs to reprimand him, it will have to be someone more senior than him.

3. Option A (telling their senior) is a bit better because you are involving someone who can make a difference and they will try to get to the bottom of the problem with your colleague. This will include investigating any particular problem that may be causing the delay. You might not find out by yourself what is causing the delay but at least someone will and the problem should get resolved. There are other things that you can do though before you get to this stage.

4. Option B (discussing with other juniors) is slightly better because at least you are trying to see if the team has any ideas about the reasons behind the delay and whether there are solutions that can be found. Your other colleagues will undoubtedly also be affected by his late arrivals and therefore it makes sense to discuss the matter with them. Please note that this option is only ranking high because it mentions "junior doctors". If it mentioned "nurses" instead, then it would have no impact whatsoever and could be considered as gossip. It would therefore rank much lower.

5. Option D is the most helpful and therefore the highest ranked option. It is seeking to resolve the matter in a helpful and supportive manner.

Scenario 12   ANSWER: 1:C – 2:D – 3:A – 4:E – 5:B

1. The issue here is that you want to ensure that patients are safe at all times but you also want to try not to ruin your entire evening for the sake of a patient who should really be handled by someone else if possible. Therefore your approach will be to show a helpful attitude but also to ensure that the system works the way that it should work. In particular, you might have been asked to review a patient (no one said it was urgent!) but since you are leaving your shift, surely the SHO on call is the one who should be handling this and who should be available to handle such matters (otherwise you will spend your entire days at the hospital).

Against this background, you also have to consider that, as a junior doctor, you have responsibilities (hence why asking a consultant to take over will not rank high for a routine case). You also have to consider the patient safety element (hence why seeing the patient quickly is not a good idea – you never know, it may end up taking much longer than you thought it would take).

2. Your first approach should be to encourage the team to function the way it should. This means getting your colleague to trace the on call SHO (C). If he is too busy for that, you would consider doing it yourself (D); the reason being that it is really the on call SHO's job to deal with the patient and not yours. The primary responsibility to delegate to the on call SHO is your colleague's, not yours.

    Some of you may find that this is not a good team playing approach, but in fact it is. It is about defining boundaries and not creating confusion by going into someone else's territory. Imagine if you were the SHO on call and you found out that another doctor has been seeing some of your patients without telling you! This could be embarrassing for you as well as unsafe for your patients.

3. If the on call SHO is not available then we are now faced with three remaining options:

    ▪ Giving the patient to the consultant (E)
    ▪ Seeing him yourself (A)
    ▪ Seeing him quickly (B)

    Giving the patient to the consultant will place you in a bad light. Option E says "Tell your consultant". This makes it a direct command rather than a request for assistance. If the option was worded as "Ask the consultant if he would not mind seeing the patient" then it would rank higher. It should be down to your colleague to tell the consultant anyway, not down to you. You will therefore have to see the patient yourself.

    Seeing the patient quickly is simply unsafe, which makes it the worst option. Once you have seen him, he may need further care which will take you longer to organise. What would you do if, once you have seen the patient, you need to stay behind? We are back to square one. In addition, B says that your family will be waiting for you in the waiting room during that time. This is bad news as they will be a constant reminder for you that you are late and this will bring extra pressure onto you.

Scenario 13   ANSWER: 1:C – 2:E – 3:D – 4:A – 5:B

In this question, you need to ensure the safety of the patient, whilst minimising the impact on your colleagues.

1. Option C is both safe for the patient and convenient for the team. It will only inconvenience one single colleague.

2. Option E sounds like a good idea though it could be embarrassing for your colleague if he is not well prepared. Still, it is a safe option, it ensures that the team gets their session and only one colleague is inconvenienced.

3. Option D is very safe but will inconvenience everyone in the team. Also, you cannot cancel educational meetings every time there is an emergency, otherwise no one would ever get trained. Still, it is better than just slipping away (at least people know what is going on and where things stand) and therefore will need to rank higher than A.

4. Option A is very safe for the patient but awful for your colleagues who will be sitting around wondering what is going on.

5. Option B is the most unsafe of all. The scenario says that it is an emergency call.

Scenario 14   ANSWER: 1:B – 2:A – 3:C – 4:E – 5:D

1. Option D is a non-starter. You simply cannot ignore such an important issue. Your colleague may lose his job as a result of this; but, more importantly, patients may be placed in danger because of his addiction. Option D therefore has to come last.

2. All the other options involve reporting the matter but in various circumstances. When faced with such a choice, it sometimes helps to rewrite the options in a clearer, more concise manner:
    -   A: Report after telling your colleague
    -   B: Report after giving the colleague a chance to address the matter by himself
    -   C: Report without telling the colleague
    -   E: Report only if you have concerns about his performance.

130

E is potentially unsafe as you should not just be concerned about his current performance but also future performance. Your colleague might be fine for now but his addiction might escalate and spiral out of control. Will you wait until he kills a patient to act?

Out of the other three, the order is fairly obvious: B, A, C.

Scenario 15 ANSWER: A, B, C

1. Potentially, the patient is asking you to help him commit insurance fraud. So there is absolutely no way you will delete the information from the notes. That means that D and E are not suitable and that C is suitable. If you ever received a court order asking to see the notes, your integrity would be questioned (remember how Dr Shipman altered his records!).

2. Option A is appropriate because, unless the patient has consented, you will not be able to give any information to the insurance company. It is appropriate because you need to be absolutely clear about the boundaries. The insurance company may subsequently refuse to give the patient any insurance but this will be the patient's problem for refusing to give consent in the first place. (Note that option A cannot be generalised. There are cases where you can divulge information to a third party without the patient's consent, most often when there is a danger of serious harm or death to others, e.g. child abuse).

3. Option F is not correct. Unless you have the patient's consent, you cannot reveal the information. Saying the opposite to the patient would just be telling a lie and would be unethical.

4. Option B is appropriate as, although you may never get consent from the patient to reveal information, you should always notify him whenever you are considering breaching confidentiality. Making this clear will reassure the patient without compromising your integrity. In reality, you would not seek to breach the patient's confidentiality voluntarily in this case. But you can envisage a scenario whereby the insurance company seeks a court order to obtain information from the GP (e.g. to check on a claim), in which case you would be forced to reveal any information the court order is asking for. Saying otherwise would mislead the patient.

5. Option G would be suitable only if you contacted the insurance company without naming the patient, say to ask for advice about whether they actually care about this type of information. As soon as you name him, you are breaching confidentiality in an unacceptable context.

Scenario 16 ANSWER: 1:D – 2:A – 3:C – 4:B – 5:E

1. Whenever you are confronted with the issue of a gift given by a patient you must look at the nature of the gift, the circumstances surrounding the gift and the impact that a refusal would have on the doctor-patient relationship. Your main concern will be to ensure that you are not being bribed by the patient and that the situation cannot be construed as bribery. On the other hand, you do not want the refusal of a gift to affect the doctor-patient relationship negatively.

2. In this particular example, the amount of the gift is unusually high, particularly in view of the short-term relationship that you have had with the patient. The wording of the question goes out of its way to emphasise a detachment (short admission, only contact was during ward rounds, patient not expected to come back). Therefore it would make sense to refuse the gift, at least in the first instance.

3. There are two options to do this: D which is polite and also shows a degree of care and empathy, and A which is a bit more bureaucratic but still acceptable. Therefore the first two most suitable actions must be D and A in that order.

4. We are now left with three options to accept the gift, with different contexts:

    ▪ Option E (keeping quiet) has to be the least appropriate. In fact it is verging on unethical and dishonest (and might actually expose you to blackmail from the patient in the worst possible scenario).

    ▪ Giving the gift to your loved one (B) might sound like a good idea but is still for personal gain. It is not as good as using the money for the good of everyone on the ward. After all, the gift was for care given to the patient and therefore rendered by the whole ward. Also giving the gift to the team will make it less likely to be construed as bribery. It is

132

also an excellent demonstration of selflessness and teamwork. Therefore C is more appropriate than B.

Scenario 17 — ANSWER: 1:D – 2:B – 3:E – 4:A – 5:C

1. The situation is tricky because on one hand you must try to respect the confidentiality of the patient but on the other hand it is not a very practical thing to do if the person he wants to keep in the dark is actually working on the ward where he is staying. In particular, you will want to make sure that the care of the other patients is not compromised by the issue (bearing in mind that the safety of the other patients will always be more important than the confidentiality of one patient). You also have to make sure that you do not give in to patients too easily, particularly if their requests appear unreasonable.

2. Based on the above, it seems sensible to try to reach a compromise with the patient in order to avoid any disruption. Option D explores the reasons behind the patient's request and constitutes the most appropriate action. You might find that his fears are unfounded or that, simply by reassuring him about the team's professionalism, he will accept having the nurse around.

3. Option B is then the second most suitable because it looks after the patient's confidentiality without disturbing any team member (or not much anyway). However, it is not as good as D, which at least attempts to eliminate the constraint of confidentiality in a diplomatic way.

4. Once you have done your best to sort out the situation without disturbance, either by reasoning with the patient or by issuing directives to the team, then you are left with three options:
   - Option A: tell the patient to put up with it (not necessarily a bad idea but could create problems).
   - Option E: transfer the patient to a different part of the ward. Good idea too and better than A; at least you are doing something concrete about the problem, with limited disturbance.
   - C: Tell the nurse to take some time off – unthinkable. She must have better things to do with her annual leave than to avoid patients!

Telling the patient to put up with the situation is not something that you should dismiss outright, however rude it sounds. However, in practice, you should be able to demonstrate that you have taken reasonable steps to maintain their confidentiality before giving up. This could include taking the patient to another ward. It could also include asking the nurse to work in a different ward for a while, though you ought to think twice about doing this as it may have an impact on patient care. In any case, it does not include sending the nurse away on holiday. If you ever need to tell a patient that there is little choice, then you should do so in a diplomatic manner.

Important note
You would score partial marks for answering DEBAC instead of DBEAC.

Scenario 18 ANSWER: 1:D – 2:E – 3:B – 4:C – 5:A

1. In a question like this, it is easy to jump to conclusions. Some may think that the consultant is behaving inappropriately with the patient; others may think that there must be a good reason for his behaviour. After all, he may have been reassuring a patient who was distraught. Never ignore the issue, but equally you don't want to take drastic action until you have got your facts right.

2. Option A (doing nothing and making assumptions) is the worst option. If there is a problem, even potentially, you simply cannot ignore it.

3. Option C (reporting to the Clinical Director) is a possibility but it is quite strong. You would have to have reasonable concerns about the situation before you can go to the Clinical Director and therefore there are steps that you should take before seeing him. The fact that it ranks fourth does not mean that it is a wrong thing to do. It is just not as appropriate as some of the other options given the scenario and its ambiguities.

4. The three remaining options (B, D and E) are all about finding out more about the situation and seeking advice. They are therefore preferred over the other two.

   ▪ D is your preferred option because it enables you to discuss the situation with the consultant in a non-confrontational manner.

   ▪ E comes next because you can get a different perspective from an appropriate trusted colleague. He may know the consultant's manner with patients more than you do and might think that it is more likely to be appropriate for that consultant than not. On the other hand, he might have come across complaints from other people before and can make a more informed decision than you can. The fact that he is running the clinic next door also means that the advice will be immediate, which is an advantage.

- B comes third because sending the patient out would be quite a brave thing to do, especially if nothing untoward was happening. If the patient was simply being reassured by the consultant, the consultant and the patient might find your actions a little bit offensive. You would need to think twice before doing this because you could irritate your consultant and the patient (hence why it comes third) but it might still be an appropriate action to take if it means that it can highlight a real problem.

Do not jump to conclusions

Generally speaking, most doctors conduct themselves ethically. If you notice something strange, there is usually a good explanation for it and you should avoid jumping to conclusions too quickly. It does not mean that you have to ignore warning signs, but that you should take a gradual approach to make sure that you do not create more problems than there were in the first place. Explore the facts as appropriately as you can before escalating the matter further.

Gauge the level of appropriateness of the physical contact

The question talks about a consultant with his arms around the shoulder of a patient. Although you should avoid physical contact with patients if possible, there may be situations where such behaviour could be accepted. If you are given a question with a more suggestive wording (such as a consultant in an embrace with a patient or kissing a patient), then your approach should be a bit less subtle since the breach of duties will be more obvious.

Scenario 19 — ANSWER: 1:B – 2:C – 3:A – 4:D – 5:E

1. This is a difficult set of options. The first task is to eliminate the options which do not deal with the problem:

   - Option E: it is true that your colleague should learn how to handle such situations in future but she is not going to learn by seeing this particular patient there and then. If she was reduced to tears by the experience she will not be the best doctor for this patient. This is an issue of personal safety but also of her fitness to practise with this particular man (i.e. she might not be thinking clearly).

- Option D is a little more difficult to spot. Seeing him yourself sounds like the right thing to do but it is the second part of the sentence which should make you rank it low. Rearranging his appointments so that he is seen early in the list will certainly reduce the likelihood of future delays for him. However, it may be practically difficult to arrange and will impact negatively on other patients. Ultimately, this option ranks very low because it effectively rewards his actions and condones his behaviour, which is just unacceptable. Option D therefore ranks fourth.

2. You are now faced with the three remaining options which are all attempting to sort out the problem safely and without giving in to the patient:

  - Option A: send the patient home, cancelling his appointment. This sounds like revenge and will probably infuriate the patient ever more.

  - Option C: get him to see another doctor or to come back some other time. This is more proactive in sorting out the problem than A but it unfairly places the problem with another doctor.

  - Option B: see him yourself and explain that his behaviour was unacceptable. This is the best option since you are dealing with the patient's behaviour as well as ensuring that he gets seen thereby not aggravating the situation further.

Scenario 20 ANSWER: 1:B – 2:D – 3:C – 4:A – 5:E

1. Option E (sending the patient home) is just plain wrong. He has already come to see you with chest pains and you have done nothing. He would be better off going to A&E if it is not improving. This is just hoping for the best. It is the most unsafe and least appropriate option.

2. Option A (searching for the instructions) is also unsafe because it is wasting time, though at least you are attempting to find a solution and no

rejecting responsibility for the patient. If you find the instructions then you will have to read them too, assuming that they can be interpreted quickly.

3. Option C is neither ideal nor totally wrong. It might work but there is a risk attached to it. Still it is better than wasting your time finding instructions that may not exist.

4. Options B and D are the two most appropriate options because they ensure that patient safety is not compromised. Out of the two, it is obviously preferable to see if the nurse can do the ECG rather than send the patient to A&E. She might appear busy with a patient but she might also be able to leave the patient on his own for a few minutes.

Scenario 21 ANSWER: B, C, D

1. There is clearly a patient safety angle here and a situation which is very serious as the nurse put a patient in danger for purely selfish reasons. Therefore option A (waiting for another incident) seems a weak option. B seems a more reasonable approach which enables you to discuss the specific event with the management team and agree on any disciplinary matters.

2. Before you can discuss the event with the management team, you will need to gather some information (D). In particular, there may have been specific circumstances that led the nurse to behave in such an odd manner. Maybe she is experiencing depression or she is unhappy at work. It is not an excuse for her behaviour, but gaining some insight will help address the problem more effectively.

3. There is also clearly an issue of training as it is not practical that only one person should know how to use the machine. Therefore C is a strong candidate.

4. This gives us B, C and D as the most likely candidates, with A having been rejected as too weak for the circumstances. What about the others?

    ▪   Going to the PCT (E) is premature since the matter has not been handled internally. Therefore it is not as appropriate as other more pressing matters such as organising training to ensure that such an incident does not reoccur. Even if you went to the PCT, the head is certainly not the right person to contact about it.

- Writing to the patient (F) looks like a good idea. However, (i) it may be more appropriate to ask him to come for a discussion and (ii) ensuring that the incident does not reoccur is more important than writing to the patient. This could be the fourth most appropriate answer if you were allowed four. But you are not!

- Warning your colleagues by email (G) is simply unhelpful. It isolates the nurse and builds tension within the team. It creates a big team playing problem and does not help create a safer environment.

Scenario 22   ANSWER: 1:C – 2:B – 3:A – 4:D – 5:E

1. The main issue in this scenario is that you need to determine the woman's wishes and that she cannot express them in a way that would satisfy you. The father is able to act as an interpreter but you cannot necessarily rely on a close family member to interpret reliably for her in such a situation. You might also need to examine the woman and it will be difficult if the father is present. All in all, your preferred choice should be to talk to the woman with an interpreter in a non-threatening environment and C is therefore the best.

2. With C gone, B is your next best choice as you are still able to get the information safely from the woman's mouth through the interpreter, though this time there is a risk that she may be influenced by her father's presence.

3. Out of A, D and E:

    - Option A is your next best choice. That is really your only alternative in the absence of an interpreter (unless a nurse or someone in your practice can interpret too, but this is not an option).

    - Option D is just unhelpful as you would not be able to determine whether that new person is any less of a threat than the father.

    - Option E is unsafe as you would never be able to determine whether she actually understands what you are telling her.

Important note
You would score partial marks for answering CBDAE instead of CBADE.

Scenario 23   ANSWER: 1:B – 2:C – 3:D – 4:E – 5:A

1. This is an old lady whom you know well who offers you a small gift with no obvious bad intentions. So there is no reason to refuse the gift. In fact, refusing the gift may upset the patient and may negatively affect the doctor-patient relationship. Hence, A and E will come last, with E being slightly better as, at least, it gives you an opportunity to discuss what would have been the right thing to do and to learn from the experience.

2. B is the most appropriate option because the nature and value of the gift are appropriate in view of the ongoing relationship that you have with the patient. The other two options for accepting the gift are:

    ▪ Option C: inform the practice manager. If you really feel that the gift is a problem for you, then this is a good way to alleviate your problems of conscience.

    ▪ Option D: tell the patient that it must be the last time. It is a bit patronising and unnecessary given the nature of the gift, the frequency and the circumstances surrounding the gift. Because of this, it is less appropriate than C.

Scenario 24   ANSWER: 1:A – 2:D – 3:C – 4:B – 5:E

It is best not to jump to conclusions, and to get your facts right first. Hence, A is the most appropriate. You never know: your colleague might have had a perfectly good reason to perform the examination but simply failed to record it.

1. Option D (seeking advice from trusted senior colleagues) is also a good idea as it ensures that you are doing the right thing and it also enables you to address the issue without being too formal to start with. It will help establish the facts before you can take the matter further. However, it would be inappropriate to go to a senior colleague without identifying first whether there is a real cause for concern or a real doubt. You cannot do

this without having any details about the nature of the problem; therefore it comes second in order of appropriateness.

2. Options A and D are the most appropriate options because there is uncertainty about whether the examination was genuine and therefore a graduated approach is required in order to get the facts right. The three remaining options are harsher in their approach and present some flaws:

  ▪ Option C is failing to get any information from the patient and involves reporting to the Clinical Director straight away. This is not necessarily a bad move, and you might consider it once you have raised the issue more informally with other senior colleagues first (D).

  ▪ Option B is more or less telling the patient that the colleague is guilty; it is therefore inappropriate. If the patient has been the victim of an unscrupulous doctor, then you would need to have a discussion with your seniors first before approaching the patient about the matter. You cannot jump to conclusions so quickly and tell the patient that the examination might constitute an assault without getting all the facts. The best that you can do in the first instance is to tell the patient that you will look into it and get back to them.

  ▪ Option E is worse than B because it is ignoring the hierarchy within your team and launching the full system against him when there may not be a cause for concern. It is not your role to go to the GMC unless your seniors fail to act appropriately. In addition, before the case can go to the GMC, it will have to go through the local complaints procedure; hence E must follow B in the order of appropriateness.

Important note
You would score partial marks for answering ACDBE instead of ADCBE.

Scenario 25 | ANSWER: D, F, G

The fact that your colleague has Hepatitis C is only an issue if he is performing procedures where he is exposing his patients to a risk. Therefore, unless you believe that he performs risky procedures, you have no reason to intervene. This makes D one of the appropriate actions.

1. Option A is not an option because, even if you noticed that your colleague performed risky procedures, you would report the matter to one of your senior colleagues and not to Personnel/Medical Staffing.

2. Option B is just rubbish. A vaccine against Hepatitis C virus does not currently exist.

3. Option C is not appropriate because you would not report to a senior colleague unless he performed risky procedures (D).

4. Option E is not appropriate because it is not the role of the senior sister to spy on your colleague. She is not responsible for his actions.

5. F and G are both appropriate because they encourage your colleague to take responsibility for the situation, to seek advice from appropriate sources and to raise the matter himself with senior colleagues so the team can identify how to deal with the issue.

Note

In practice, you would remind your colleague that he should steer clear of risky procedures and encourage him to go to Occupational Health for advice (and not for vaccination!). You should also encourage him to discuss the situation with his seniors, so that they are aware of the issue and can support him, and with his defence union, so that he is aware of the risks to which he is exposed. His defence union will also be able to advise him about the best way to approach senior colleagues.

If you felt that your colleague posed a danger to patients, and you would need some kind of proof for that (for example if he told you that he performed risky procedures, or if someone else told you, or if you observed it), then you would need to discuss the issue with your colleague and impose on him to discuss the matter with a senior colleague. You could offer to go with him for support. If he fails to do so, then you would need to discuss the issue with seniors yourself.

Scenario 26   ANSWER: A, B, D

1. One important aspect to consider here is that your role is to support the secretary in getting the issue sorted out but not necessarily to sort it out for her. Hence A and B are appropriate. She has senior colleagues that she can approach to start the process.

2. Alternatively, she could also approach the HR department about it but it would not be your place to do it for her. Therefore F is not the most suitable.

3. There will be little value in confronting the consultant directly about the issue as it would lead to confrontation. So C is not the most appropriate. G is also inappropriate as it feels like public humiliation for the consultant in question and is unlikely to lead to any substantial result.

4. Approaching another senior colleague (D) would be more constructive as it would enable the senior team to become aware of the problem and to find a suitable way of approaching the consultant in question (rather than the confrontational style of C).

5. Contacting the GMC (E) is just wrong unless the situation has reached such proportions that the local systems cannot handle it. It would thus not feature as one of the "most appropriate" options in such a situation.

Important note
You may score partial marks if you answered ABC instead of ABD as C is a possibility in some cases (e.g. if you know the consultant in question well), though the outcome is fairly unpredictable.

Scenario 27   ANSWER: A, B, G

1. This question tests your integrity. If you have made a mistake then you must own up to it, whether it has any consequences or not.

2. Option C is not safe as you simply cannot wait until the patient has a reaction to the drug in order to take any action.

3. Option D shows that you are being honest with your team but you must also tell the patient if you have injected them with the wrong product, even if this means taking the consequences (hence why A is appropriate).

4. Option E might be open and attempting to minimise the stress on the patient but it is dishonest. It is NOT a procedure that is sometimes carried out. It is just a mistake that sometimes happens.

5. Option F blames the nurse. Whoever brought the wrong product, you are the one who injected it so you must take responsibility for your mistake. If there is a problem with the nurse then you can sort it out later with her but do not involve the patient with such interpersonal staff matters. This will look unprofessional and can reduce the patient's confidence in the medical team.

6. Option A is the most honest answer. You will just have to bite the bullet. Option B ensures that a senior colleague is informed and that the right course of action is being followed. Option G ensures that the team can learn from the incident.

Scenario 28 ANSWER: A, C, D

The simplest approach is to proceed by elimination:

-   Option G (critical incident form) is not an answer to someone who is washed out. You should complete a form whenever a critical incident occurs, regardless of how tired the doctor is. In any case, by the time you complete the form and it gets processed, he will have had plenty of time to make other mistakes. This is a red herring.

-   Option F (contacting Occupational Health) is also ineffective. Firstly, if you are going to contact someone about it, it should be one of your seniors. Secondly, Occupational Health are not responsible for that registrar so they would not be able to do much.

-   Option E (locum through Medical Staffing). Getting a locum should not be your decision. If a locum is required to relieve the pressure on the registrar then it should be done through the proper channels, as a result of a discussion between your registrar and his seniors. You are interfering.

You are now left with A, B, C and D. All of them are possible candidates but you need to eliminate one of them. Option B stands out because it feels harsh, patronising and not very supportive in relation to the other answers. If he ends up actually placing patient safety at risk then you may resort to discussing the situation with the consultant, but you should aim to achieve this without having to threaten the registrar.

Scenario 29   ANSWER: 1:D – 2:B – 3:C – 4:A – 5:E

1. This is a really awkward situation because the patient is new and you do not want to destroy his confidence in you at the outset. On the other hand, you must also find a safe approach.

2. Option E is very unsafe. You are taking a big gamble. You can't have a patient walking around the streets with a week's worth of methadone. Some GPs who have done that in the past have ended up being struck off (it came to light when the patient took the whole dose in one go and died). It has to be the least appropriate.

3. Option A is also unsafe to the extent that it relies on the patient to tell you what their normal dose is, but it is safer than E because you are only giving one dose.

4. Having eliminated the unsafe options, we are now left with:
   - B: send the patient to A&E
   - C: Wait until the notes arrive
   - D: Call the previous GP.

   The order D, B and C seems logical. Calling the previous GP will give you a reliable way to identify the correct dose. Sending the patient to A&E is not ideal because doctors probably have better things to do there but at least it is a safe option for the patient. They can check that he is a heroin addict through a urine test and prescribe one dose. Waiting for the notes and prescribing nothing feels a bit like a cop-out but it is sometimes better than taking a risk. The patient always has the option to go to a local rehabilitation centre.

Note
Sending the patient to a local rehabilitation centre was not an option, but if it had been an option it would take precedence over sending the patient to A&E.

Scenario 30 ANSWER: 1:C – 2:D – 3:B – 4:E – 5:A

There is a definite problem so you cannot do nothing. Therefore option A comes last.

1. Option E (confronting the colleague at the team meeting) is the least effective of the remaining options. It will probably ensure that it never happens again but it will humiliate him and will create a problem within the team.

2. Option C: as ever, you should try to discuss the situation with the colleague first and make him realise that he has done wrong. He must understand how such behaviour affects the team and that it is not acceptable. Because there is no effect on patient safety, there may not be a need to report the matter straight away, hence why warning him is a better option.

3. Option B is harsh and does not give your colleague the opportunity to redeem himself. Because it is an issue which has affected the junior doctors (since they had to cover for him), it makes sense to address the situation as a team (D). The team can then decide how best to address the matter, whether this is by having a strong word with the colleague, or by reporting the matter to a senior colleague (particularly if it happens often!).

Important note
You may score partial marks if you answered CBDEA instead of CDBEA.

Scenario 31 ANSWER: 1:D – 2:E – 3:B – 4:C – 5:A

1. Option A: the fact that he is watching the images on his own computer makes no difference. It is the act of looking at the child pornography that matters. Therefore option A should rank last in appropriateness.

2. Options B (police), D (senior colleague) and E (HR department) are fairly easy to rank. You can start from within your team and go towards the outside. So, in order of appropriateness, you should first consider talking to a senior colleague, then HR and then the police. You do not want to undermine the people you work with, so you should always go to a senior

first. If they are not available or are not doing anything about the problem, then you may consider escalating to a different level (first at Trust level, then outside). Ranking the police as the least appropriate of these three options does not mean that it is inappropriate to call them. We are simply saying that it is not necessarily your role to call them and that, before the police are called, a range of internal people (senior, HR) should be involved.

3. The main problem is with option C (sending an anonymous note) because, although it looks like you are doing something, it is rather counterproductive. You are introducing fear in your colleague (which may have an impact on his performance), you are not actually trying to resolve the fundamental problem and you are introducing a climate of suspicion within the team (he will forever be trying to identify who sent him that letter). So, essentially, you are not really doing anything useful and it is just about marginally better than doing nothing at all. The real issue here is child protection. No need to be too subtle about it.

Scenario 32 ANSWER: B, D, E

1. Adult pornography is not illegal. However, it would certainly be seen by both patients and staff as very unprofessional to watch it in any workplace environment, particularly a hospital, where patients can become exposed to it. Your colleague is acting unprofessionally by watching it in an inappropriate place. He is going against hospital policy, but in many ways that is his problem more than yours. However, it is likely to become a real problem if it starts to offend others, particularly patients.

2. Because it is not illegal, a gentle warning about problems the registrar might encounter is probably the first thing that you would do. Hence B is one of the most suitable options. The issue of patient safety also cannot be ignored and therefore E is appropriate too.

3. Option G (police) is irrelevant since it is not illegal. Option C (confronting him as a group) is just humiliating when there is no need to do so. If possible, you should take a tactful approach.

4. Options A and F might become an option later on but they would need to be initiated by a senior colleague on your team if they felt that the problem

needed further investigation or action. It is not for you to make such decisions.

5. This leaves us with D, which seems a sensible thing to do. If you have real concerns about someone's professionalism because of the way they act then you should feel free to approach a senior colleague about it. The senior colleague may act or they may not, but at least you have raised the issue. In the chronology of events, you would tactfully seek to sort the problem directly with the registrar first before going to the consultant.

Scenario 33 ANSWER: 1:A – 2:B – 3:C – 4:D – 5:E

1. This question is a trick question where doing nothing is actually the right thing to do! This is gossip about someone you don't know getting drunk at a Christmas party at which you were not present. Why bother…? Option A is therefore the most appropriate.

2. The rest follows in the order of escalation, i.e. the higher up you go and the more people you involve, the less suitable the option.

Scenario 34 ANSWER: 1:A – 2:C – 3:B – 4:D – 5:E

Before you do anything (and this includes reporting her), you need to get more information about the nurse's actions. There is no doubt that taking antibiotics for personal use from the trolley is unprofessional and she should also be made aware of this. Hence option A should come before you address the problem at a more senior level.

1. Writing a critical incident form (E) will achieve nothing at all. It has to be the least appropriate option as there is nothing critical about it.

2. The other options (B, C, D) involve reporting to various people. You should start with the nurse's immediate superior and escalate on the nursing hierarchy. However, going to the Director of Nursing is quite a strong action to take and, before you do this, you may want to seek advice from your own consultant. In any case, he may be able to play a role in resolving the matter within the department rather than making a big fuss

about a relatively small issue (it would be different if she were taking controlled drugs instead of antibiotics).

Important note
If the scenario stated that, as a result of the nurse's actions, the patient's health had been compromised then the ranking would be CBDEA, i.e. all options in the same order except for A, which comes last.

Scenario 35 ANSWER: A, C, F

1. As part of a team it is important that you show some flexibility in your relationship with your colleagues, particularly if they have requests that are not unreasonable. Do to others as you would want others to do for you! However, you should ensure that patient safety is never compromised.

2. Option D (insist he stays) seems harsh in a context where all the jobs have been done and this is a special occasion, particularly if he clears it with a senior before and if you can cover for him for the remainder of the day.

3. Option E (Medical Staffing) seems pointless since it will take time and they will only tell you to clear the matter with a senior colleague (which is option A).

4. Option B (let him slip away) is the optimum flexibility but it is not very safe. What if the registrar needs to get hold of him urgently? Also, the registrar or someone else may have had plans for him, thinking that he would be around, and therefore it would be best practice to let someone senior know.

5. Option G (redirecting bleep to on call) is unsafe as the on call hasn't started. In any case, if you take the responsibility to let your colleague go then you should take the problems that come with it.

6. In this context, options A, C and F seem the most logical options to retain.

Scenario 36 ANSWER: 1:B – 2:A – 3:C – 4:D – 5:E

Most people would tell you that they would just ignore it. However, since we are in a medical selection context, you could at least make an effort to see if he is okay! It does not cost much and no one could fault you for doing this. Hence B has to be the most appropriate option.

1. The truth is that you would not want to launch a full medical team after every drunk person in the street if there is no real emergency. Therefore C, D and E, which are quite involved when there is nothing to suggest an emergency, would be over the top (he is only vomiting, there is no mention of blood or anything drastic). Option A is therefore second best.

2. If you did decide to do something then E would be pointless since you are near A&E and the tramp hardly justifies monopolising an ambulance in such circumstances. Therefore E comes last.

3. After that, it is a case of choosing between taking him to A&E yourself or fetching someone from A&E to take him in. If you want to be a Good Samaritan, do it in a way that is least disturbing for your colleagues. There is no need to take an A&E member out of A&E for this. You should do it yourself.

Scenario 37 ANSWER: 1:D – 2:A – 3:E – 4:B – 5:C

1. Option D is the most sensible and the safest approach since you are well trained and have practice. Whether you can get away with it will very much depend on the consultant's ego.

2. Option A is also safe (in fact this is what would happen if no one in the team had ALS training). However, it comes second to D because you are only providing basic care to the patient (albeit safe care) and not the maximum care that is provided under D.

3. Option E is unsafe because you have to wait for help and you are doing nothing in the meantime to stop an unsafe situation; but at least expert help should be quick arriving.

4. Option B is unsafe and you are not acting in the patient's best interest.

5. Option C is chaotic. Team members will get confused between mixed messages. The consultant will be undermined and all this will build resentment. In fact, the patient is likely to be worse off than if the consultant handled the whole event by himself (option B).

Scenario 38   ANSWER: C, F, H

1. Option A would only be an option if you felt that you were being bullied (in which case hospital procedures may indicate that you should complain either to a senior colleague or Human Resources). However, there are many options that you can choose before making a formal complaint. The question suggests that it is a one-off incident or a first occurrence. If it had suggested that it happened frequently then A would be a possible appropriate action; but in the absence of more details, we can leave it out.

2. Option B is not appropriate because this is a matter between the consultant and you. By complaining to a senior nurse you are seeking support from someone who will not want to interfere in this hierarchy and who really has nothing to do with the problem. At best she can have a word with the consultant but the consultant will feel aggrieved that you have involved people who are unrelated to the incident.

3. Option C is non-committal and encourages you to think properly about your actions before going ahead. This should certainly feature in the list of appropriate actions. Generally, in conflict situations, it is best to step out and think with a clear head.

4. Option D is the "tit-for-tat" response and will only inflame the situation. Your consultant probably does not realise that he is out of order and therefore any attempt to respond in a similar manner will achieve nothing. Besides, sorting out the problem in front of the patient is not the best solution. Your consultant will never forgive you for embarrassing him.

5. Option E not only involves the patient in a conflict which is really none of their concern, but you are also undermining the consultant's credibility at the same time. This is probably one of the worst actions that you can take in the circumstances. If you need to involve external parties, make sure you involve people who can actually help resolve the problem. The patient is not one of them.

6. Option F is a sensible course of action. If you have a problem with someone, talk to them. It may not be a nice meeting but at least they will know how you feel and they may even learn something about themselves in the process. This is the best approach to regaining a sensible working relationship with the consultant and you may find that he respects you for this.

7. Option G is just inappropriate. To complete a critical incident form, there needs to be a critical incident, i.e. an incident that had or could have had an impact on patient care. The team must be able to learn from the incident so that a concrete solution can be implemented to prevent future occurrences. They do not deal with personality issues.

8. Option H belongs to the "Involving a third party" category, but this time your education supervisor is one of the most suitable people to involve. There are three reasons for this: (i) he is responsible for your education and the incident was part of the educational process; (ii) he is a consultant and part of your hierarchy; (iii) he is in a position to intervene or provide advice at a relevant level.

Scenario 39 ANSWER: 1:D – 2:A – 3:E – 4:C – 5:B

1. We have a situation where we don't know if the colleague has had one sip or more, why they were drinking and whether they have a drink problem or just a temporary weakness. Therefore it is important to act with a degree of diplomacy.

2. On the other hand, there is an issue of fitness to practise. In the worst-case scenario, the colleague may be unsafe. In the best-case scenario, he may not be unsafe but he will smell of alcohol, which can be construed as unprofessional.

3. Options B and C both encourage you to drop the matter and are therefore the least appropriate options. In cases of alcohol intake whilst at work, you cannot ignore the patient safety aspect. Therefore dropping the matter is out of the question. Out of the two options, C is slightly better than B because at least you are warning him that you might do something in future, whilst in B you are simply giving up.

4. Options A and D are both appropriate options as you demonstrate that you understand the gravity of the situation and that you are (i) talking to your

colleague about it and (ii) involving senior colleagues. D has a softer approach than A and is probably more appropriate in the circumstances described. If the question had actually said that the colleague was visibly drunk then you may have preferred the stronger approach dictated by A.

5. We know that D should be the first option and that C and B should be the bottom options. The main problem is whether A is better than E or vice versa. The dilemma is as follows: option A is slightly harsh whereas E allows you more flexibility by making you seek advice from other colleagues. On the other hand, E also means spreading rumours/gossips about your colleague, which could undermine his standing in the team.

6. The key to the dilemma is in the level of efficiency achieved by each option in helping the matter progress. In option A you are being upfront with the colleague and, with your colleague's knowledge, you are going to a relevant person who will be in a good position to discuss and resolve the matter. With option E, you are going to the rest of the team behind your colleague's back. Furthermore, those colleagues will only be able to advise you and once you have received that advice you will be on your own again to make a decision. E therefore looks attractive but will yield little, whilst A, although slightly harsh, will ensure that something gets done. It is also the more open approach of the two.

Scenario 40 ANSWER: A, C, E

1. Option D is not acceptable. The fact that the mistake had no impact on the outcome does not mean that you do not have to act.

2. In such a situation, the consultant (who is ultimately responsible for the patient) should be informed. A critical incident form should also be completed as it is a mistake that could be avoided with better processes in place. An investigation into the process is required to determine where it went wrong and how future occurrences can be prevented. Option A is therefore the most suitable option. Option B can be dismissed because you should not wait until mistakes have been made several times to raise the issue and/or take corrective action.

3. Informing senior Trust managers (G) is not strictly relevant unless there is a serious risk of the Trust being sued as a result of the mistake (in which case it would be important that the Trust lawyers are informed as soon as

possible). If the relatives had threatened to sue, for example, then you would need to go to your Clinical Director as soon as possible so that he can involve the relevant managers. In the context of this particular scenario we are not told of any particular threat and the relevant Trust authorities will be informed via the critical incident form, which should be enough given the circumstances.

4. Informing the rest of the team (C) is an important factor because they will need to learn from the situation at an individual level. It will not have any impact on the patient who died but the team will become a lot more aware of the type of issues that can arise. They can then play an important role in implementing changes within the team to make sure that such a mistake does not reoccur.

5. Options E and F both raise the issue of talking to the relatives. The options imply that the consultant was not present at the time of the incident and the scenario states explicitly that the relatives are upset (though we are not sure whether they are upset only because of the death of the patient or because they became aware that a mistake was made). Waiting until the consultant comes back could take a while and it would be careless to let the relatives wait around for any length of time. If there are sensitive issues to discuss, you could always let them know that you would like to talk to your consultant before going into detail but, in the absence of the consultant, you will need to meet with the relatives sooner rather than later (unless, of course, there is a registrar around, but this is not an option here). Option E is therefore more appropriate than F.

Scenario 41 ANSWER: 1:C – 2:B – 3:D – 4:A – 5:E

1. The question says that the patient is 17. She is therefore technically still a minor (being under the age of 18) and you have a child protection responsibility.

2. This scenario deals with a sad situation but there is no hint that you must deal with it at this very minute. Therefore, in doubt, and given that you have time in front of you, you should seek advice from other members of your team before doing anything. If you are about to breach a patient's confidentiality, it is always best to make sure that you have got it absolutely right. Therefore option C is ranked at the top.

3. Your duty will be to protect the patient. Had the patient been over 18 and with old small bruises then you could argue that the onus would be on her to make a decision for herself and that all you could do would be to provide advice. However, the scenario is quite clear that she is only 17 and that the bruises are severe. Therefore there is some justification for breaching confidentiality to ensure that she is not placed in danger physically, socially or mentally. Options B and D are both possible candidates. Option B is very harsh but you are breaching confidentiality with the patient's full knowledge. Option D takes a softer approach which is more in line with what one would expect, but it finishes badly by mentioning that you will go behind the patient's back. Although not strictly unethical, it should certainly be avoided if possible as it could impair the relationship and trust that the patient has with you. Therefore B, although harsher, is more suitable, closely followed by D.

4. It remains to allocate A and E to the last two places, which means having to decide whether it would be best to have a discussion with the patient's partner or to do nothing. Going to the patient's partner could have disastrous consequences. He may feel threatened and, given that we are told that he is a violent criminal who takes drugs, one could ask what would be achieved by such a discussion other than more trouble for the patient. We can therefore conclude that, on balance, it would be safer for the patient if you did nothing than if you had a discussion with her partner. By giving her time to reflect, she may well come to a safer decision by herself later on. This places options A and E in fourth and fifth position respectively.

Note
This is a rare example when doing nothing may actually be better than taking an action which, on balance of probabilities, could prove very detrimental to the patient.

You may score partial marks if you have answered CDBAE instead of CBDAE.

Scenario 42 ANSWER: A, D, F

One of the key factors in this scenario is the fact that the problem is recurrent and that the registrar has a fairly casual approach to it. It is a clear potential conflict situation where one of the parties is having problems recognising that there is an issue and therefore fails to take steps to address it. In dealing with such issues, there are a number of factors that you need to consider:

- Guaranteeing patient safety
- Trying to sort it out directly with the individual if you can
- Escalating the process to an appropriate senior if necessary
- Minimising the impact on the team as much as you can.

1. Option D is the most appropriate of all options since you are attempting to resolve the matter in the most personal manner.
2. Option A is appropriate once you have failed to resolve the matter directly because the consultant is responsible for patient care and he will need to be able to influence the situation so that patients are safe.

3. Option F is appropriate because the registrar failed to review a very sick patient and therefore patient safety was compromised. There are lessons to be learnt and completing a critical incident form will assist the learning process.

4. Options B and C both advocate that the problem should be ignored but that you should compensate by asking others to step into the registrar's shoes instead. This would probably make the patients safer to a degree as they would get a quicker review (maybe) than with the absent registrar, but it is certainly not a guarantee. In any case, it is not a solution that can be adopted permanently.

5. Option E is inviting colleagues to gossip and introduces the notion of mistrust. This is simply not a good team playing attitude and you should be more open in your dealings with others.

6. Option G is not appropriate because a senior nurse has no direct hierarchical responsibility over the registrar.

Note
If option B had been "Ensure that you seek help from another registrar whenever yours is unavailable" (i.e. not making any mention that you would ignore the problem), then it would have featured amongst the most suitable options for ensuring the immediate safety of patients. The answer would then have been ABD (to an extent the critical incident form can wait, relatively speaking).

Scenario 43 ANSWER: 1:B – 2:C – 3:A – 4:D – 5:E

1. This question not only deals with the manner with which you handle the referral process but also about the manner with which you deal with the patient's expectations. In your answer, you should take account not only of the efficiency with which you handle the problem in a busy environment but also the impact of your actions and the reward that you are likely to get in return for the amount of effort that you put in. For example, B does not take long to do but it may actually achieve the desired effect.

2. Option A is the theoretical answer to the question in that, ideally, if the patient wants to seek a specialist opinion for what is not an emergency, he should go back to his GP and ask for a referral. However, before you do that, there are easy steps that you can take, which may resolve the problem once and for all. Your first steps would be to show the patient that you are confident (B) and, failing this, to get another colleague who is present for a second opinion (C). This will save everyone a lot of trouble if it works.

3. Option D is failing to address any of the patient's worries and is slightly dismissive. However, it does attempt to get a second opinion (if the patient can afford it or has insurance). Option E is equally dismissive but, worse, it simply postpones the problem to another day and to another doctor. By not sending the patient back to the GP or to a dermatologist then you are not actually making the matter progress. Option E therefore has to be the worst possible option, which places D in fourth position.

One of the points of the question is to get you to think about what is best for the patient as opposed to what is best for you as a doctor (within limits). By trying to resolve the problem by yourself in the first instance (i.e. without referring to others systematically) then you demonstrate initiative and also a recognition that you could actually save the patient and other doctors a lot of trouble. For example, referring the patient back to the GP may inconvenience both the GP and the dermatologist who will see the patient subsequently. A little investment of your time will save others (and the NHS) a lot of time.

Scenario 44 ANSWER: 1:D – 2:C – 3:B – 4:E – 5:A

1. As a junior doctor you are not entitled to speak on behalf of the Trust, however good your intentions. The press can easily misquote you or quote you out of context (even if you ask for reassurances) and you must ensure that the journalist contacts the right person. This means that option A should come last. Similarly, E comes in fourth place as it implies that you will be answering the journalist's questions.

2. Options B, C and D are all realistic options and the ranking can be determined as follows:

   - Option B is the rude option, when such an attitude is not strictly necessary. It does not reflect well on the Trust and you may find a comment in the article about no one being available for comment except for rude doctors. Since the other two options are more helpful and polite, B should come in third place.

   - Options C and D both boil down to sending the journalist to a more appropriate person; however, in D he must do the work himself to find the right person whilst in C you are doing the work for him. In this situation, it is not exactly your responsibility to do the journalist's job for him (surely your patients should take priority) and therefore you should prioritise D over C. Most Trusts have one person responsible for press enquiries and the journalist should follow the right channels.

Scenario 45 ANSWER: 1:B – 2:C – 3:E – 4:A – 5:D

1. Option D is dishonest and will make your work entirely useless. It has to be the worst option.

2. Three of the options refer to the way in which you would handle the data:
   - Photocopy and anonymise (B)
   - Copy on paper (C)
   - Take notes home (A)

   Option A is the worst of the three. Taking the notes away from the practice not only risks a breach of confidentiality if they were to fall into somebody else's hands; but there is also the small but possible risk that you may lose these notes for good. Option C would be acceptable in principle but rushing the exercise makes it prone to error. Option B is definitely the best option as it provides you with a reliable record together with a good protection of the patient's confidentiality. Therefore B, C and A should appear in that order from most suitable to least suitable.

3. This leaves us with the issue of option E, which should appear in third position: it is more appropriate to cancel a meeting with your supervisor about the audit than to get the data input done by taking the notes home. Your supervisor would not appreciate hearing how you got it all done on time by acting unprofessionally.

Note on option B
Many candidates would be hesitant to rank option B as first. However, the fact that the photocopies have been anonymised makes it both a professional and safe option. If B did not mention that any patient-identifiable information would be removed then you would need to consider cancelling the meeting before taking the risk of taking identifiable patient data home. In that case, the answer would be CEBAD.

Note on options A and D
Some candidates may wish to rank D as more appropriate than A since they feel that a patient's confidentiality is more important than the results of a small audit's project i.e. a few made-up data points changing the results of a whole audit is not such a bad thing in contrast to the potential disclosure of patient confidential information to an unauthorised third party.

In this case, you have to step back and think about the probability of these events occurring and their likely impact. On the face of it, creating results for 20 patients in an audit may seem insignificant; however, 20 patients may form a substantial number that can skew the results of the audit. Audits, as an essential component of clinical governance, are intended to assess and guide clinical practice. Therefore, falsifying results will undermine this and could impact negatively on future practice. On the other hand, the potential disclosure of patient information from taking notes home with you is only a potential risk if several unforeseen circumstances were to occur, e.g. your house being burgled or the notes being picked up and read by a family member. Furthermore, it is only likely to be of significance if the notes are comprehensible to a third-party and, in particular, if they knew the patient concerned.

This will always remain a conflict between the ethical principles of Justice and Autonomy; however, on balance, more damage can potentially be done by falsifying the audit.

Scenario 46 ANSWER: A, B, F

1. Options B and F are two obvious contenders as you would try to address the issue first with the colleague in question and then with the consultant.

2. The problem then is that there does not seem to be any other option that would be suitable:

- Option A feels like you are rejecting responsibility.

- Option C is just pointless. Why do you need to do a survey to determine if someone has strong body odour?!

- Option D is public humiliation.

- Option E is also humiliating for the colleague though he will not feel the effect straight away. It is also difficult to see what discussions would take place at such a meeting.

- Option G is a coward's approach.

When faced with such a dilemma, you need to look at the option which is most likely to achieve a result and appears to be the least insensitive. Ultimately this problem is best addressed on a one-to-one basis with the colleague in question. Option A is best placed to achieve this (even though you are pushing the responsibility to sort it out onto the consultant – though one may argue that this is part of his remit anyway).

Scenario 47 ANSWER: 1:D – 2:C – 3:B – 4:A – 5:E

1. As in most cases, it is best to sort out any situation directly with the individual concerned. However, you must ensure that the problem is handled sensitively too. Therefore D is the obvious candidate for the most appropriate response.

2. Option A (the heavy approach) is dangerous. Not only will you embarrass the receptionist in front of the other patient but you might end up looking silly too, particularly if you have misunderstood the situation. Option A is therefore likely to feature towards the bottom in order of priority.

3. Option E looks tempting because it brings an element of patient communication into the process but it is, in fact, a red herring. This is the type of incident that you want to play down. Apologising to all patients will not only embarrass the receptionist, it will also raise the profile of the incident and will certainly not help matters. Therefore option E will rank last. It ranks lower than option A because it maximises the receptionist's embarrassment.

4. This leaves us with B and C to rank. On the basis that the clinic manager will have influence on the receptionist and that this is not really an issue that can be ignored, C will rank higher than B.

5. To confirm that we have the right order we also need to validate the fact that B (do nothing, but talk to the clinic manager next time) is ranked higher than A (telling the receptionist to stop there and then). Such ranking suggests that it is better to let the matter lie until next time rather than risk embarrassing the receptionist in front of everyone. This makes sense since, although the matter is not trivial, it is not something that needs to be addressed there and then at the risk of the receptionist losing face or motivation for the job. Also, you may want to establish a pattern of behaviour before reporting the issue.

Scenario 48 ANSWER: A, B, E

1. There are two issues to consider in this scenario: your consultant's integrity and the fact that two doctors have potentially fake CVs and therefore pose a possible danger to patients by misrepresenting themselves to future employers. The issue is further complicated by the fact that you still need to work with your consultant and therefore need to be careful in your handling of the matter.

2. Talking to your consultant privately would be a good start, which makes option E a good candidate. During the meeting you should ensure that you do not become an accessory to the fraudulent activity that is taking place and you will need to refuse to add the names to the publication unless

these individuals have had some input into the process (option A). It would be tempting to go ahead with the publication with the extra names in for the sake of an easy life (option C) but you must think about the consequences of your own actions and also the consequences of helping two doctors fraudulently representing themselves. Whether it is a case report or a more important publication is not what the problem is. It is a matter of personal ethics and duty towards your patients and society.

3. Reporting your consultant to the GMC will achieve little. Although his approach was unprofessional, you would need to discuss the matter with the Clinical Director first. The issue is not of extreme gravity as far as your consultant is concerned and the Clinical Director is likely to handle the matter by himself without involving the GMC (unless this is a recurrent problem). However, you may want to contact the GMC about the two other doctors (option B) as their fraud is a potential risk to patients.

4. Checking with others (option D) sounds like a good idea but it will just be spreading rumours. In any case, if he had been trying the same trick with other colleagues, the next step would be to contact the Clinical Director and not the GMC. So, option D is not suitable.

5. Warning the paper (option G) is pointless. There is little they will be able to do about it. And you may get sued by the other two doctors for slander.

Scenario 49 ANSWER: B, C, D

1. Agreeing to make the change (A) could lead you into great trouble (possibly being struck off). You are responsible for your own decisions and therefore the only option open to you is to refuse to make the entry (B).

2. Your next step would be to contact your defence union (C) and to make sure that you keep a note of the conversation that you had with your consultant as you may need to testify in future.

3. Following on from that, you will need to report the matter to a senior colleague. Your Clinical Director is the obvious candidate for this (option D). Informing the GMC (F) is a little premature. If there is cause for concern, the Clinical Director may well do that but later in the process. As for informing the police (G), this is also a possible course of action but not one that you will need to take by yourself. If need be, the police will be

called following a decision made at Trust level (e.g. by managers, the Medical Director, the Chief Executive) but not by you.

4. Informing the patient that a mistake has been made is a good idea and should be done. However, option E also says that you should tell the patient about the consultant's attempt to modify the notes. If a decision is made to tell the patient about the consultant's request then it will be made in consultation with the Trust's management (as there is a legal risk). You should stick to the clinical aspect of the work and let the managers handle any situation that has possible legal implications. This makes option E inappropriate.

Scenario 50   ANSWER: 1:B – 2:A – 3:E – 4:D – 5:C

1. This question is primarily about confidentiality. As a rule, you can breach the confidentiality of an adult patient in a few circumstances only, e.g. there is a risk of serious harm or death to a third party or you are the recipient of a court order. Such exceptions are not relevant here and confidentiality must be maintained. Option C is the only option that clearly breaches confidentiality and therefore must be the least suitable option.

2. Option D is deliberately misleading since it is falsely confusing competence with confidentiality. Competence dictates whether you can take consent from a patient. Taking option D will also mislead the father. However, since this leads to a favourable outcome i.e. not divulging confidential details to him, it is the not least suitable option. Letting the registrar take the call would be more appropriate than misleading the father; hence option E ranks third.

3. Options A and B are suitable for the top two places. However Option A is slightly harsh and dismissive towards the father whilst B is more compassionate and is less likely to cause communication problems later on during this admission.

Note on confidentiality
Telling the father that his daughter is "fine" would not be seen as a breach of confidentiality. The term "fine" is very vague and serves to reassure the father rather than provide any meaningful information. After all, he has reasons to be concerned and if there are ways in which you can reassure him without compromising your integrity then you should use them. This assumes that the

father knows that his daughter was admitted in this hospital in the first place (which the question implies).

If the question said "a man is on the phone asking if his daughter is in your hospital" then you would not be able to divulge the information as you would then confirm to the father that his daughter is receiving treatment, which he wasn't aware of.

Scenario 51 ANSWER: 1:B – 2:A – 3:E – 4:D – 5:C

1. Three of the options relate to the same topic – the extent to which you would breach confidentiality: A, C and D.

    - Option A is clearly the least suitable option as you would blatantly breach the husband's confidentiality whilst, at the same time, not benefiting the wife in any way.

    - Option C also makes you breach confidentiality, but only on the subject of whether the husband came to see you rather than what he came to see you for. Although not best practice, this is lot more acceptable than option A, particularly if you feel that she already knows that he came or you feel that she is almost certain he did. One of the dangers with this approach is that, once you have revealed that the husband did come to see you, the wife will ask more questions about the reasons.

    - Option D is the best approach as you are ensuring that you maintain the husband's confidentiality at all costs. This is justified because all the wife needs to know is that she has an infection that needs treating, regardless of where she got it from. The rest is a matter between her and her husband.

2. Option B (asking advice from colleagues) will become an appropriate option when you realise that you are out of your depth, i.e. it should be ranked just before the option in which you start making a mistake or acting unprofessionally. We have ranked D, C and A in that order and have identified that C is slightly unprofessional because you have revealed that the husband did visit your surgery. Therefore B should rank before C.

3. Option E is an interesting one. There isn't really a conflict of interest. You can perfectly treat both patients for whatever infection they have and work

on each of the two individuals to achieve joint counselling. It is also a bit melodramatic; the situation is not very extreme and, if you sent the patient to another GP, she would only start asking similar questions again. Having to register at another GP practice may also add unnecessary delay in the management of her medical condition.

It is ranking fourth because it is not something that would achieve very much but it is still better than breaching the husband's confidentiality.

Some may feel that options C and E should be swapped since option C divulges some information about the husband (i.e. that he has come to the surgery at all). This in itself is a breach of confidentiality. However, by stating in option E that there is a potential conflict of interest, you will also imply that there is some problem and that you are aware of information about her husband. This, on top of the upheaval of changing GP practice, will cause more problems than good.

Scenario 52   ANSWER: 1:A – 2:B – 3:C – 4:D – 5:E

1. This is a very serious issue which could lead to unsuitable student qualifying. It is therefore important that the problem is addressed as soon as possible. The deanery needs to investigate the extent of the problem and, if necessary, will need to write a new exam paper. In order to investigate, they will need to contact those who came into possession of the paper and therefore option A should rank as the most suitable option.

2. Option B (reporting without naming the student) would also be effective as it would raise the issue at the highest level where something can be done about it. By not naming the student, you are protecting him (which could be interpreted in many ways) but at least you are giving others in charge the power to sort the problem out. Note that there is no issue of confidentiality here. The student is not a patient. You must treat the incident sensitively but if need be you can name the culprits.

3. Option C is a feeble attempt at resolving the problem. It is almost guaranteed to fail, but at least you tried (which is not the case for the two remaining options D and E).

4. Option D (ignoring the matter) is fairly bad as there is an obvious cause for complaint here. But it is not as bad as propagating the fraud to continue by

encouraging him to distribute the papers further (option E). One may think this is a good option since everyone would have access to the questions. However, you could not be sure that the papers would be distributed to everybody in the year group. Ultimately, this is a bad idea since the whole purpose of an exam is not just to test the content of the paper but to ensure that, through the process of revision, candidates have covered a significant proportion of the syllabus.

Note on ignoring problems

Doing nothing is often the worst option because in most cases you are expected to be proactive in resolving problems. However, doing something that makes things worse is obviously less appropriate than remaining passive.

Scenario 53 | ANSWER: 1:D – 2:C – 3:A – 4:B – 5:E

1. Option D: Until you have all the information about the patient you cannot judge how important the call is and how urgently you need to attend. You already know the patient is conscious and has a low blood pressure but there are a number of causes of this (including a peri-arrest situation and a wrong blood pressure measurement!). You should always listen to a request from the nurses and, only then, decide the priority of that request.

2. Option C: If you are overwhelmed with work and are struggling to cope, or if there is likely to be a long delay in attending a sick patient because you are busy with other sicker patients, you should always call on your team for help. Ensuring that you have the contact number of a doctor who can help the nurses will ensure they can contact them quickly. You should only do this once you have all the information and know the patient is not at immediate risk (i.e. after option D).

3. Option A: A patient on CCU is usually a "sick patient". A hypotensive patient on CCU could be in a peri-arrest situation and if you cannot get any more information or there is no one else to help, you should attend as soon as you can. You must however ensure the patient you are with is "safe" and ideally walk quickly, rather than run. It would be much better to get the information from the nurses first (as in option D) as this would allow you to assess the priority.

4. Option B: If you are busy and cannot attend a patient in a reasonable amount of time, it is important that the nurses who requested your

attendance are aware of the potential delay. This will allow them to decide whether they need to call someone else, or if the patient can wait for you. You should always try first to get the full information about the patient (as in option D) before refusing to attend. In addition, be careful about 'telling' nurses what to do. They are valued members of the multidisciplinary team and should be respected. A much better way is to explain why you are delayed, offering them an alternative doctor to help (as in option C).

5. Option E: A crash call should only be used if a patient requires the crash team's input, not because you cannot attend.

Scenario 54 ANSWER: 1:E – 2:A – 3:D – 4:B – 5:C

1. Option E: When a patient doesn't take their medication, it is important for you to find out why. If you ask her the questions and give her all the information relating to her medication, you can then assess if she has the "capacity" to make an informed decision. If she has capacity, based on the ethical principal of autonomy, it is the patient's right to choose whether they take it. You should always then offer the patient a follow up appointment in case they change their mind.

2. Option A: In this option you have not assessed her capacity or asked about her medication, (as in option E), but offering her a blood test in 3 months time is a good thing to do to allow you to assess her thyroid function at that time. It also ensures a follow up appointment in case she changes her mind.

3. Option D: It is not ideal to do nothing. You should always try to engage with the patient (Options E and A) to gain their trust. In this option you have offered a follow up. They may change their mind.

4. Option B: Telling patients to take their medication often doesn't work, it is much better to listen and then to negotiate with them. Offering a re-referral to the endocrinologist is a possible option if you are concerned about her thyroid control but in this case it would be better to try and build up a rapport with the patient (option E) to enable them to come back for a regular review (options E, D and A).

5. Option C: This is the worst option. Even if you do not believe in homeopathic medicine, you should not impart your own beliefs onto the

patient. If they have capacity it is then their choice. If you do judge patients choices, you are likely to loose their trust and the patient is unlikely to return to see you. .

Scenario 55 ANSWER: 1:E – 2:D – 3:C – 4:B – 5:A

1. Option E: Calling language line is the best choice. This means you can see the patient knowing with certainty that the interpretation is correct. A 6-year-old child is too young to translate effectively.

2. Option D: Whenever possible, it is best to offer your patient their choice of interpreter, although using a young child who is unlikely to understand the conversation, and who you cannot be certain will translate appropriately, should not be the first choice. By asking if anyone else can help, you give the patient choice.

3. Option C: By engaging with the child and grandmother, you can assess fully whether it is appropriate to use the child; although it would be better to try to find an alternative (as in option D). It is highly unlikely that you will be able to use the 6-year-old, but at least you will not antagonise your patient. Telling her not to use the child again also ensures that you will not face the same problem a few weeks down the line.

4. Option B. Simply refusing to use the 6 year old is not helpful. How are you then going to communicate with the patient?

5. Option A. You should never refuse to see a patient just because they require a translator. By simply looking at the patient – even if you do not communicate with words – you will be able to tell if they are acutely unwell. Always try to find alternatives.

Scenario 56 ANSWER: 1:C – 2:B – 3:E – 4:D – 5:A

1. Option C: Even though your shift is ending, there are times when, as a doctor, you will have to work late. We have a duty to all our patients, both alive and after death, and to their relatives. It is always essential to document fully any clinical contact with a patient and before breaking bad news you must ensure you are in a fit state to face the family. You are of

no use to them if you are upset, tired or in a rush and you may affect their grief reaction in the long term if you break the news badly.

2. Option B: It is important to inform relatives as soon as you can but you must document the clinical episode and ensure you are "ready" to face the family as in option C. Handing the task over to someone else (Options E and D) should only be done if you have no alternative

3. Option E and D: It is never ideal to hand over a difficult situation to another colleague but if you do decide to hand this task over it MUST be to someone of equal or greater experience than you. Option E is therefore preferable to Option D.

4. Option A: Sending a cup of tea to the family, whilst commendable, is not addressing the issue at all. It would be better to offer the tea AFTER the news has been broken.

Scenario 57   ANSWER: 1:E – 2:A – 3:D – 4:B – 5:C

1. Option E: It is important to remember we have a duty of care to our patients (and their relatives) in death as well as in life. Writing the death certificate as soon as you are able to will help the family organise the funeral and help with their grief reaction. We also have a duty to teach the next generation of doctors; and so asking your junior doctors to attend as a teaching tool is ideal which makes this option better than option A.

2. Option A: The only difference between option A and option E is that you are also teaching the next generation of doctors in option E, which makes it a better choice.

3. Option D: There is no reason to go to see the body of a deceased patient to write a death certificate. Only if they are being cremated do you need to see the body. By going to see the body, you are delaying the writing of the death certificate. It is better to attend as soon as you can (options E and A).

4. Option B: If you accept the task of writing the death certificate you should complete it as soon as possible for the reasons stated above.

5. Option C: The doctor who certified the patient did not treat the patient during his illness and was a locum doctor. It is your duty to complete the form. This is therefore the worst option.

Scenario 58   ANSWER: 1:B – 2:C – 3:A – 4:D – 5:E

1. Option B: The fact that a drug is on repeat prescription does not mean you have to continue to prescribe it. If you sign the prescription you are responsible for the issue of that drug. It is good practice to review the notes and ensure that the patient knows the risks involved is good practice. Offering an alternative to addictive medication is a positive consultation. The patient may refuse the alternative today, but at least they will have been given the option.

2. Option C: It is always important to ensure that any medication such as sleeping tablets is being used appropriately; but in this option, no alternatives or explanations were given. Option B offered alternatives which makes it a better choice.

3. Option A: It is important to monitor the use of additive drugs such as sleeping tablets and so at regular intervals the patient should be reviewed. In this option you have assessed whether the patient is using the medication correctly. Options B and C are better choices as in this option you "tell" a patient they do not need to waste GP's time in the future. This infers that they are wasting your time today. Statements such as this may break down the doctor-patient relationship and are not helpful.

4. Option D: Giving the patient the prescription they request just because they tell you it is on repeat is not ideal. It is your responsibility to check this when issuing a script and so you must ensure the notes and medication history are reviewed as in options A, B and C above.

5. Option E: Sending the patient to another GP does not address their problem and is "wasting" another appointment. In situations such as this, if you are not happy to issue the full repeat script, you may wish to issue a small quantity of the medication and then ensure their next appointment is with their regular GP.

Scenario 59 ANSWER: 1:C – 2:B – 3:A – 4:E – 5:D

1. Option C: Building a relationship of trust between the doctor and patient in a situation like this is imperative. You are allowed to break confidentiality in cases such as this as the patient is "at severe risk of harm", if, after trying to negotiate with the patient they still refuse to tell the police themselves, or allow you to tell the police.

2. Option B: As stated in option C, you are allowed to break confidentiality in cases such as this (as the patient is "at severe risk of harm") if after trying to negotiate with the patient they still refuse to allow you to tell the police. However, you should only break their confidence if there is no way you can convince them otherwise. "Telling" them you will go to the police is not as good as option C where you "ask" the patient to allow you to make the call.

3. Option A: The police need to be informed of the threats but it is better to engage with the patient and get them on board as in options C and B.

4. Option E: Supporting the patient is imperative, but "wishing her luck" effectively ends your support. You need to let the police know one way or the other, ideally with her support (options C, B, A).

5. Option D: This is nonsense. There are many things you can do, as demonstrated above.

Scenario 60 ANSWER: 1:E – 2:B – 3:D – 4:A – 5:C

1. Option E: It is essential in cases such as this to assess capacity. If a patient has capacity, based on the ethical principle of autonomy, it is their right to choose.

2. Option B: Once you have assessed their capacity (option E), you can then offer alternative ways of helping, paying particular attention to their comment that they want to die.

3. Option D: In this option you have not assessed the patients capacity or offered help in any way. (As in options E and B)

170

4. Option A: Any doctor can assess capacity although if you have not been trained to do so, or do not feel able to then a psychiatrist will be able to help. This patient should only be referred if options E, B and D do not help.

5. Option C: It is illegal to assist patients to die in the UK.

Scenario 61   ANSWER: 1:A – 2:E – 3:D – 4:C – 5:B

1. Option A: If a minor (under 16 years of age) has capacity, can understand the pro's and cons of taking the COCP, she is deemed as having "Gillick competence" as based on a court case in 1986. It is therefore acceptable to prescribe the COCP in this case.

2. Option E: It is better the child (if she is at risk of an unplanned pregnancy) is commenced on the COCP than not, but in this option her capacity has not been assessed as in option A.

3. Option D: If a 13 year old has asked for the COCP, it is usually best (not always) to start them on this and review them after a couple of months (options A and E). You could "discuss" the implant at this appointment to see if they are interested but not "insist". Even though she is only 13, it is still her choice. as in options A and E.

4. Option C: If a child has "Gillick competence" / capacity then they do not need an adult with them although you should ask them if they are willing to tell a responsible adult (parent/ guardian).

5. Option B: although it's "illegal" for a 13 year old to have sex, our job as doctors is to ensure the child is safe, ensure they have capacity and to prevent unwanted pregnancies. This option should therefore never be used.

Scenario 62   ANSWER: 1:C – 2:D – 3:E – 4:B – 5:A

1. Option C: It is important in medicine to admit your mistakes and to always ensure you act in the best interests of the patient. (First do no harm). You must document your clinical findings, always explain to the patient and inform your consultant of the problem.

2. Option D: It is always better to keep the patient informed (as in option C). In this option, you tell your consultant and document your findings but the patient is unaware of the problem.

3. Option E: It is unlikely that the echo lab will be able to perform an echo at such short notice and even if they were able, your consultant and the patient should still be informed as in options C and D.

4. Option B: Although the anaesthetist does (usually) listen to the patient's heart, you are essentially "passing the buck". Having discovered an issue it is your responsibility to deal with it.

5. Option A: You should never ignore a clinical finding, it must always be documented. Option B is marginally better than this one, since you are leaving the clinical findings in the hands of the anaesthetist. In this option, there is no way of knowing if the murmur will ever be detected by another clinician preoperatively.

Scenario 63   ANSWER: 1:B – 2:C – 3:E – 4:D – 5:A

1. Option B: You should never request a patient's consent for a procedure that you do not fully understand. By asking your consultant for help you will learn how to consent a patient for this procedure (although in reality it is such complicated surgery you are unlikely to ever be asked to perform such a consent). In addition, rather than simply saying that you don't know, showing some initiative by using the internet to do some "self-directed" learning in preparation will be to your credit.

2. Option C: You could of course ask your registrar to help, but as the consultant asked YOU to perform the consent, it is better to approach them directly (as in option B) rather than ask an alternative team member. In addition, this option is more "passive" than Option B as you are not showing any personal initiative to learn about the procedure and are simply relying on a senior colleague.

3. Option E: This option does not address the problem that the consent needs completing although is much better than options D and A where you perform the consent yourself.

4. Option D: It is inappropriate to teach yourself from the internet about a complicated surgical procedure and then perform a consent. You must ask a senior colleague as in options B and C

5. Option A: You must never consent someone for a procedure that you do not know about.

Scenario 64   ANSWER: 1:E – 2:B – 3:D – 4:C – 5:A

The bottom line for this question is that assisting someone to die is illegal in the UK, whether you are doing it directly, or arranging for it to happen. As such, all options which suggest that you should do so should be ranked lower than others.

1. Option E: In this situation you firstly need to assess if the patient has capacity and can therefore make a sound judgement, and then always assess the patient for depression. It is very common for the elderly to have an element of depression.

2. Option B: Although you do not need a psychiatrist to assess their capacity, you may wish to refer them to a psycho geriatrician if, either you are unsure of how to assess capacity or if you are worried about depression. You should never "assume" a patient is depressed. Always assess them first (as in option E).

3. Option D: It is important to assess their capacity but it is illegal to assist a patient to die in the UK. This includes giving help and advice about assisted suicide clinics overseas although since you assessed their capacity, this option is better than option C.

4. Option C: It is illegal to assist a patient to die in the UK. This includes giving help and advice about assisted suicide clinics overseas.

5. Option A: This option is nonsense and illegal. It is ranked last as it recommends direct intervention as opposed to simply advising a patient.

Scenario 65 ANSWER: 1:C – 2:E – 3:A – 4:B – 5:D

1. Option C: You should always explain to patients the reason for not prescribing antibiotics. In this case because her examination is normal and the likely cause of her symptoms (a viral infection) will not be cured with antibiotics. By offering her an appointment in 48 hours, she also has an easy way to be reviewed if she develops a chest infection as she fears.

2. Option E: An alternative to a follow up appointment is to issue a delayed prescription. This is where you issue a prescription to the patient but they cannot get the medication from the pharmacy immediately (in this case, not for 48 hours, and then only if their symptoms get worse). Although this is a valid alternative, you have not explained the reasons for not issuing the antibiotics today, which is why option C is better.

3. Option A: There is no indication for antibiotics in this case, but it is preferable to give an explanation rather than just refuse.

4. Option B: Sending her to see another GP the same day is a waste of an appointment if there is no indication for the antibiotics. It will simply push the problem onto someone else.

5. Option D: Giving antibiotics when there is no clinical indication (as in this case) is not good prescribing practice and will only make the patient believe that she can demand antibiotics every time. Always think about antibiotic resistance when prescribing and only ever prescribe when necessary.

Scenario 66 ANSWER: 1:C – 2:D – 3:A – 4:E – 5:B

1. Option C: Your priority is the patient in front of you. This man could have lung cancer and so you must investigate him.

2. Option D: This man may have an infection although a cough present for 6 weeks is suspicious in this man for lung cancer. In an A&E situation, AFTER investigating the man, antibiotics would be an appropriate treatment if there were signs of infection. By referring him back to his GP, you also ensure follow up. However, it is obviously better to investigate the man whilst he is in A&E in order to prevent any further delays (option C).

3. Option A: This man may have lung cancer but until you have investigated, you cannot be certain. You must investigate first (as in option C). Admission is also unlikely to be a suitable solution for this man; indeed, he could be treated as an out patient, since the question states clearly that he is "otherwise well".

4. Option E: You cannot refer someone to oncology without any investigations or a diagnosis. This is not a good option, but it is better than option B which does not address the man's illness at all.

5. Option B: This is the worst of all the options as it does not address the man or his illness at all. By calling the GP, you are waiting time and energy which could be used to investigate and treat the patient in front of you.

Scenario 67 ANSWER: 1:A – 2:C – 3:B – 4:D – 5:E

1. Option A: A nurse practitioner is trained to order investigations and to interpret those investigations. If she ordered the ECG, it is her right to be able to review it and to ask for help if she does not know what it means or if she cannot then treat the patient. The question states that the patient is stable; there is no indication that the nurse practitioner in unavailable, unwilling to interpret the ECG, or struggling with it. By offering to attend immediately if the nurse practitioner requests it, you ensure that the patient is not put at risk whilst respecting the nurse practitioner's role.

2. Option C: By asking for more information about the patient and the urgency of this review, you can determine how quickly you need to attend. It would be more appropriate in the first instance to allow the nurse practitioner to review the ECG (Option A).

3. Option B: This could be a myocardial infarction: but, unless you ask for more information about the patient (as in option C), you will not be able to make that judgement. One of the most important tasks as a doctor is to prioritise your caseload.

4. Option D: Putting a patient with chest pain at the bottom of your list of things to do without having more information (option C) is poor prioritisation. Its is far better to over-prioritise chest pain (option B) than to under-prioritise it.

5. Option E: The nurses who called you did not request the ECG; it was the nurse practitioner so this option is unhelpful and may result in no action being taken by anyone, thereby potentially placing the patient at risk. It is also condescending.

Scenario 68   ANSWER: 1:D – 2:A – 3:E – 4:C – 5:B

1. Option D: Since you have seen the fax, you have a duty to that patient. Although no one is usually at the practice at 9pm (option B), A haemoglobin of 5 is consistent with profound anaemia and needs treatment as soon as possible. The best way of getting that treatment is to arrange for the patient to be admitted to the local hospital.

2. Option A: Someone needs to organise the admission so that the patient is safe and treated. If you do not do that (option D), then the haematologist at the hospital (who has sent you the fax) should organise that by contacting the on call team.

3. Option E: It is much better to organise an admission directly with the on call team (options D and A) than to send the patient to A&E. Indeed, the A&E team will not be aware of the full picture. If the patient arrives in A&E without prior warning or any kind of referral letter, this may cause confusion and delay care.

4. Option C: This patient needs treatment as soon as possible (options D, A, and E). By placing the fax on your desk, at least you are planning to action it the next day rather than ignore it completely (option B)

5. Option B: Since you have seen the fax, you have a duty to that patient. By ignoring it completely you are putting the patient at risk.

Scenario 69   ANSWER: 1:E – 2:A – 3:D – 4:C – 5:B

1. Option E: Since this patient has a temperature, you need to ensure that there is no other cause for it than their dental pain. Once you have ruled out a medical cause, you can attribute it to dental cause/ abscess and they can be referred to and assessed by a dentist the same day. The question

clearly states that it is 9am in the morning so there is ample time for this to happen.

2. Option A: If it is clear to you that this is a dental abscess, then you could treat it with antibiotics but you need to rule out other medical causes for their temperature first (option E).

3. Option D: Simply giving them pain killers without medical assessment (option E), or treatment for the abscess (option A) is not ideal.

4. Option C: Even though as GPs we are not trained in dental treatment, it is fairly common to see patients with dental pain / abscesses. Often, patients do not have an NHS dentist, or are worried that they will not be able to afford the treatment. If it is obvious that it is a dental abscess then you can treat it (option A). It is better to give them painkillers at least (option D) than do nothing as in this option.

5. Option B: Simply telling a patient to see a dentist is often not helpful, which makes this the worst option. In option C, at least, you explain to the patient why you cannot treat them.

Scenario 70 ANSWER: 1:E – 2:D – 3:B – 4:C – 5:A

1. Option E: Your first port of call whilst in General Practice should be your trainer. If you cannot resolve the problem directly with them, only then you should seek help elsewhere. By asking them rather then telling them (as in option D) you are using better negotiation skills and are likely to achieve a better result.

2. Option D: Again, the first port of call should be your trainer, but asking them (option E) is much better than telling them as in this option.

3. Option B: If you cannot resolve the problem with your trainer (options E and D) directly, then it is much better to ask another GP to help you, (who may also then be able to talk to your trainer), than to go outside of the practice as in option C below.

4. Option C: Reporting your GP trainer to the deanery should only be undertaken if you cannot resolve the problem locally. Thankfully, the

standard of training in General Practice is high so it is very rare to have to take things this far (although it does happen).

5. Option A: Doing nothing is not addressing the problem and potentially is putting your training at risk.

Scenario 71   ANSWER: 1:B – 2:E – 3:A – 4:D – 5:C

1. Option B: Treatment of anaphylaxis includes, A (airway), B (breathing), C (circulation) and treating with ADRENALINE. This is usually followed by hospital admission and so an ambulance would need to be called.

2. Option E: If you do not have adrenaline or are not confident giving it to a patient, your next option is to call an ambulance. You must always assess the patient's "A,B,C" as you may need to start basic life support (BLS) whilst waiting for the ambulance. It is better to proceed and give the adrenaline if you have it (option B).

3. Option A: Getting help from the paramedics is a good option, but as a doctor you should also assess their "A,B,C" (options B and E) to allow you to start basic life support if required.

4. Option D: Basic life support starts with the assessment of ABC, but this does not address the need for adrenaline (as in option B – yourself, or options E and A- from the paramedics)

5. Option C: Atropine is the wrong choice of drug and so is an inappropriate treatment.

Scenario 72   ANSWER: 1:A – 2:C – 3:E – 4:B – 5:D

1. Option A: This is a neurosurgical emergency. In order to prevent permanent neurological damage, immediate referral is essential.

2. Option C: The neurosurgeons will want an MRI, but you must talk to them first (option A) and make the referral. They will usually organise the MRI to ensure it has all of the views that they require.

3. Option E: The patient will need admission but ideally needs the MRI and neurosurgical input as in options A and C above. Admitting under the medical team is better than options B and D below because, at least, if the patient is admitted to hospital then the medical team will refer the patient onwards.

4. Option B: There is no indication for a back X-ray in this case.

5. Option D: This patient should not be discharged home. He needs admission. This is the worst of all the options. At least, in option B he is still in the hospital even though a back X-ray is useless.

Scenario 73 ANSWER: 1:E – 2:A – 3:D – 4:C – 5:B

1. Option E: As long as a patient has capacity and all the information (including the advantages and disadvantages of both having and not having the procedure) it is their right to choose whether to proceed with surgery or not (ethical principle of autonomy).

2. Option A: You need to ensure the patient has capacity first (option E) but offering to re explain the surgery involved is good medicine. It also gives the patient time to ask any questions they may have. If you do this before talking to your consultant, you will be better prepared to present the case to him/her.

3. Option D: You must inform your consultant, but as an F2 you do have some clinical experience and therefore you can assess the patient's capacity and talk to the patient about their options (options E and A). This way you will be better prepared when you inform your consultant of the patient's decision.

4. Option C: It is the patient's choice, but you should always ensure the patient has capacity (option E) and all the information (option A) first. You must also inform your consultant (option D).

5. Option B: You should not insist that any patient has surgery. It is much better to assess them, talk to them and then involve your consultant. This is therefore the worst option.

Scenario 74 ANSWER: 1:D – 2:C – 3:B – 4:E – 5:A

1. Option D: Even though the child is not your patient, as doctors we all have a duty towards the protection of children. If you have noticed something you are worried about, you must act on it immediately. The child's GP will know if the child is on a child protection register and will be able to follow the child up for you, or inform the health visitor.

2. Option C: Asking the mother about the state of the child is a possibility, but it is better to be armed with facts before doing this (as in option D).

3. Option B: Without information from the GP (option C) or from the mother (option B), it is difficult to know whether there is any need for admission. If there was any bruising or you witnessed abuse from the mother, it would be appropriate to admit the child for further investigation (in which case Option B would be ranked higher) but the text of the question does not refer to any bruising and there may be a justifiable reason for the child to be in the state that they are. Always ask questions before making judgements.

4. Option E: In some hospitals, a clinic letter can take over 2 weeks to reach the GP. If you have concerns about a child's welfare, such a delay is too long. It is better to telephone the GP (option D), confront the mother (option C) or admit the child (option B) than to leave the child "at risk" with no follow up.

5. Option A: This is the worst option. If a child is at risk, it does not matter if they are not your patient; it is your duty to act.

Scenario 75 ANSWER: 1:B – 2:C – 3:A – 4:E – 5:D

1. Option B: The health visitor sees patients in their own home at approximately 10 days post birth and is a primary source of help for new mothers. She will have seen the mother at least once by the time that baby is 5 weeks old (as in this scenario) and so will have more information about how the mother and baby are. By contacting the patient after receiving this information and offering to see them is extending their circle of support at a difficult time.

2. Option C: Seeing a new mother in her home at a difficult time will give you and idea of how she is coping. This is a good option, but you do not have the added advantage of the information form the health visitor as in option B above.

3. Option A: You will ideally contact the patient (options B and C) but if you decide not to, coding the diagnosis in the patients notes, means that whichever GP sees the baby for their routine 6 week check (which will be in 1 weeks time since the baby is already 5 weeks old), will be aware before the child enters the room. This will enable them to be prepared and to offer better support to the mother.

4. Option E: Since the 6 week check is only a week away, the letter may not arrive before the patient is seen in the surgery for the routine 6 week check. Option A is slightly better as at least the diagnosis will be coded in the notes for whoever sees the patient rather than risking the letter not arriving before she comes in for her appointment.

5. Option D: Expressing "sympathy" at a diagnosis of Downs syndrome is inappropriate until you have found out how the parents feel. What most parents need is positive support, not people feeling sorry for them to enable them to cope better. "Sympathy" is the worst of all of the options.

Scenario 76   ANSWER: 1:A – 2:E – 3:C – 4:B – 5:D

1. Option A: The patient's safety is paramount in this scenario. One lung has disease / fluid in it (the side you should have aspirated) and you have just compromised the other side by attempting the aspiration. Once you know they are stable, the patient needs to be informed of the mistake as does your consultant. In potential medical negligence cases such as this, seeking your consultant's help at the earliest opportunity is very important. That is why option A is better than option E.

2. Option E: It is better to seek your consultant's help as early as you can. Taking your consultant with you when you apologise to the patient may help to fend off a complaint.

3. Option C: There is no apology here, which is why this is not as good as options A and E.

4.   Option B: This option does not include any explanation (as in options A, E and C) or apology to the patient (as in A and E).

5.   Option D: You must acknowledge the mistake and inform your consultant. Proceeding to aspirate the other side before ensuring there is no pneumothorax is potentially dangerous and this is therefore the worst option.

Scenario 77   ANSWER: 1:E – 2:B – 3:A – 4:D – 5:C

1.   Option E: If patients are on medications that require regular review, such as sleeping tablets, or medication that requires regular investigations such as anti-hypertensives or thyroxine then it is your duty as the prescribing doctor to ensure that those checks are done. It is usual for GPs to prescribe a maximum of 3 months at a time. Some primary care trusts are also trying to encourage 28 day prescribing only.

2.   Option B: If your practice has a protocol, you must follow it. Option E is better than this as it includes an explanation to the patient in addition to issuing the script.

3.   Option A: In this case it is safer to refuse to prescribe them a year of medication as in this option, than to issue it (as in options D and C below) since their medication includes drugs that require monitoring. In addition, there are rules with regard to how long you can be out of the country before your entitlement to NHS care ceases and so it would be justifiable to advise the patient to submit their NHS card to the PCT.

4.   Option D: It is inappropriate to prescribe 12 months medication in this case but if you did, a thorough assessment of the patient notes as in this option, is better than simply issuing the script as in option C.

5.   Option C: This is the worst option. It is inappropriate to issue a years worth of medication in this case but if you did, you should review the notes thoroughly as in option D.

Scenario 78 ANSWER: B, C, E

It is likely that this man is having another heart attack and so needs hospital care immediately. If the paramedics arrive, they can assess him and if he still refuses to go to hospital you could do an emergency visit at that time.

1. Option B: This would get the paramedics there at the earliest opportunity and therefore be the best treatment for the man.

2. Option C: If you cannot get him to agree over the phone and he lives close enough, you could do an emergency visit and try and convince him in person to go into hospital, on your way to visit him call the paramedics and meet them at the house.

3. Option E: This is essential as the gentleman needs to know how serious this chest pain could be. It may help him to agree to go back into hospital.

The other answers: (In no order of priority)

*   Option A: This man cannot wait until the end of surgery.

*   Option D: This man needs emergency treatment in A&E or a cardiac centre. Admitting him under the medical team with a non-urgent ambulance to take him is not addressing urgency of his need.

*   Option F: In 30 minutes, he may not be in a fit state to pick up the phone. More urgent action is needed.

*   Option G: He needs urgent care. Making his fate depend on how busy your morning clinic is not appropriate in such circumstances.

Scenario 79 ANSWER: G, C, B

You have a duty of care to this patient to ensure that he is reviewed and treated as soon as possible. This is a difficult situation as you will have to point out a mistake to your supervisor and so tact is essential.

1. Option G: Referring the patient immediately is essential to ensure their illness is treated, even if this is in the middle of a teaching session.

2. Option B: Showing your trainer the results will flag up the mistake to him and you can then use the case as a teaching tool, contact the patient and refer them immediately.

3. Option C: This is a significant mistake and should be investigated to ensure the same mistake is not made again. Filling in an incident form is the first step in that investigation.

The other answers: (In no order of priority)

*   Option A: Your duty is to the patient, not to your trainer

*   Option D: The practice manager will find out through the incident form and investigation that follows. There is no need to specifically inform them at this stage.

*   Option E: The senior partners will find out through the incident form and investigation that follows. There is no need to specifically inform them at this stage.

*   Option F: All mistakes/ complaints should be investigated at a local level before escalating them to the GMC. Obviously if your trainer is repeatedly making mistakes and the practice manager, senior partners and the primary care trust do not act on it, then you should take the matter up with the GMC.

Scenario 80 ANSWER: C, A, F

As a doctor, even if you are not at work, you have a duty to help if someone is injured or unwell. Acting in this way (out of work) is covered by your medical defence union and is entitled a "Good Samaritan Act".

1. Option C: Attending immediately to help and assessing the A (airway) in ABC (airway, breathing and circulation) is essential.

2. Option A: You do not have any resuscitation equipment (e.g. oxygen, mask, etc) with you and so calling an ambulance to help is essential. Unless the collapse is inside the hospital building the arrest team will not be available to you, so the paramedics are required.

3.   Option F: An alternative is to ask the friend to call 999. This allows you to proceed and assess the patient without delay.

The other answers: (In no order of priority):

•   Option B: You have a duty to the patient and should never walk past.

•   Option D: You should never give rescue breaths (part of BLS) until you have assessed their airway and breathing.

•   Option E: You do not have facilities for ALS (which includes defibrillation and drugs) in a hospital car park. You will need to await the paramedics.

Scenario 81 ANSWER: C, G, F

It is essential to be aware of child protection issues and to safeguard the well being of all children in your care. You must always listen to a child and document everything they say.

1.   Option C: It is essential to listen to the child and clearly document everything they say.

2.   Option G: Once the child has explained everything, asking if this has ever happened before gives them the opportunity to talk about other abuse.

3.   Option F: Having a nurse with you gives the child extra support and gives you a witness of what the child is saying.

The other answers: (In no order of priority)

•   Option A: You need to give the child time to talk and if they have chosen you to open up to you should listen to them. Admitting them immediately and informing the child protection registrar may break that trust and the child may not say anymore. It may become necessary to admit the child but you should talk to them first. As such, although it would be an appropriate action to consider, it does not feature in the top three here.

- Option B: Always believe a child when they talk about abuse. NEVER tell them or imply that they may be lying. A full investigation will follow any allegation of abuse.

- Option D: Always document every allegation a child makes. They may never repeat it again. By ignoring the first allegation, you may send the child back into an unsafe environment.

- Option E: You do not need to wait for mum to return to talk to this child. He has obviously waited for his mother to leave before opening up to you. Respect that and act on it.

Scenario 82   ANSWER: F, D, C

Although you are not officially on duty, you still have a duty of care to your patient. You will need to address the issue of their diet at some point but it is essential to maintain confidentiality and not discuss this in front of other people/ in public and to maintain your doctor patient relationship/ trust.

1. Option F: By calling the patient to come in for a review, you are dealing with the problem but you are not breaking confidentiality in front of his friends (you do not know if he has told them about his diabetes) and are therefore not placing the patient in a difficult situation.

2. Option D: Saying hello ensures that the patient sees you, but he does not have to tell his friends who you are or talk about his illness. By calling them to come in for review, you are addressing the problem.

3. Option C: Saying hello ensures the patient sees you, but he does not have to tell his friends who you are or talk about his illness. You will have already organised a follow up with a new type-1 diabetic; and so waiting until that follow up (as long as it is soon) is an alternative option.

The other answers: (In no order of priority)

- Option A: Whether on duty or not, he is still your patient and has a problem if he is eating these things. You need to do something.

- Option B: Confronting the patient with his friends present is inappropriate and is breaking confidentiality.

- Option E: In this option you are not addressing the problem that you have witnessed with the patient's diet / diabetes. There is nothing wrong as such with this option; however there are others that are more suited to the situation.

Scenario 83 ANSWER: E, B, A

If someone is attending for their 4th termination of pregnancy at the age of 21, then she needs some degree of sex education and a form of long term contraception such as the coil or an contraceptive implant.

1. Option E: It is important that this lady is told that repeat surgical TOP is potentially dangerous and knows that it is not a form of contraception.

2. Option B: Offering to insert a coil at the time of TOP means the lady will have a long-term (5-10 year) reversible contraception and will not have to worry about the procedure of inserting it, as she will be under general anaesthetic.

3. Option A: Offering her an alternative long-acting contraception such as the implant (3 years) is another option.

The other answers: (In no order of priority)

- Option C: The combined oral contraceptive pill is less protective than with the coil or implant and is not long term.

- Option D: Condoms are important to protect her from sexually transmitted diseases, but are less reliable than a coil or implant from a contraceptive perspective.

- Option F: Counselling may help but does not address the need for contraception.

Scenario 84 ANSWER: C, F, E

Repeated DNAs are a fact of life in all areas of medicine. In General Practice you have the advantage (usually) of knowing your patients and being able to contact them. By addressing the issue of the non-attendance you may find out that there is a problem (eg. depression, abuse) that the patient wants to talk about or decrease the number of DNA's in the future.

1. Option C: By calling the patient yourself and asking if they are OK, you are not accusing them of anything and are giving them the opportunity to tell you if there is a problem.

2. Option F: Writing to the patient makes them aware of the number of appointments that they have missed. Ensuring you ask if they are OK in that letter gives the patient the opportunity to contact you if there is a problem.

3. Option E: By flagging the notes, you are ensuring that in the future the patient is advised about how to cancel their appointments. If this fails you can act at a later date.

The other answers: (In no order of priority)

- Option A: Annotating the notes is not addressing the problem in any way.

- Option D: By "demanding" information from a patient you are putting them in an awkward situation which will make it difficult for them to "open up" to you in the future.

- Option B: Telling the practice manager is simply involving another person in the problem. If you are unable to resolve the situation yourself, then you can go to the practice manager.

- Option G: It is inappropriate to remove a patient form your GP list without a serious reason, and never at F2 level.

Scenario 85 ANSWER: E, D, B

A one off blood pressure recording of 190/90 without symptoms in an otherwise well patient should not be immediately treated. Only sustained hypertension needs treatment.

1. Option B: Review the patient's notes and medication fully to assess previous blood pressure readings, blood results, medication and investigations. This will help you ascertain whether this blood pressure reading is an isolated one.

2. Option D: By performing serial blood pressure readings at home (as long as the machine is correctly calibrated) you can determine whether she suffers from hypertension.

3. Option E: A 24-hour blood pressure monitor is an excellent way of checking a patient's blood pressure, especially those who have so called "white coat" hypertension.

The other answers: (In no order of priority)

•   Option A: Although you should believe your patient, you need to be certain that this is an isolated reading (options B, D and E).

•   Option C: There is no indication for admission here.

•   Option F: Without reviewing her notes or performing serial blood pressure measurements, you cannot decide whether she requires medication for her blood pressure.

Scenario 86 ANSWER: G, E, C

A patient with an INR of 8 is at risk of a serious bleed and needs to be assessed as a matter of urgency.

1. Option G: This is your mistake and you must act on it. By contacting the patient yourself and bringing her in for review you can assess her, take a repeat INR, and admit her if necessary.

2. Option E: This patient needs a repeat INR today.

3. Option C: By calling the patient and telling them to stop their warfarin you will prevent the problem getting worse. They need to be seen the same day; if you cannot see them yourself, A&E is the next best place.

The other answers: (In no order of priority)

•   Option A: The anticoagulation clinic needs to know about the elevated INR, but the patient must be review and assessed first.

- Option B: Telling the patient to stop their warfarin without any follow up is not a good idea. You do not know what their INR is today or if they have had a bleed, and the patient does not know when (or if) to restart their warfarin.

- Option D: This patient needs to be assessed with a repeat INR as a matter of urgency. It cannot wait until tomorrow.

- Option F: The patient's GP does need to know, but the patient should be assessed and treated first. You can inform the GP in the discharge letter.

Scenario 87 ANSWER: E, C, B

The occupational therapists are professionals and are present in our hospitals for a reason. They are an essential part of the multidisciplinary team and should be respected.

1. Option E: By contacting the OT and asking when they can do the visit, you will have a better idea of when the patient will be discharged.

2. Option C: The consultant needs a bed as a matter of urgency and so the sooner they are aware that this patient cannot be discharged, the sooner they can try and find an alternative.

3. Option B: Taking the notes with you to show the consultant is also advisable.

The other answers: (In no order of priority)

- Option A: The ward manager will need to know but the consultant and OT are the first people you should talk to.

- Option D: By telling the OT the patient is being discharged is not respecting their clinic decision written in the notes.

- Option F: OT's are busy professionals and as with all of us, will not unduly delay a discharge. Even if the home visit took place today, the patient would not be discharged and so this will not help your consultant.

- Option G: By discharging the patient, you are not respecting the occupational therapists clinical decision written in the notes.

Scenario 88   ANSWER: B, A, D

If you are concerned about a patient and want the patient to be seen by the medical team at the hospital the medical team should never refuse to see them. In this case, a suspected subarachnoid haemorrhage is a medical emergency and your duty is to the care of the patient.

1. Option B: The first thing to do if an admission is refused by a junior doctor (i.e. F1, F2, SHO or registrar) is to refer the case to the consultant on call.

2. Option A: If this is a subarachnoid haemorrhage the patient needs to be reviewed as soon as possible. Although it is always better to refer patients directly to the on call team, occasionally a patient may need to be sent to A&E. You should always send a referral letter with the patient.

3. Option D: If you work in an area where you are lucky enough to have 2 hospitals in close proximity, then you could always refer the patient to a different hospital. The essential fact is to ensure the patient is seen and investigated with the minimum delay.

The other answers: (In no order of priority)

- Option C: If you are concerned about a patient and want further investigation, then follow it through. Your duty is to the patient; if you do not have the resources in General Practice or the patient is too sick, they must be sent to hospital.

- Option E: Although you would be justified in complaining about the registrar, calling the hospital manager is unlikely to help. Firstly you must ensure the patient is safe (options B, A, D)

- Option F: if a registrar has refused to accept the patient it would be wrong to go to a junior member of staff. Always go to a more senior member of the team (option B)

- Option G: This would be lying to get your own way and is not an acceptable way to proceed.

Scenario 89 ANSWER: D, E

If you have spent a long time stabilising a patient in the community, it can be very frustrating when a patients drugs are altered by the hospital. When they have been in patients for a long time, you can be certain that the hospital has monitored the patient and that they are then stable on the new drugs. In this case since the patient has only been in hospital for 3 days, it is highly possible that this is a mistake. Anything that appears strange to you (such as significant changes to drugs in a short time) should be clarified with the hospital.

1. Option D: By calling the team, you can discuss with the medics what medication that have changed (if any) and then ensure the correct drugs are prescribed.

2. Option E: Many hospitals now have dedicated ward pharmacists who often prescribe the medication to take home from the drug chart. By calling the team/ ward pharmacist, you can clarify the medication that the patient should be on.

The other answers: (In no order of priority)

- Option A: Making no changes could compromise the patients care. Until you have the information you need from the hospital teams (options D and E) you cannot decide what to do.

- Option B: By immediately changing the medication back you may compromise the patients care. Until you have the information you need from the hospital teams (options D and E) you cannot decide what to do.

- Option C: Slowly changing the medication you may compromise the patients care. Until you have the information you need from the hospital teams (options D and E) you cannot decide what to do.

- Option F: Until you have all the facts, you cannot make a complaint as you do not know if it is justified. Get the information first, then ensure your patient is stable and if there is a complaint to be made you can address that afterwards.

Scenario 90 — ANSWER: C, E

Although, at the current time, there is no official screening programme for prostatic cancer, it is a test that is requested by patients on a regular basis. Before performing the test, the patient must be aware that if the blood test is positive they will need to be referred to the urologists who are likely to perform prostatic biopsies. They also need to be informed that the test is not a perfect screen for prostate cancer. A positive test does not mean they have prostatic cancer (false positive) but means they need further investigations and a negative test does not mean that they do not have prostatic cancer (false negative). This, together with the comments set out below, means that Options C and E are therefore the most appropriate answers.

The other answers: (In no order of priority)

- Option A: If a man is worried enough to come to see you to request the blood test it is not good to simply refuse to perform it. Counsel the man fully and if he still wants to take the test, organise it.

- Option B: You must counsel the man fully before performing the test. You need to ensure they understand the risks involved.

- Option D: It is part of the clinical assessment for prostate cancer to perform a digital rectal examination and this should be offered to the gentleman. You MUST however counsel the man before performing the blood test (options C and E)

Scenario 91 — ANSWER: C, E, F

The clinical picture presented to you is highly suspicious of metastatic breast cancer.

1. Option C: This woman needs admission to assess her and to start treatment.

2. Option E: Prior to admission as an A&E doctor you should perform basic tests to include liver function.

3. Option F: The patient needs to know that there is something wrong with her liver as proven by the jaundice and hard craggy liver. At this point, you

do not know 100% that this is metastatic breast cancer (although this is highly likely). If a patient asks you directly about the connection with her breast cancer you have to be honest. At this point it is possible / likely that it is connected.

The other answers: (In no order of priority)

- Option A: You cannot be 100% certain that the breast cancer has spread (although it is highly likely) and you must not tell the patient this until investigations have proven it.

- Option B: This lady will be referred to the palliative care team in time, but until the diagnosis is confirmed it is premature to do this.
- Option D: This lady does need urgent tests, but a liver MRI and mammogram are not indicated at this time.

- Option G: The patient needs admission and work up.

Scenario 92 ANSWER: A, F, G

If you have concerns about the welfare of a child you must protect them. If someone is not listening to your concerns you must try alternative routes to ensure the safety of that child.

1. Option A: If the duty social worker does not listen to your concerns, there is always a senior social worker on call. They are the first people to approach in this situation.

2. Option F: By clarifying your concerns in writing, you are making your concerns official and there is then a formal paper trail for future reference. Always file a copy of your report in the patient's notes and follow up written requests if there is no response in 24-48 hours. Sending these urgent referrals by fax or email is essential.

3. Option G: If the social work department do not take your concerns seriously, you can always ask the named doctor for child protection for help and advice. Every hospital trust and every PCT has a named doctor who is there to help.

The other answers: (In no order of priority)

- Option B: If the duty social worker does not accept your concerns as genuine then insisting is unlikely to make a difference. Inform them that you will speak to a senior colleague of theirs instead.

- Option C: If you have genuine concerns about the welfare of a child you should always persevere to ensure the child's safety. Do not accept it if your referral is refused.

- Option D: If you have concerns, you need to act on them as soon as possible for the benefit of the child. Delaying the referral is not acceptable.

- Option E: By putting your concerns in writing by post, it delays the referral and you have no way of knowing if the letter arrived. Fax or email is always better for urgent referrals.

Scenario 93 ANSWER: D, F

If you have information that could alter the clinical decisions made by the team you must share them.

1. Option D: By immediately informing the team of what you know, it will become apparent that the CT scan being discussed is not that of the patient; or that there is something other than the uterus in the pelvis. It may alter the clinical management and so is essential that you share the information.

2. Option F: If you do not feel able to share the information to the whole group, you could approach your consultant and inform him/her of the hysterectomy allowing them to share the information with the rest of the meeting.

The other answers: (In no order of priority)

- Option A: By doing nothing you are not helping the patient or the clinical management.

- Option B: You could return to the patient and discuss the hysterectomy but it does not address the problem in the meeting and is unlikely to help.

- Option C: You need to tell the team at the time the scan is bein discussed (options D and F).

- Option E: It is important to review the notes to determine whether th information that the patient gave you is correct but by waiting until later the day, you have missed the ideal opportunity to affect the clinic management of the patient.

Scenario 94 ANSWER: E, F, G

There are patients who repeatedly request admission to hospital for "soci reasons" but these patients can still get ill. This man may have previously lie about the chest pain, but this time it could be real. Never ignore patien symptoms. Always examine them.

1. Option E: You need to assume that this patient does have chest pai even though he is a repeat 'attender'; and therefore you must see him a an emergency.

2. Option F: Anyone presenting with chest pain will get a standard set investigations to rule out a cardiac cause. These should be repeated c this man.

3. Option G: In every medical history there is a section for "social history". this man has admitted to you before that he is lonely, by spending som time listening to him and trying to work out who he has for support cou help prevent unnecessary repeat attendances in the future.

The other answers: (In no order of priority)

- Option A: You do not know that this man does not have chest pain. Yc must see and review him.

- Option B: Anyone presenting with central crushing chest pain is assume to have a myocardial infarction (heart attack) until proven otherwise. Yc cannot determine that he is non-urgent until you have seen and review him.

- Option C: Until you have seen and reviewed him you do not know wheth his pain is real this time. Even if his pain is not real, it is unlikely to help I reprimanding him for wasting NHS time and money. This man needs help. Whether that is medical or social help, you have yet to determine.

- Option D: You cannot refuse to accept the gentleman. You must see and review him.

Scenario 95 ANSWER: G

Option G: By the time most GPs call secondary care to request a referral they have exhausted all of the options available to them. Never refuse to accept a referral. Until you see the patient, you do not know how sick they are. In paediatrics, it is also important to "treat" the parents as much as it is to treat the child. You must ALWAYS listen to the mothers' concerns: they are usually right!

The other answers: (In no order of priority)

- Option A: The GP has requested your help now. Delaying the referral for a few hours is not helpful.

- Option B: If this mother is concerned about meningitis, an out patient referral is not going to help. See the patient now.

- Option C: The GP has requested your help now. Delaying the referral until the next day is not helpful.

- Option D: If a mother has concerns about her child's health you must always listen. Review the patient and ensure the child is well.

- Option E: The GP has requested your help. Respect their judgement and accept the referral.

- Option F: Never refuse a referral.

Scenario 96 ANSWER: F, A, C

In inner city areas particularly, it is common for people to request home visits simply because they do not have transport to get to the practice. Each GP practice will have its own protocol for home visits. Most will refuse to do visit unless the patient is seriously ill, immobile or very elderly.

1. Option F: By requesting more information about the child and their illness you will be able to triage the request.

2. Option A: By discussing other ways of the patient attending the practice you are not refusing their request, but negotiating with them. It may be that during your discussion the patient realises that they can after all attend the practice.

3. Option C: If there really is no way that the mother can bring the child to the surgery and the child is ill, you may need to accept the visit and go to see the child.

The other answers: (In no order of priority)

- Option B: It is unlikely that the GP practice has a fund for taxi fares for patients. Even if it had, you would not want to encourage patients to take advantage of such situations unless there was really no other choice.

- Option D: If the mother really had no way of getting to the practice and after trying to negotiate with her, she still states that she cannot bring the child, insisting she attend is not going to get you anywhere.

- Option E: By sending this child to A&E you are wasting valuable NHS resources. You need to find a way for you, as the GP, to review the child.

- Option G: By advising her to call an ambulance you are wasting valuable NHS resources.

Scenario 97 ANSWER: D, A

It is a sad fact of life as a doctor that you will come across violent or dangerous patients. From the information on the letter, you do not know the background to the attack, whether it was verbal or physical or how serious it was. You must get more information before seeing the patient (unless they have a life threatening injury/ illness).

1. Option D: The GP who referred the patient will have the information you need to ensure your own and the department's safety.

2. Option A: If a patient is violent either physically or verbally, to ensure your own safety and for a witness, you should always use a chaperone.

The other answers: (In no order of priority)

- Option B: You should not refuse to see patients who "have been" violent. They have a right to be treated by the NHS. Ensure you have all the facts, use a chaperone, and refer to the department manager for the "violent/ dangerous patient" protocol if required.

- Option C: You need information first (option D) before deciding if you need security, police or any other help. In most cases, the help of a chaperone will be sufficient to keep patients calm; calling security will only really be needed in extreme cases. You may score partial marks if you selected option C instead of option A.

- Option E: You need to see and assess the patient. Calling the GP in this way is not going to help. You need information from the GP first (option D).

- Option F: For your own safety, you need information regarding the previous attack. Never ignore a warning such as this.

- Option G: If you are frightened, you can always ask another doctor (junior or senior) to accompany you for support or you could ask a senior member of the team for help. However it is not fair or correct to pass this to a junior member of the team.

Scenario 98 ANSWER: B, A, C

People present to A&E with a multitude of problems. To this man, his testicular lump is an emergency and you should treat him with dignity.

1. Option B: If you are certain (as stated in the question) that this is a benign epididymal cyst then you do not need to refer this gentleman for further tests or for any treatment. By suggesting he should see his GP if he is concerned, he has the opportunity for follow up if he chooses.

2. Option A: If you are certain (as stated in the question) that this is a benign epididymal cyst then you do not need to refer this gentleman for further tests, or for any treatment. Sending him home is the correct management.

3. Option C: By informing the man of his benign diagnosis, you have hopefully put his mind at rest. Sending him to his GP for follow up is a good suggestion and it may be that an ultrasound is warranted IF clinical examination has not eased the man's worries or if the clinical findings change. Be careful about telling patients to "tell their GP to send them" for an investigation. The GP will decide if an investigation is needed and request it if necessary. Always advise your patients to "ask" if an investigation is required rather than "demand" one.

The other answers: (In no order of priority)

- Option D: Benign epididymal cysts do not need referral to urology if small and causing no symptoms.

- Option E: If you are "certain" of the diagnosis, an ultrasound is not required.

- Option F: If the man has presented to A&E, he has a right to be seen. To him, this probably is an emergency.

Scenario 99   ANSWER: C, G, B

It is not uncommon for patients to confide in you whilst you are treating them for an illness or injury. You should always pay attention to what is being said!

1. Option C: If someone talks about suicidal ideation to you, you must assess them fully from a psychiatric perspective, paying particular attention to their suicidal risk.

2. Option G: Once you have assessed her psychiatric risk, if you are not concerned she can be discharged but MUST have follow up of some kind. The easiest way is to inform her GP.

3. Option B: If you are not certain of her risk, then a psychiatric referral is necessary.

The other answers: (In no order of priority)

- Option A: It is unlikely that she will be admitted under psychiatric care. Refer her and let them decide.

- Option D: If her sprain does not require hospital treatment it is inappropriate to admit the patient under orthopaedics. The nurses on an orthopaedic ward are not trained to assess suicidal risk.
- Option E: You must always take threats of suicide seriously until you have fully assessed the patient (options C and G).

- Option F: If the patient is at risk of suicide she needs a psychiatric referral, if she is not at risk then having someone stay with her for 24 hours is not necessary.

Scenario 100   ANSWER: D, F, E

Vaccination in the UK is not compulsory. It is the parent/ guardian's choice.

1. Option D: It is the parent/guardian's choice as to whether their children are vaccinated. If you are certain that the parent/ guardian understand the risks involved then you must respect their decision.

2. Option F: You must ensure that they have all of the information that they need to make an informed choice and then respect their decision.

3. Option E: Offering them a follow up appointment ensures that the parent or guardian has the opportunity to change their mind if they wish at a later date.

The other answers: (In no order of priority)

- Option A: There is no need to refer this child on. Vaccinations are not compulsory in the UK. If the parent has made an informed choice then you must respect their decision.

- Option B: Unless you are a Chinese medicine expert, you cannot be certain that it will not work. Do not belittle other people's beliefs. Ensure you maintain open communication in case the parent changes their mind.

- Option C: There is no need to refer this child on. Vaccinations are not compulsory in the UK. If the parent has made an informed choice then you must respect their decision.

Scenario 101 ANSWER: F, E

The GMC (General medical council) in its publication "Good medical practice" 2006 states that you should seek independent medical advice" for yourself and for "those close to you" i.e. friends and family when they are unwell and need treatment.

1. Option F: Since your friend is not your patient and you have not seen and examined them, the first step is to help them get an appointment with their own doctor for assessment.

2. Option E: Following the GMC's guidance is essential. You must therefore refuse to prescribe for your friend.

The other answers: (In no order of priority)

- Option A: You should not prescribe for friends and family. (See above).

- Option B: Taking antibiotics from the A&E stock is stealing NHS supplies and you should never do this.

- Option C: You should not prescribe for friends and family (see above).

- Option D: Your colleague does not know your friend and neither of you has seen or assessed them. This would be putting your colleague in an awkward situation and should be avoided if at all possible

- Option G: By telling your friends GP you are certain it is tonsillitis, you would not be telling the truth since you have not assessed your friend. Lying in this way is not professional and should be avoided at all costs.

Scenario 102 ANSWER: E, B

This referral was urgent and you would expect the patient to have heard from the hospital within two weeks. It needs following up urgently.

1. Option E: Calling the hospital whilst your patient is present is the best option. This ensures the patient knows you are chasing the appointment and that they know the outcome (which is hopefully an appointment date) immediately.

2. Option B: If you are unable to call the hospital whilst the patient is with you then you must do this the same day. This is an urgent case.

The other answers: (In no order of priority)

- Option A: You cannot be certain the referral has been lost and without calling the hospital you will never know (Options E and B). By simply resending a referral and relying on the standard process you are further delaying this urgent care.

- Option C: Telling the patient to chase up the appointment would be unfair. This is an urgent referral and is best done directly to the medical team by you (options E and B).

- Option D: This is not true. There is always something you can do about delayed or missed appointments.

- Option F: If you are concerned about a malignant melanoma it needs to be seen by the local dermatologist or plastic surgeon. This should not be excised by an in house GP.

OTHER BOOKS IN THIS SERIES

GPST STAGE 2 – Clinical Problem Solving
300 MCQs (Single Best Answer) for GPST / GPVTS entry
4th edition: ISBN 978-1-905812-20-2
David Phillips, Nishali Patel

GPST STAGE 2 – Clinical Problem Solving
1400 EMQs for GPST / GPVTS entry
4th edition: ISBN 978-1-905812-21-9
Nishali Patel, Lisa Hamzah, Ruth Reed, David Phillips

GPST STAGE 3 – Selection Centre
Ultimate Guide to the GPST / GPVTS selection centre
4th edition: ISBN 978-1-905812-23-3
Gail Allsopp

ISC MEDICAL GPST ENTRY COURSES

**Optimise your chances of success by attending an
ISC Medical GPST Entry Course.**

- **Run regularly through the GPST recruitment period**
- **Maximum 12 participants**
- **London & Birmingham venues**
- **Cover all relevant stations**
- **Practice under exam conditions**
- **Choice of Stages 2 + 3, and Stage 3-only courses**

204

Chapter 3

How Stories are Written

An education

Accepting the Gullibility of Being a Writer

One year, I started an experiment on my blog. Instead of long, ~~opinionated~~ thoughtful posts on events going on in the publishing industry, I started posting numbered lists. Just silly ways of saying, "Write with your brains, folks."

Wow.

My stats doubled the day I started and tripled a couple of days later. And they kept rising after that until they took an exponential leap and I went into blogosphere hyperspeed, where one of my numbered posts went viral.

Who would have guessed?

People love lists.

I was particularly impressed by the response to the first one, in which I claimed to know "107 Things You Should Know About Being a Published Author." Now, I don't know 107 things about being a published author. *Nobody* knows 107 things about being a published author. Even Stephen King doesn't know 107 things about being a published author.

But we're willing to believe that someone does!

"Hot dog," we're thinking. "The whole instruction manual! I can now plan my life. *Finally.*"

Granted, those of us who are so into such things are writers, not readers. We're just a tiny bit gullible because we're *striving so hard* to get somewhere, not simply looking for a temporary escape. It's our intense need to *become something* that drives us, not our intense need to *stop* being quite so much ourselves for just a while.

Those really are different needs.

Because working in fiction makes us a bit crazy. I know this. You know this.

We're concentrating, we're concentrating, we're concentrating on something we want with our whole souls — to be really good writers — until we lose track of little things like perspective and, you know, maybe our native horse sense. It becomes quite easy to believe that someone has figured out all 107 things we need to know about what's going to happen to us when we get published, thereby simplifying our lives down to just this part, the part about *creating* something to publish.

And that is an enormous gift in this day and age, when absolutely everyone and their grandmother is stampeding toward publication, and we're just running along with the herd hoping we don't get trampled under thousands of little cloven hooves.

Besides, what can writers *not* believe? Our greatest joy is hanging out with imaginary people.

We *like* believing things we know for a fact aren't true.

Reviewing the Definition of a Story

So what is the definition of a story?
And who gets to say?

There are a couple of well-known angles on this time-honored question, pointing at it from different directions.

First, there's Flannery O'Connor's wonderful discussion in the essays in *Mystery and Manners*—collected from her papers and edited by her friends Robert and Sally Fitzgerald after her death—in which she defines a story as 'a full action with a point.'

Then there's the canonical example:

The king died, and then the queen died. (**plot**)
The king died, and then the queen died of grief. (**story**)

This example illuminates two essential aspects of the difference between plot—an action or series of actions—and story—a *full* action with a *point.*

One essential aspect is causality. **Cause-&-effect**.

And the other essential aspect is **character**. Story is not just plot. Story is plot *plus* character.

Story is based upon cause-&-effect.

And story is based upon character.

Which, if we look at it from the right angle, are almost exactly the same thing.

Plot

King Rupert learns he's dying. However, he has no heir. He tells Queen Isabella he has an illegitimate daughter. He introduces Isabella and Maggie. He dies, and Isabella becomes ruler. Isabella is hit by a bus.

Character

King Rupert is suffering from a terminal disease. This is tragic not only because Rupert is king of a small principality without an heir, but also because Rupert's a darn nice guy who takes good care of his people. The only thing nobody knows is that Rupert has an illegitimate daughter, Maggie, from a liaison with a close friend of adolescence. Oh, yes, and Rupert is deeply, madly in love with his wife, Queen Isabella.

Isabella is a hot-headed but basically good-hearted activist, prone to launching herself into confrontations on a whim without pausing for little things like diplomacy. As much as she helps some of her people, she tends to alienate others, so she definitely does not want Rupert's job, now or ever. Her and Rupert's childlessness is an issue for the kingdom, but in fact it means she is not manacled by motherhood as so many women in her position are. What Isabella really wants is to be an adventurer. She sublimates her hunger for excitement in her profound, sincere love for her husband, King Rupert. Right up until the day she gets hit by a bus.

Story

King Rupert learns he's ill and most likely dying. This causes him to re-think his situation regarding his kingdom, his wife, and his illegitimate daughter, Maggie. This causes him to face the possibility that Maggie could cause complications for Isabella when he dies. *This* causes him to go to Isabella to confess Maggie's existence to her.

Isabella learns Rupert is ill and most likely dying. This causes her to become more hot-headed than normal. This causes her to tangle with embryo-rights activists over stem-cell research. *This* causes her to create a national incident.

Maggie is a medical intern at the kingdom's major medical research facility. She learns King Rupert is ill. This causes her to throw herself into her stem-cell research, staying up night after night without sleep, desperate to find a cure for her country's leader and patron. This causes her to become unstable. This causes her to attend a major embryo-rights demonstration in a less-than-reasonable frame of mind. This causes her to give an impromptu speech. This causes Isabella to use her speech as a rallying point for a passionate — if slightly incoherent — expression of her own anguish. This causes Maggie to mistake Isabella for an embryo-rights spokesperson. And *this* causes Maggie to turn on Isabella, sparking the national incident. . .

Do you see how we're heading for the last conflict — the scene in which Rupert confesses Maggie's existence to Isabella — loaded for bear?

Character is the basis of all fictional cause-&-effect.

Why?

Because we read to learn how some folks *will* do. We like human nature! We find it endlessly fascinating. Why *do* people go and do things? Why *don't* we all just stay home twiddling our thumbs?

And — most importantly — when we *don't*, how are we supposed to handle the inevitable crises we bring crashing down upon our own heads?

So we've got this last conflict set up, and we go into it:

Story Climax

Rupert goes to Isabella, who has just come home from causing the national incident and is in her boudoir being cleaned up and first-aided by her ladies, wishing she were in the Himalayas dealing with something reasonable like a nice, quiet avalanche. Rupert sends away the ladies and is about to confess to Maggie's existence.

Meanwhile, Maggie arrives at the castle gates, prepared to take down the queen for interfering with essential stem-cell research that could possibly save the life of the king, but on her way to Isabella's chambers she learns from the servants that Isabella was, in fact, *defending* Maggie's research. This causes her to break down in tears, so when she is finally shown into the queen's and king's presence, she's a stumbling, sobbing wreck.

This causes Rupert to run to her and throw his arms around her.

This causes Maggie and Isabella to go into shock, which gives Rupert a chance to tell them Maggie is his daughter. This causes Isabella and Maggie to be reconciled (faux resolution), but the effort of confession causes Rupert to collapse, and he croaks in their arms.

This causes Isabella, stunned and devastated, her whole life a shambles, to run raving with grief into the street and out into traffic. . .

. . .which causes her to be hit by a bus.

Do you see how it is the characters' personalities — their needs and desires — that create the cause-&-effect that fuels the story? If we gave them different personalities, different needs, different desires, the cause-&-effect would be something completely different. And the plot (the king dies, then the queen dies) would be a completely different story.

This is how we can tell basically the same plots over and over again throughout history — there really aren't that many — and yet continue to tell an endless panorama of stories. This is what Honoré de Balzac was attempting with his gazillion hilarious little stories: an infinitely entertaining and touching and educational portrait of *The Human Comedy*.

What would this story have been if Rupert were a lovable psycho? A loser? A mad scientist? A warmonger? Secretly a wizard with power over life and death?

What would it have been if Isabella were a useless wimp? A monster? A madwoman? An exhausted mother? A schemer? A brilliant leader?

What if there had been no Maggie, but a legitimate heir of Rupert and Isabella with their own needs and desires? Or both? If the people were a force pitted against the royalty? If there were yet other forces involved that we haven't even *thought* of?

Why — someone would have to tell that story!

Reviewing the Definition of Fiction

We've started off with the definition of story through *cause-&-effect* based on *character*. As it should be! Now let's review the definition of **fiction**: storytelling through the written word.

One day, I was talking to my son's tutor about how I'd gotten back in touch with my old college chum Craig Bartlett and was planning to interview him as soon as the hoopla over Craig's new PBS children's cartoon *Dinosaur Train* had abated a bit. We chatted about Craig's early work in pioneering claymation at Will Vinton Studios in Portland, Oregon, and my son's tutor mentioned nostalgically that wonderful 1974 Will Vinton/Bob Gardiner classic of all claymation classics, *Closed Mondays*.

What he loved about it, he said, was the morphing you can do with claymation, the way one thing can magically turn into another without any break in credibility — because realism and surrealism are *equally believable* in clay.

Have you ever heard of Firesign Theater? They made surreal radio programs in the 1970s — not music or commentary, just stories exploring the possibilities of sound. And I can't tell you how we loved them when I was a teen. We had their records memorized, most particularly *Waiting for the Electrician or*

33

Someone Like Him and *Don't Crush That Dwarf, Hand Me the Pliers*. My brother and I used to go to shallow 1970s teen parties and sit in the corners being wallflowers and quoting Firesign Theater *shtick* to each other.

Just like clay, sound can magically turn one thing into another as we listen. A horse whinnying behind the wavering voice of 'Tiny Dr. Tim' saying, "It's a horsey! Let's give the horsey a *sugar cube*," turns unexpectedly into a trumpeting elephant and thunders furiously away.

Great stuff, this playing with the eye of the mind!

And, just as with clay and sound, words can also magically turn one thing into another with no break in credibility.

We must use this to our full advantage. Zoom in on details — the protagonist is wearing argyle socks and playing obsessively with her wedding ring. Does our reader care if her hair's normal? That she's medium weight? That she has a 'pleasant' smile? *No.* They can guess all that for themselves. They want a close-up of the chip in her front tooth, the tear in her screen door that lets in the mosquitoes she's always slapping, the mole on her neck that the secondary protagonist is going to spend a lot of time thinking about touching or not touching.

In fact, fantasy and sci-fi are popular genres precisely *because* we can mix fact and fiction so cleanly with words.

Whatever fiction genre we love, our medium — words — gives us the surreal ability to create absolutely anything we want to create.

This is our lodestone, writers. This is our magic wand.

Reviewing the Purpose of Storytelling

So we come to our story with a question: *"What's going to happen to these fascinating people in my head?"* And we spend hours, weeks, years exploring the answers. . .because there are myriad answers. There are almost *infinite* answers.

And the exploration of those answers — the long, glorious hours feeling our way through them as though blind, discovering which ones are right, when, where, in what way, and why — is our purpose in doing this work.

However, our reader comes to our story with a different question: *"Why should I care?"*

I learned this from the *Gormenghast* fantasy trilogy by Mervyn Peake, of which I read more than half in my early twenties at the behest of a friend. They're the quintessential blending of the real and surreal. Gormenghast is a castle as big as a city, which its inhabitants rarely leave. It's sprawling, ancient, *gothic*. Rats crawl in the dungeons, and bats fly around the belfries. Ivy covers the crumbling stone walls, and the furniture and draperies inside are tattered and dusty. The royal family is a collection of freaks — all except the youngest members, who are, against all odds, completely believable, emotional, multi-faceted.

Human.

Tell us a story about someone we've never met, but we'd love if we did. Someone interesting and funny and droll, but also baffled and clumsy and sometimes downright stupid. Someone whose life is weird and unexpected enough to be fascinating, while their reactions are ordinary enough to be poignantly familiar. Someone who screws up just like us, but handles it better than we do, who can fall over a footstool and land on their feet still walking, the eternal Dick Van Dyke. Someone who hits bottom, bounces up, hits it again, bounces up again, hits it *again*, bounces so hard they knock a hole in the ceiling and wind up flying, arms and legs waving, into the ether.

Make their story unexpected but credible — startling but satisfying — something new and exciting everywhere they turn, but always completely coherent within the context of their own personal fictional dream.

And *keep them in the center* of that story, forever falling over footstools and landing on their feet.

I was enjoying *Gormenghast* tremendously clear up until Fuschia Groan dies.

What?

Fuschia isn't supposed to die! What was Peake thinking? She's the character I was reading for! Cranky and obstinate, but decent and feeling inside, she has all the qualities of a true sympathetic character. *Bang!* She hits bottom. *Bounce!* She goes flying. *Bang!* She hits bottom again. *Bounce!* She goes flying again. I loved the castle, sure. But I was reading for Fuschia.

Peake could go on designing traps for the other characters as long as he liked, but I quit reading *Gormenghast* the minute Fuschia disappeared.

Writer beware! Never forget: *we're storytellers.* We may think that everyone knows stories take a lot of words, that fiction is longer than oral storytelling by very virtue of the medium, and that therefore our reader understands implicitly why they must hang on and keep reading, reading, reading this story we're so in love with. But the magic and flexibility of fiction are *always* submissive to the reader's investment.

Why should they care?

We must make our reader believe. But, even more than that, we must make them *want* to believe.

Chapter 4

Character Arc/Narrative Arc

The rainbow

Character arc: *someone living their life*

Narrative arc: *the things that happen when someone lives their life*

When I worked with children, the first thing I'd do on the first day was review the basic parts of speech, grammatical points, stuff I knew they probably already knew. Then I taught them the very simple, straight-forward, zen fact: every sentence has a **subject** and a **verb**.

Someone does something.

Subject. Verb. That's all there is to it. That's all they needed to know.

I'd look at them. They'd look at me. I'd nod.

And then, *I'd mess with their heads.*

I'd tell them, "From this you can learn that all storytelling is holographic. Do you know what a holograph is? It's a document written entirely in the handwriting of the same person who signs it. A *whole* or *holistic* graph or piece of writing. And a holo*gram* is a picture made out of light, of which every little tiny bit is actually the whole big picture in miniature." I'd wave my hands around, showing them little-tiny and whole-big.

Then I'd say, "I think. Or the other way around. But, anyway, they're both very cool.

"Because a story — just like a sentence — has a subject and a verb: someone does something. And everything *in between* the big picture of the overall story and the tiny picture of the individual sentence has a subject and a verb. No matter what the granularity — cosmology to quantum mechanics — it's all designed the same. A subject and a verb."

Now, these children didn't know what holographs, holograms, granularity, cosmology, or quantum mechanics are, but that's okay because I didn't mind telling them. And kids love that! What cool ideas! It's not listening to a teacher drone on and on and on about participles and imperatives and the pluperfect, much less calling on them to parrot anything. They're bemused, but entertained. *When is she going to go back to drilling stuff into our heads?*

All f big words and concepts make subject-verb, frankly, laughably easy. Geez. Just two things stuck together. A person. And what they do. Anyone can remember *that.*

I liked picturing the looks on their parents' faces when they'd go home after an hour with me and say, "Did you know a holo-something is something that's the same in its tiniest parts as it is in its biggest parts? And atoms are characters and what they do are verbs? And it has something to do with other stuff about writing too, but I forget what because I 'm starting a novel?"

I loved working with kids.

Character arc. Narrative arc. Subject. Verb.

Someone does something.

We're working on our story, living with these characters in our heads, hearing their voices speak to each other, watching them move around the rooms of their houses, the places they go, the wildernesses of city or forest or desert or small town ingrown like a toenail. And they're doing things (things they shouldn't), making decisions, taking trips, running into each other under inconvenient, embarrassing, or even dangerous circumstances. They're doing, doing, doing, and it keeps twisting back on them, thwarting them, turning their carefully or not-so-carefully laid plans inside out, tossing them cavalierly, time after time, out of the frying pan into the fire.

What are their *arcs*?

Well, *we* go through arcs. We go to a child's basketball game, maybe, and some kids there are mean to other kids, and we don't like it.

It sets up an internal conflict inside: we have our own personal issues about confrontation and control over other people and public situations and, maybe, our own experiences on the basketball court as children. And at the same time we have this dearly-cherished value that *we don't let people hurt kids*. Not if we have anything to say about it. So how do we resolve this internal conflict?

That's our character arc.

Meanwhile, this trigger to our character arc also sets off a domino effect, a series of events sparked by that original event. We go to the game, which causes us to see the kids being mean, which causes us to make a decision. Maybe we decide to hide our head and shuffle out in embarrassment. Maybe we decide to go along with the kids and pretend it's all fun and games. Maybe we decide to blow our top, and the police arrive. Maybe we decide on something else.

Whatever we decide causes another event, which backs us into a more specific corner, about which we must make a new, more refined decision, which narrows our options even more.

That's our narrative arc.

So the further we work our way through our character arc, the more focused our narrative arc becomes, and the more inevitable become the events we face. Until we reach the point after which the life we were leading before this chain of events (this narrative) came along has been irrevocably altered into something different (by our character).

Who's your story about? What's going on inside them that sets them up for this original decision with which they must cope throughout the rest of the story? What's on one side of their internal conflict—what *need* in their character forces them to make this particular decision? And what comes along and creates the conflicting side—what other need *contradicts* that original need, turning this one aspect of character into a narrative?

What values, beliefs, fears, hopes, prejudices, assumptions, secrets, denial, habits, and history bear in on this character constantly from all sides, forcing them to be able to react to stress in just the one way? What's the core of their internal conflict, the Gordian Knot, the inescapable toe-stubber beyond which they simply cannot continue? How does this core illuminate their two mutually-exclusive needs, the clues to their basic character and to how all of us—every single human on earth—live with irreconcilable paradox in our souls?

We must ask ourselves all of this every time we find ourselves dealing with internal conflict of our own. How we resolve the conflict matters less than what we learn about ourselves in dealing with it.

We're not just revealing characters when we create fiction. We're revealing the key to being human.

And what are the dominoes that keep falling on us or out from under our feet? What scenes occur, one after another, other characters coming in and out, days and nights passing, outside events happening, conversations, gestures, activities, *milestones in a life?*

We're not just chronicling stories when we write. We're chronicling the inevitable forward motion of being alive.

Chapter 5

Graphing in Three Dimensions

Theme

We can think of storytelling as (x,y,z) graphing, which is drawing an image through three-dimensional space with a single line, using two sets of coordinates: one for one end of the line, the other for the other. Computer graphics engineers write these $(x1,y1,z1)$ and (xn,yn,zn), where n represents the furthest possible point at the end the line.

A character must make a journey through an experience in their life. That's a story. It can be either an outer or inner journey, with other characters or without them, but they must start at one point, and they must wind up at another point, and those two points encompass everything in between.

The protagonist's conflicting, overwhelming needs are the two diametrically-opposed points that define our x coordinates. Those needs get our protagonist through space in one dimension, which is their character arc.

The plot begins with a Hook and ends on a Climax, which are the two structurally-opposed points that define our y coordinates. That structure gets our protagonist through space on exactly the same journey in a *second* dimension, which is their narrative arc.

And our major and minor themes contain those aspects of life we're exploring through this story. We want more than one theme so that we can create tension between them, and the two most powerful are defined by our z coordinates. They get our protagonist through space on that same journey in the *third* dimension, which is the progress of our exploration of themes.

You'll notice there are multiple points — an infinite number, actually — between the first and last sets of (x,y,z) coordinates, and at each of those points we must be able to define the coordinates of all three planes. For every step of our character arc, we must know the corresponding step in our narrative arc, which illuminate — all on their own — the corresponding step in the progress of our themes. That's (x,y,z).

Now, I'm not going to explicate theme, and this is on purpose. I have a Taoist perspective on theme. I believe the less said about it the better for everyone, especially the reader. We must focus on our storytelling — on developing truthful, gut-wrenching characters and believable, hair-raising plot — and forget about theme while we do it.

Then when we throw our reader off the rainbow into their own epiphany at the very end of our story. . . they find the full illumination of our themes, the part we didn't know we knew, the art lying at the core of the craft of fiction.

When we have written our story and polished it in exactly the right way, we will have illuminated everything we have to say about these particular themes.

Let the reader be one to put them into other words.

Chapter 6

The Only Two Stories

Relationship & Quest

Mining Yourself

There are no new stories, only new perspectives.

Has anyone ever told you that? It's true.

There are two ways in this world to get into trouble: with other people and on our own.

If we want to get our protagonist into trouble with others, we give them a **relationship**. If we want to get them into trouble on their own, we give them a **quest**.

How many kinds of *relationship* are there? Well, there are romantic/sexual relationships (with women, with men), family relationships (with children, with parents, with siblings, with extended family), friendships (individual, group, crowd, close, distant, estranged), business relationships (with bosses, with subordinates, with peers, with allies, with competitors), and antagonists (original enemies or any of the above gone bad). We can also have relationships with things, as the narrator does in Marie Redonnet's *Hotel Splendid*, but unless they also involve either other people or a quest they're going to become boring pretty quickly.

How many kinds of *quest* are there? Two. The kind where we actually go somewhere, **external**, and the kind where we stay in one place, **internal**.

See? Only a handful.

So how do we write something new, something unique, something that wasn't already beaten to a fruity pulp long before we were even born?

These days everyone knows about Monty Python, that pillar of British non-sequitur and daftly logical conclusions. And many of us are even conversant with *The Meaning of Life*. But how many actually know the lyrics to *The Galaxy Song*?

Along with a plethora of cosmological facts (apparently first disproven and then re-proven, causing Eric Idle to demand 'the bastards' make up their minds), the song gives us that nihilistic reminder how amazingly unlikely were our births. And although it's meant, in context, to scare us, I for some reason have always found it rather encouraging.

After all, if my birth was amazingly unlikely — which isn't debated by scientists on either side of the argument — that means I'm unique, doesn't it? And if I'm unique, then my experience of life can't be duplicated by anybody, anywhere, at any point in history, can it? At least, not without my express written permission.

Take this to heart. *You are unique.*

We may have to paw through the minimalist slush pile of potential stories to find the one that strikes our fancy, but once we do we've got unlimited rein to do with it what we will.

Mine yourself.

No matter what story we want to tell, relationship or quest, we must look to our own lives to teach us how to tell it uniquely.

We must be alert wherever we go, whatever we do. There is only one person in human history in a position to perceive and note down the specific, telling details of this life—nobody else's—in all their extraordinarily singular significance.

Does cheese remind us of telephone wires because of our cheese-slicer? We give that to a character. When we're scared, do we finger our buttons? Some people do. When the one we love tells us they don't love us anymore, is our first thought of tango'ing off an Argentinian cliff to the anguished wail of Tito Luisardo?

Does it, in fact, inspire us to travel to Buenos Aires and there meet the ravishing grandson of Tito, who tells us of the secret *amor* of his grandfather and the violet-eyed Amelia Bence? Is it our passion for 1930s Argentinian music that teaches us, in its complex, magnificently-detailed, ultimately poignant way, what it means to be alive?

There is only one person who can discover the links between one detail and another that illuminate the workings of this one bizarrely-convoluted human brain. (Have you ever seen a human brain? Convoluted doesn't even *begin* to cover it.) There is only one person who loves the strange conglomeration of hobbies that each of us loves in exactly the way we love them. There is only one person who will ever come up with the weird and unusual meanings that each of us knows, in our heart of hearts, lie just beyond the surface of everything we do, everything we say, everything that ever happens around us.

It's not getting our books on a bookstore shelf that makes writing worthwhile. Believe me, I know.

It's getting to spend our writing time scrutinizing ourselves and our own lives for the devastating, electrifying, inherent beauty of living that is the essence of us—all that we will take with us to the grave.

Differentiating Between Together & Alone

So the first thing we need to know is that writing itself is a quest, and if we don't know this when we first start out we sure will by the time writing is done wrestling us to the floor.

A *quest* is a journey, external or internal, the solitary path that is the true path of each of us throughout our life.

A *relationship*, on the other hand, is an accumulation of the consequences of people's influence upon each other, the mingling of individual paths that creates community between all of us out here rattling around in the world in the same place at the same time, social animals that we are. (This is, oddly, the act of publication — quite different and in some ways the opposite of writing.)

Is our story focused upon the characters and how they interact? Is it mainly about the ways in which these people relate to each other, how they come to signify to each other all things dreadful and ignoble and all things great and glorious, how they reach into each other's hearts and souls and rearrange the furniture to produce something new and unusual, something poignantly true to life, something none of them has ever been before?

That's a story of relationship.

Or is our story focused upon one character, one goal, one twisting, staggering, marvelous, and infuriating struggle to come to grips with what it means to be alone inside a single brainpan on this planet?

Yeah, that sounds like a quest to me.

Fyodor Dostoevsky's *The Brothers Karamazov* is a novel of relationships, the story of three brothers and a half-brother who struggle, in their different ways, to come to grips with each other and with the mysterious death of the father who has made their lives hell. It's a mystery, and as a mystery it involves the infinite permutations of human interactions, all the ways in which we move and breathe and behave around each other and create — in the act of creating our own lives — the world in which we all live.

On the other hand, Dostoevsky's *Crime and Punishment* is a quest. Again, there's a suspicious death, and again there's a search for some resolution to the crime. But in this case, there's no mystery. We know who committed the crime, how, and why, because we were there with him when he did it. Now we're learning all about what happens to a person who does such a thing — just an ordinary man, a mediocre man, someone with faults and virtues no better or worse than our own, but a man who has done something beyond the pale that now he can't undo. We are learning what the first step is for him, how this leads to the death and everything after, and by the end of the novel we learn how it turns out for him — what one person makes of this extraordinary act of character and how their goal (escaping punishment) twists around on them at the last moment and becomes something completely different from anything they could ever have predicted.

What about a story like the movie *Galaxy Quest*? Is it, in fact, a quest?

First, may I say to you: Enrico Colantoni? Tony Shalhoub? Sam Rockwell? Alan Rickman? Four of the great comic actors of our time, all in one place, all in one ludicrous, hilarious, death-defying spoof on *Star Trek*? Wow!

Ship's captain Jason Nesmith and his crew are the has-been stars of a science fiction TV show with all the overweening schmaltz and cliché of the original *Star Trek*. They're living off their fading fame making appearances in malls and shopping center parking lots across America. It's a hard time to have no talent except a surprising ability to conquer the galaxy.

There's a Hook (Jason makes a fool of himself at a sci-fi convention, in a spoof on a *Saturday Night Live* shtick starring William Shatner). There are Developments (aliens co-opt the whole kit-&-caboodle to save their planet from Sarris, the Darth Vader of Reptilia). And there's a Climax (Sarris wins! Oh, *no!*). There's also a Resolution, which is of course the feel-good moment at the end of the story.

Throughout the plotline, the characters mess with each other's heads, save each other's butts, and come a cropper of each other's failings. In the end, they have all learned something significant about themselves and each other and had a *darn* good time, to boot.

They have changed each other.

This is a story of relationship.

Graham Greene's *The End of the Affair*, on the other hand, while it purports to be about a woman and a man involved in an illicit romance during the bombing of London in World War II, isn't actually about the affair at all. The reader follows Maurice through the years after Sarah inexplicably dumps him, digging deeper and deeper into his own character, until he learns not only the long-buried truth about the end of their affair but the truth about himself — the one person he hasn't thought to confront all along.

This is a solitary journey into the very heart of what it means to live alone in a human soul.

This is a quest.

Molding & Being Molded By Relationship

There's a legend that after Faulkner left Hollywood someone found a piece of paper in the garbage can by his desk that said repeatedly all the way down the page: "Boy meets girl. Boy meets girl. Boy meets girl."

This is a take-off on the standard romance plot, "Boy meets girl. Boy loses girl. Boy gets girl."

And, sexism aside, that's the basic issue behind all relationship stories: meet someone, lose them, regain them.

The purpose of relationship stories is the exploration of the ways in which human beings, thrown together as we are on this increasingly-crowded planet, alter and reinforce and form each other's lives even as we are formed. We might each start out alone in our own little squished post-natal heads, and we might, indeed, spend our time in this mortal coil isolated inside those heads, which is the whole point of the quest story and the point of writing in general.

But the time we spend here *itself* forces us into proximity with others so, unless we check out the minute we check in, our fate is the fate of all co-existing substances: to mold and be molded in turn. (Which, as it happens, is exemplified in the practice of publication.)

If a story is a full action with a point, then the point of a relationship story is whatever the writer finds significant in that relationship.

The entire history of a relationship, like the history of a life, is generally random and really quite boring unless it's designed specifically around significance.

Therefore the full action is: the beginning of the significant part of the relationship, through the significant developments, to that one thing that the writer wants to say is significant about this particular relationship.

In **mystery, horror**, and **thriller**, what is significant is who did or does what to whom and *why*. As mystery writers are so fond of saying, "Show me the why, and I'll show you the who."

While some mysteries, horror stories, and thrillers explore the potential for danger in us all, many are less discerning — they can be about any type of threat, on any kind of flimsy grounds (and some are really flimsy), so long as they explore why people do things to each other.

Edgar Allan Poe and Wilkie Collins gave us the original Western mysteries (although the Chinese have been telling mystery stories for 2,000 years), while Horace Walpole gave us the original gothic romance, which is the basis of horror, which is the basis of thriller. And those darn resilient genres haven't met their untimely ends yet.

In **romance** what is significant is the sexual energy between people. As we all know, sex is the single greatest motivator in the Animal Kingdom. It would have to be, wouldn't it? Any species that *wasn't* designed specifically around sex would simply find procreation far too difficult and die out in a generation. (Have you ever given birth to the next generation? It's *hard!*) This is why romance has been and remains one of the all-time massive-selling genres in fiction. Nobody ever gets tired of thinking about sex, especially its powerful emotional ramifications, which in romance we are pleased to call 'love.'

Emily and Charlotte Brontë, Jane Austen, and — much later — Jean Rhys laid the groundwork for all modern romance stories.

In a **buddy** story what is significant is the ability of two or more people to bond to each other above and beyond the confines of family — overcoming the plethora of differences between us, but without the magnetism of sex — to find a deeper meaning in that human bond. We need each other. Even when we sometimes can't stand each other, we still need each other.

Interestingly, most of the earliest novels that might have been buddy stories are, in fact, quests: *Don Quixote, Moll*

Flanders, Tom Jones. Fascinated as we are by bonding, buddy stories lack either death or sex and therefore typically need more plot than just the relationship to carry them all the way through to a Climax. So instead we use layering — multiple purposes — to explore the eternal greater truths.

The mystery duo Sherlock and Watson are buddies. The Japanese 'Western' *The Seven Samurai* is a buddy story. Mary Shelley's classic sci-fi novel *Frankenstein*, oddly, is the story of what happens when we try to build our own buddy.

In a **family** drama the significant lies in the many ways in which family members create, influence, and infect the life they all must share. Family is our original tribe. We are a social species, and our brains are organized to find gossip, intrigue, and conflicting agendas interesting as all get-out.

Eudora Welty went to the wall with *Delta Wedding*, but before her we had Emily Brontë, Ivy Compton-Burnett, Faulkner, and James Thurber's hilarious *My Life and Hard Times*. Rebecca West wrote the extraordinary *Cousin Rosamund* trilogy as a fictionalized account of her own family.

And in a **parent-child** story what is significant is the special power imbalance between parents and children and how this sets the participants up for conflict and union more fundamental to character than any other relationship.

Thus we get fairytales and their great dependence upon parent-child relationships: mothers, fathers, step-parents, runaway children, lost children, obedient children, disobedient children, dominated and dominating children. In many cultures, the royal family serves as the archetype of the nuclear family for fairytales, laying the groundwork for fiction and storytelling in general.

It's especially effective if we can combine several of these stories into one. Almost any story — even William Gibson's geek sci-fi classic *Neuromancer* — gets more exciting if we add romance.

So what about the plot structure of the relationship story: meet someone, lose someone, gain someone?

In modern culture — after the rise of the romantic concept that we might choose whom we spend time with rather than simply take what we get — we find ourselves especially drawn to that act of choosing. This means the beginning of the relationship.

But all stories need conflict. It's not enough to say: "They met and lived happily ever after." I mean, what kind of story *is* that? Remember, the reader wants to read about when things go wrong.

So it must be: "They met, they were prevented from being together, they triumphed over their obstacles, and *then* they lived happily ever after." Frankly, once we get to the triumph, nobody's even interested in the happily-ever-after. That's why we can cram it all into one phrase like that: "Whatever."

This, of course, lends itself very tidily to the standard plot structure for all stories: Hook (they meet or are reunited after a separation), Development through a sequence of Conflicts of rising tension to a Faux Resolution (separation, reunion, separation, reunion, *big* separation, *big* reunion!), and Climax (insurmountable obstacle to their union — oh, dreadful day, they can never be together *again*). And the Resolution: either they never will be together again, or somehow, based upon some clue dropped early in the story, they manage to surmount the insurmountable and triumph over ultimate separation.

And that, my friend, is the whole point of this story. I could have told you how it ended in the first place, but it wouldn't have been nearly as much fun, now, would it?

Aiming Past Ecstasy through Quest

I had a great conversation with a client one day on the subject of *Galaxy Quest,* which, it turned out, is one of both our favorite movies.

My client made the good point that a quest has an *aim.* In the story of a relationship, what seems to be the aim is really only the locus of a framework, within which the author explores humanity and its infinite disgrace and glory. While, in the story of a quest, the aim really *is* the point.

In a quest, the protagonist is driven relentlessly forward toward their aim, through punishment and reward, trauma and reprieve, until they reach it and *in reaching that aim* discover what lies beyond it.

Although an entire lifetime could, theoretically, be framed as a quest (remember *Don Quixote, Moll Flanders, Tom Jones*), the bildungsroman is rarely today considered a viable storytelling format, which means the quest itself becomes the tidy storytelling framework, good for all themes and seasons.

The complete action is: the beginning of the quest, through the significant developments, all the way to the aim or at least destruction of the quest.

An **external quest** is the easiest to design—we send our protagonist on an **adventure.** Such stories are riveting for the details of new and unusual places. It's the Marco Polo experience of learning, the tidal wave of new information about what kind of planet this is, who lives here besides us, what they're like. When we write such a quest, the bulk of the work is the research. We must go where our protagonist goes, learn what they learn. And, like Marco Polo, we bring our findings back with us to share with our reader.

Our protagonist must have a reason for this adventure—storytelling is always about cause-&-effect. They must have an aim to accomplish, a reason for ending their adventure (unless we do something fancy like ending on the realization that this particular adventure will never end). And things must happen to them on this adventure.

It's not enough to take a guess at what the adventure is like. Unless we're writing fantasy, our readers can guess just as well as we can, and they do not come to writers for anything they can do themselves. Mrs. Radcliffe, the nineteenth-century English blockbuster author of such grand gothic epics as *The Mysteries of Udolpho*, is reported to have lifted entire pages of description out of travel books for the foreign settings of her characters' travails. Now, that is of course very bad manners. (*Mrs. Radcliffe.*) And today we would get busted. But she did demonstrate her solid understanding of the need for authentic telling detail.

The purpose of an external quest, an adventure, is to go somewhere. The external quest has a geographical aim. And whether or not the protagonist actually gets there, coming to grips with that destination is the point of telling this particular story.

An **internal quest**, on the other hand, is often more powerful but much more subtle. Our protagonist's character arc itself is the adventure—who are they in the beginning, what happens to alter them in the crucible of life, wherein lie their hopes, wherein their climactic despair?

An internal quest is concerned, on all levels, with the resolution of the protagonist's unresolved needs. *They need something.* Naturally, all protagonists do, but an internal quest must be designed to keep those needs clear and alive in the protagonist's perspective. In other types of stories, those needs can be subsumed into actions, complications, the interplay between one character's needs and another's. In an internal quest those needs are the be-all and end-all of the story. And the protagonist's drive to meet those needs is the aim.

In the relationship story *Pride and Prejudice*, Jane Austen can, in the interests of true love, cavalierly toss aside Elizabeth's powerful need to make snap judgments, which has motivated her throughout the novel. But in Henry James' quest story, "The Aspern Papers," the nameless protagonist must either acquire the papers or resolve his emotional need for them in a way that allows him to live out his life without being emotionally destroyed.

Like a relationship story, any quest fits very nicely into standard plot structure: Hook (aiming at something), Development through a sequence of Conflicts of rising tension to a Faux Resolution (danger of failure, averted, danger again, averted, *big* danger, *big* success! maybe the protagonist will just pitch a permanent tent?), and Climax (*impossible danger of failure*, this quest must end in complete and utter disaster!). And the Resolution: either the quest ends entirely unexpectedly, or somehow the impossible danger is averted and the quester safely achieves their aim.

In this way, the protagonist of a quest discovers, in the end, not the interdependence of humanity in all its infinite entanglements and permutations. Not even the dichotomy — the release or ecstasy — they expected.

But only, in the final hour, a deeper understanding of their own life, after all.

Chapter 7

Reading with Attention

Learning your form

Reading for Plot Design

I love vintage mysteries—those cheap, battered little paperbacks of the 1930s, '40s, and '50s—and I spend a lot of my time scouring the West Coast for them in all the obscure bookshops I can find between San Francisco and Portland. So now I've got hundreds of pulp mysteries to work my way through.

It's a *pulp avalanche*.

And as I fly through these—I read almost one a night—I've devised a reading exercise for the study of their structure, which I've assigned to my local teenage creative writing students and I'm going to assign to you, too.

Whatever book you're reading right this very minute, let's take a quick second to look in the back and see how many pages it has. Rounded, I mean. A lot of these early mysteries are in the 180-240 range, but nowadays novels are expected to be actually quite long by comparison, in the 280-400 range. (This has to do with the shift from general-purpose novels to strictly genre fiction in recent decades, mega-volume fantasy and series fiction pushing the envelope right to the limit and beyond into the infinite abyss, as well as a growing neglect of the editorial craft of cutting and trimming by many publishers. No wonder we suddenly need flash fiction.)

Let's find a scrap of paper or a used envelope and jot this down at the bottom: total number of pages.

Now we'll divide that into: $1/8$, $1/6$, $1/4$, $1/3$, $1/2$, $2/3$, $3/4$, $5/6$, $7/8$. We can knock it right down into all the eighths and sixths if we like, but these are the main divisions. We scribble those numbers vertically above the total.

Now—as we work our way through our current read—every time we come to one of those pages, we'll make a note of whatever big, important plot point is going on *right there*. At least within a few pages.

Depending upon the type of novel we're reading (and in some cases how recently it was written), the Climax may be shoved all the way to within spitting distance of the last page. And that's fine! That's an excellent way to end a novel. So when we get to the Climax, we go ahead and scribble that down, too. We can give it its page number if we like or, if the Resolution really is negligible, just let it roll with the final page number.

We label it at the top with the title of the book. Then throw it on a box on our desk and start a new scrap for the next book.

Eventually, we're going to have a whole *raft* of these little lists.

And. They. Are. Priceless.

We take them out every now and then to study.

What do we see?

Act 1

Hook (the beginning to $1/8$-$1/6$)
Conflict #1 ($1/8$-$1/6$ to $1/4$-$1/3$)

Act 2

Conflict #2 ($1/4$-$1/3$ to $1/2$-$2/3$)
Conflict #3 ($1/2$-$2/3$ to $2/3$-$3/4$)

Act 3

Faux Resolution ($2/3$-$3/4$ to $5/6$-$7/8$)
Climax ($5/6$-$7/8$ to the climax near the end)

Now, writers will joggle this a bit. Sometimes there are mini- and midi-Faux-Resolutions at the ends of Conflict #1 and Conflict #2, a little pacing to give each element punch, although they're often truncated in mid-stride by the hook to the next Conflict. And sometimes the Hook is a bit shorter and Conflict #1 closer to the beginning to make room for a longer Conflict #2, or vice versa. (That's only by some small number of pages, though, not huge chunks.)

Some writers use a pattern based on quarters ($1/8$, $1/4$, $1/2$, $3/4$, $7/8$), while others prefer a pattern based on thirds ($1/6$, $1/3$, $1/2$, $2/3$, $5/6$). Occasionally I stumble across someone who skews the $1/2$ point to $3/5$ (rare) or even $2/3$ (even more rare).

Some writers also trim the Faux Resolution down to a single page before they kick their characters off the moving train into the hook for the Climax, while others drag the Faux Resolution out a bit to shove the Climax farther toward the last page.

That's why this isn't formula, it's structure. A house with many rooms is just as livable as a house with only one room, but a house with no supporting walls at all falls down. Once we've tracked the structure through several entire novels, we develop a nose for it. Just keep an eye on those fractions.

So let's lick a pencil and scrabble for whatever's handy. All those novels we've been reading all these years?

All structured properly.

You're going to be *amazed.*

Reading for Character Development

Now I'm also going to assign a *second* exercise for our current reading material. Because I don't believe in doing things halfway.

Let's flip over that scrap of paper or used envelope on which we're jotting down our plot design research and scribble the name of the protagonist of whatever we're reading on the back. If there's more than one protagonist, we'll scribble the name of the main one. We'll chew our pencil for a few minutes (don't eat the paint—just destroy the little metal bit that holds the eraser) and ask ourselves, "What does this character *need* more than anything else in the entire world?" When we've got it, we'll write it down under their name. "And what do they need that *conflicts* with this need?" We'll write that down too. Put a big blocky square all the whole thing.

Got it?

Good.

Now, every time we reach one of those milestones we've outlined on the other side of this paper, we'll jot down on this side *what happens to the protagonist and their conflicting needs.*

I can guarantee something does.

Is one need satisfied in some partial but slightly fulfilling way? Just enough to keep the character addicted to the search for total fulfillment?

Is their search for fulfillment of one need thwarted in some way? Enough to freak them out, but not enough to make them think, "This is for the birds. I'm giving up"?

Are their needs ever totally fulfilled?

Are their needs ever totally thwarted?

Scribble, scribble, scribble. We do our scribbling. We're scribblers.

Then — you knew I was going to say this — we chuck it in that box on our desk. And start the whole thing over again with another book.

When we're ready, we'll take these scraps out of the box and study them. What patterns do we see? How do all these different authors lead their characters by the nose through the hoops that have been set for them, feeding their needs, denying their needs, feeding their needs again, denying their needs again? How does this rhythm build to a crescendo by the end, driving both character and reader nuts with frustration and anticipation?

How have these authors kept their reader *addicted*?

Do you ever watch fireworks — for Chinese New Year, Mexican Independence, a hobbit's eleventy-first birthday?

Every time I do, I'm thinking about how it would feel to have them go off inside my heart. Then I think about how all of these authors have made the Climaxes of their novels feel. . .

Exactly. That. Way.

Chapter 8

___

Creating Reader Addiction
Tension

Creating the Basic Tension in Character

Let's talk reader **addiction**. Let's find out why some stories can hold sway over the imaginations of hundreds of thousands of readers for generations, while others vanish without a whimper almost before they're read.

Let's take a look at character tension, the inherent tension inside a single character that must, eventually, cause them to collide with themself.

Internal conflict.

I was working with a client once on a Middle Grade (MG) novel in which a main character must become romantically entangled with one of the villains. At the same time, one of the major events involves that character turning their back on that villain, in a last-minute switcheroo that allows them to win a major triumph for the protagonist's side.

But then the character has to turn *back* to that villain, in order to set up the Faux Resolution that leads to the Climax. It's a whole sequence of unbreakable cause-&-effect to make a Superhero weep. And it has to be *perfect*.

How did we do it?

With internal conflict.

The part about being romantically-attracted to the villain is easy for the later MG audience. Those people are pre-pubescent, just beginning to sprout hormones, and it's a big surprise to them to discover themselves feeling irresistible urges to consort romantically with others.

So all we need for this story is show how this character is swept off their feet by the villain in a romantic tsunami that takes them completely by surprise and writes their doom in indelible ink all over their face.

We've all been there.

But at the same time, we need to show how this character *manages to break with* this overwhelming romantic attachment at the crucial moment. And what drives that break?

It has to be that character's fundamental *need*, the need that shapes their personality, fuels their journey forward through the plot, makes them who they are. What kinds of things serve as character need?

Well, what kinds of things serve as *ours*?

We all need love and acceptance. And we tend to choose one of a handful of basic avenues toward satisfying that need:

affection

intelligence

work

self-protection

self-promotion

self-deprecation

power

humor

tragedy

mystery

There are others, but these are some of the biggest. We all strive toward certain stations along the track of that universal Love & Acceptance Train.

Say we've got a character who needs *affection*. Affection is what gains them love and acceptance. So this character's basic, driving agenda is to *get affection from people*. Anything that interferes with this agenda gets tossed by the wayside. Obstacles are never taken seriously, detours are always hijacked, arguments are just so much babbling in the wind.

"Don't try to get affection out of *her*," the other characters cry, aghast. "She's got a knife in her pocket!"

"Don't stand in my way," this character yells back belligerently. "She's got the manna I need!"

While, at the same time, someone *else* is maybe sporting the ever-popular hormone flag.

Whom to choose?

This quandary gives our character devastating internal conflict.

Or say we've got a character who needs to be *self-deprecating*. Advertising their own failings is just their thing—it's what makes their life, oddly enough, worth living. This is a tricky protagonist to pose, because self-deprecators tend to be victims, and victims are boring. Nobody wants to read about a boring protagonist.

But let's say this character isn't a victim, they're actually quite forceful and entertaining and full of beans. But there it is: they need to be, above all things, self-deprecating.

This can get them into a *whole lot of trouble*.

"You're tall and handsome!" gushes Eve Arden.

"You're near-sighted," Groucho shoots back (*A Day at the Circus*).

Groucho can get away with this because the vast suspension of disbelief in 1930s comedy audiences left him plenty of room to continue romancing the woman in all good faith in spite of his self-castigating one-liners. But a modern fictional character must remain faithful to their agenda, so when they need to self-deprecate, god help them, they need to *self-deprecate*. And when the survival of all they hold dear depends entirely upon them accepting the role of hero, they're going to get themself into some mighty hot water shucking the cape over and over again.

Princess Leia says she'd prefer to kiss a wookie, which Han Solo says he's willing to arrange. At the same time they both desperately need other things — she needs the rebellion to succeed, and he needs to watch out for Number One. And so their romance struggles and struggles and struggles to get off the ground, until he's being dropped into carbon-freeze and she has only seconds to admit *she'll do anything* to get him safely out again. (Just in case hers is the first face he sees when he's unfrozen, so he won't throw her through a wall.)

It's too bad they didn't say in the first place, "I love you, and you love me. Let's go kick some cosmic ass."

But no.

Or say we've got a character who needs to be *mysterious*. It's simply how they style themself. It's their personal fetish. So when it comes time to trust, they don't trust the ones who could make their lives so much easier. And when it comes time to divulge secrets, they never divulge them in time. And when it comes time to put their life in the hands of someone who has *also* made it their mission to hide the truth about themself. . .they can't bring themself to do it.

Which means that this need to be mysterious is going to constantly trip them up in their pursuit of whatever *other need* we've laid at their door.

Jane Austen's *Emma* is so busy rushing around playing matchmaker that she never has to admit her own secret romantic needs — until her machinations lead her to wreck her own chance at love.

Internal conflict comes from dual, opposing needs. No matter what happens in a story, our protagonist's fundamental conflicting *needs* keep them from achieving the aim they've set for themself and, even worse, force them into the nightmare they so desperately want to avoid.

This is what makes our characters addictive to the reader.

And addiction is what keeps them turning the pages long past midnight, gripping our books in their hot, sweaty palms, hoovering up our words like little human vacuum cleaners.

Creating the Basic Tension in Plot

One of the things I love about fiction is that craft is craft, and what works for one particular genre actually works, in a very fundamental way, for all genres. It's funny how the arts can be so convenient.

So let's examine plot tension now, the inherent tension between two disparate plotlines that must eventually cause them to collide.

External conflict.

Every story is the story of more than one intertwining plotline. Genre fiction is kind of fun because we can twine plotlines from different genres, and when we're done we've mixed genres, like *The Color Kittens*, and come up with something new.

Every story is the story of how two plotlines run *almost* parallel from beginning to end, only to collide in a stunning display of fireworks at the Climax.

Think of those plotlines as railroad tracks.

In **mystery**, those two plotlines are the unraveling of what *really* happened in the context of what *appears* to have happened. The Climax is the point at which the detective or seeker-for-truth seems to be almost tricked into believing that what *appears* to have happened is in fact what *really happened*, and they are suddenly proven to be, in the immortal words of Poirot, 'such an eediot!' So when they pull a rabbit out of their hat the reader unexpectedly understands the entire story from the opposite side of the tapestry.

In **horror** and **thriller**, it's the same thing except both plotlines are occurring simultaneously and there's enormous pressure upon the protagonist to sort them out before something dire occurs.

In **romance**, those two plotlines are generally the protagonist's and the nemesis/lover's conflicting searches for whatever it is they're after. (It could be anything, but when we mix genres to come up with a significant conflicting need we make this one especially powerful.) The Climax is the point at which those searches bring the two inevitably together in conflict, where the clash of agendas throws them both top-over-teakettle so that, when they come back upright, they discover they're in love.

In **fantasy**, those two plotlines are generally the paths of good and evil (or, in the versions I prefer, between fantasy and reality or between two conflicting fantasies). The Climax is the point at which evil triumphs (or chaos triumphs, or deconstruction triumphs), throwing the protagonist into an impossible state of existence from which, when they extricate themself, they find they're living in unforeseen harmony between either fantasy and reality or those two conflicting fantasies. They hope!

In **science-fiction** those two plotlines are generally two paths *toward* the perceived future and *away* from that future. The Climax is the point at which those two struggles reach their inevitable point of stasis, where the tension between them exceeds capacity and the break throws the protagonist into the *worst possible* future so that, when they re-orient themself, they discover an extraordinary new way of coping with the future as it really is.

In **commercial fiction,** it's all the same except everything that happens could, conceivably, happen to the average reader.

And in **literary fiction,** this is all done exactly the same way only with meticulous attention to language.

The issue to keep in mind is that those two plotlines, because they are different plotlines (and we make them as different as we possibly can, so the fireworks will be really impressive), contain an inherent tension between them.

"You are not I," said Paul Bowles. This is the basic tension of all human existence.

So when we set our protagonist on these paths of self-destruction, the reason they're paths of self-destruction is that the character must simultaneously cope with two conflicting agendas. And they're going to discover — in the long run and exactly when they can *least* afford it — that those two conflicting agendas are irreconcilable.

Up until then, sure, there've been glancing collisions, there's been damage, there've been sparks. . .but there was always hope of reconciling those two agendas.

The Climax is here to prove: there will be no reconciliation.

Write toward that Climax. Set your characters off down their road to hell, paved so lovingly with attractions that no reader in their right mind could resist. Let your characters round corners and scare the wits out of themselves when they catch glimpses of where they're going. Then let them round more corners — complications — after which they lose sight of the game.

Keep them moving, always moving toward the collision that they have no idea is coming.

And in the last conflict before this collision occurs, (Conflict #3) give them one extra push.

Increase the incline.

Now, *that's* tension.

Chapter 9

Creating Reader Fulfillment

Resonance

Touching Your Reader's Core with Resonance

A client brought up a good point in the comments one day when we were talking about not introducing a pivotal character too late in the story.

She wanted to know: "When is too late too late?"

The truth is the sooner we introduce our essential characters, the better the **resonance** when our Climax (featuring those characters) wraps back around to where they first appeared. Make your wrap *big*. Make your wrap *loooooong*. A wrap of twenty pages — or even 100 pages — isn't worth it to the reader when there are writers out there managing wraps of 200, 300, 400 pages or more. Readers *love* resonance.

But what does this mean?

You know those period-piece movies about the 1930s where everyone goes to some fabulously rich, fabulously isolated house together, and they're all scurrying around in the middle of the night in clinging ankle-length sequins and cummerbunds, their wrists at shoulder-height, uttering noises that should by rights be coming out of rodents?

Those houses that are all dark, carved staircases and crackling fireplaces and Persian rugs, where someone is bound to come tumbling down the stairs at some point and land dead at the feet of the heroine in the front hall?

I *love* those darn movies.

And one thing you'll notice (this has nothing to do with the movie plots, by the way) is that those houses are usually decorated in a pastiche of Oriental imports in brass and cloisonné.

The absolutely best part is the enormous brass gong in the front hall.

They used those gongs to sound the alarm to get dressed-up in your fanciest knickers for formal dinner every night, then twenty minutes later to call the cattle down to the trough. However, if I'd been around I'd have stood there bonging that thing all evening simply for the joy of the **resonance.**

Resonance is how we reach out of the pages, through the words, past the reader's intellectual appreciation of our story, and touch their very core.

It is the essence of storytelling — creating a visceral response in the reader.

In technical terms, resonance is when something happens late in the story that reminds the reader of something that happened earlier in the story and creates a link between those two events to illuminate the hidden essence of both.

Remember in *Art & Craft of Writing Fiction: First Writer's Manual* when we talked about looking for the **links** between two disparate things to reveal a fundamental truth about life inherent to both? How that's the basis of all art?

This is the technique for doing that through structure. (There are dozens of aspects to linking truths — structure is only one.)

When two things resonate, they automatically include everything between them, just like a gong. So if we have a significant object that turns up in Chapter 7 and we repeat it in Chapter 9, the reader forms an unconscious mental link between its appearance in Chapter 7 and its other appearance in Chapter 9, and the pages between take on an incredibly subtle ambience of a united episode.

If we have an event that happens in Chapter 3 and something related happens in Chapter 10 and again in Chapter 19 and again in Chapter 31, the reader begins to build (unconscious) associations in their mind between these chapters, making them milemarkers for where our story is going. (If we've got 50 chapters, and this series of milemarkers ends in Chapter 31, we've either made our point or dropped the ball.)

And if we have a character who turns up in Chapter 1 and then reappears under extraordinarily significant circumstances in the Climax — that character has enormous *resonance*.

Can we get away with a character vital to the Climax who *doesn't* have resonance?

In *Jane Eyre*, her secret cousin Stuffed-Shirt St. John is wildly significant to the Climax, in which Jane must choose between either marrying him and becoming a missionary in the wilds of — I don't know, some ancient culture the Brits of the nineteenth century thought was primitive because they hadn't invented scones — or going back to that decrepit, blinded old rascal Rochester and taking care of *him* instead.

But was this a real predicament? Did Charlotte Brontë have the reader on the edge of their seat over Jane's decision?

Heck, no. St. John only appears in the last portion of the novel, while Rochester has been lurking in the bushes since barely a fifth of the way in — a sixth, even, if we count him as a rumor.

When Jane goes back to Rochester, everything between their first and final meetings begins to vibrate with an inner life of its own, created by the verification of what the reader suspected in the first place — Rochester is essential. However, when Jane gives St. John the old heave-ho (and St. John's fate — even his words — gets the premiere spot actually closing the novel), nobody even notices.

But what about mysteries and thrillers? Doesn't the culprit remain invisible until the grand unveiling in the Climax?

In my first mystery they sure did. No matter how many times I read that story through — and it's a pretty good story, with high tension, strong cause-&-effect, three-dimensional characters — it just didn't *work*. Until I found a way to slip the culprit in on page two. Suddenly! Resonance.

So how late is too late?

In the mystery canon it's spelled out for us: all essential characters must appear in Act I, within the first quarter-to-third of the story. And we would all do well to abide by this guideline.

We must know who our main characters are (this seems obvious, but a lot of the time 'pantsers' — those optimistic little critters writing by the seat of their pants — actually have no idea), and know who is essential to our Climax. Then we think of some way to show their faces somewhere in the early chapters (the first quarter to third of our story). They don't have to stick around. The protagonist doesn't even have to meet them. But we must get them in there, and let the reader imprint on them, even in the most delicate, fleeting way.

Alec D'Urberville, the ruin of Tess, makes only a handful of appearances in her life. But he is there at the Climax, just as he is there in Chapter 5 to show his face for the first time, when he starts the dreadful chain of obsession that eventually, in the end, catches her in its monstrous knot.

Playing Fair with Resonance

I'm reading Ellery Queen, after a whole pile of other pulp mysteries, and I've also started re-reading *Hillary Waugh's Guide to Mystery & Mystery Writing*. Waugh was one of the great American mystery authors of the twentieth century (he died only a few years ago), and he dissected the mystery genre with great insight and intelligence.

One of the things he discusses is a crucial aspect that was missing from some (but not all) of Edgar Allan Poe's seminal works, from which the entire Western mystery genre sprang, "The Murders in the Rue Morgue," "The Mystery of Marie Roget," "The Purloined Letter," "Gold Bug," and "Thou Art The Man":

Fair Play.

But what is Fair Play?

Fair Play is letting the reader know what's going on. Even more than that, Fair Play is planting the clue to the solution early — preferably on one of the first pages.

Now, the general understanding of Fair Play is that we have to do it in order to keep the reader's loyalty. If we don't Play Fair, the reader gets mad at us and goes away. Birdcages throughout the ages have been papered with books written by writers who ignored the Rule of Fair Play.

However, Fair Play has an even more important job than that. After all, writers get away with *all kinds of crap* with their readers, and if they're good enough writers the readers take it, pay for it, and keep coming back for more. No. Fair Play is based on something even closer to the reader's heart than fairness, and that is. . .

Having a good time.

As an Australian friend of mine discovered when he visited me years ago in downtown San Francisco, a grand adventure, whether real or fictional, is all about having a good time.

Whatever else goes on in our story, our reader wants to *enjoy the experience of reading it.*

Of course, people's ideas of enjoyment vary widely, and readers in general tend to enjoy a lot more of being ejected from their chairs, dragged around, thrown against the walls, and smacked silly than you'd ever believe.

But, more than anything else, readers enjoy resonance.

That's when they get to the end of the story and find there, unexpectedly and yet inevitably, the beginning of it. That clue the writer planted on the early pages.

Putting our reader inside that brass gong and giving it a good, hearty *clangngngngng.*

Readers love this! It's possibly the single most important reason for the popularity of mysteries throughout the past 150 years.

A devastating event.

And the key to that event.

Give the reader a whiff of something tantalizing, lead them a merry chase in all the wrong directions, and then smack them in the face with the whole tantalizing pie.

It's that wonderful, visceral sense of familiarity, that whisper in the back of the mind: *this ending was inevitable.* It's the seductive implication that, if they'd just paid close enough attention (and they will the next time they read it, they promise themself!) the reader could have figured the ending out before we showed it to them. It's that magical authorial sleight-of-hand, creating a positive emotional response in the reader by what we've left out as much as what we've put in.

Planting a clue to the Climax in a story's Hook is the simplest, most powerful fiction technique I know.

It makes the story a relentless progression always forward toward a Climax both unexpected and inevitable, a living, breathing thing in the reader's hands, the story of an ending that appears to have been manifested out of thin air by sheer genius.

Chapter 10

Drawing an Analogy

Step by step

Drawing a Logo

I'm going to draw an analogy for you now. So please bear with me.

One Saturday years ago my husband and I spent the whole day creating a logo for the publishing press we invented to publish my first book on writing, *Art and Craft of Writing Fiction: First Writer's Manual.*

I wanted to use an icon of my childhood for the logo, a cardboard cut-out advertisement for a festival dated 1899. It's the head of a young blond woman in an enormous hat with violet ostrich feathers, her arms clad in soft leather gloves from elbow to fingertip, her hands to her face, her chin resting thoughtfully on one fingertip. She's gazing up as though admiring the ceiling. Her name — in overly-elegant nineteenth century script under her elbows — is *La Favorita.*

My family found her hanging on the wall of an hacienda in the Ecuadorian countryside where we lived for two years while I was growing up. My parents moved her to a prominent spot in the hacienda dining room and photographed her for posterity, and by the time we left she had become a *de facto* member of the family. La Favorita hangs in a frame right now in my mother's living room, her cardboard face over 110 years old and still fresh as a girl.

When I told my mother what we wanted to do for the logo of my press, she sent me the original photograph of La Favorita, and we scanned it. Unfortunately, it turned out that she's got far too much detail and shading to work as a tiny little spine logo. We tried shrinking her down, and my son loved it, but from a distance of two feet she looked like a grey blob.

So we set to work turning her into a piece of art that would work.

My husband and I sat side-by-side on the couch all day while he Photoshopped La Favorita into a line drawing. She needed enough big dark elements to be recognizable at a casual glance—even tiny—but she also needed her itsy-bitsy little facial features to show up with their soulful gaze. We blacked in her hat and gloves (although the gloves have wonderful highlighted wrinkles in the soft leather) and exaggerated her eyes and mouth. We erased all of her from chin to gloves and then went back, meticulously re-creating only those lines absolutely necessary to give her definition. She has a lot of ruffles around her face, which looked weird when they disappeared. We had to get just enough of them in to remove the weird without competing with her more important elements.

The *pièce de résistance* turned out to be not even a part of her, but the shadow her cardboard cut-out cast on the wall when she was photographed. It's only behind one arm (the light came from an angle), but it's a lovely calligraphic line that thins and thickens as it goes around the curves of her sleeve. We sharpened it up. Then we looked at her other arm, which has no such line. We paused.

We were going to flip the line and use its opposite on the other side.

But then I remembered a fascinating fact about stylized images: what the eye knows should be there it will see *even when it's not there*.

So we deliberately left off the other arm.

And this is something all writers must remember — what the reader knows should be there they'll supply *even when it's not there*. Not only that, but the simple act of the reader supplying the essential last detail is what engages them, sucks them in, pins them down, makes them part of the story.

When we look at our favorite logos, our eye doesn't keep going back to them because it's found every single spec of information it needs. It goes back because there's something missing, and our eye knows what it is. Triumph! Over and over and over, we feel the satisfaction of supplying the missing piece. Over and over and over, there is the sense of completion, the instant of epiphany. *That's exactly right.*

Why?

Because that's what stories are — the unique, telling details that create the anchor points of our characters and plots, and everything in between the reader fills in from their own imagination.

We must focus on those unique, telling details. Make them as wonderful and vivid and telling as we possibly can. Then sit back and let the reader fill in the rest.

Have you ever wondered how the ancients got the constellations out of tiny handfuls of stars?

By reading them.

Applying the Analogy to Storytelling

So let's take the analogy between logo and storytelling the rest of the way.

She needed enough big dark elements to be recognizable at a casual glance. . .

This is our structure. We need a Hook, we need things to happen, and we need a Climax. And we need cause-and-effect leading inevitably from one event to the next. If we leave out any of these elements, we don't have a complete story.

But we can't use *everything*. There will always be mountains of notes, questions, interviews, cut scenes that nobody ever knows about but us. The entirety of our imaginary worlds? It will always be privately ours.

. . .but she also needed her itsy-bitsy little facial features to show up

We also need supremely interesting characters for our protagonists. Who are they? What matters most in the world to them? How did they get into their predicaments, and how do they wish they could get out? They can't get out the way they want to — that's a given. The tension lies between what they *wish* they could do and what they actually *manage*.

They can't always get what they want. So they try and try and try until they get what they need.

We blacked in her hat and gloves. . .

This is establishing the anchor points of our structure. What is this story *about*? What's the Climax, the premise in a nutshell? And when did it start being about that, at the Hook? What's going to happen between the beginning and end of this story, how is the Climax's shadow going to fall backward over the characters as they struggle to make their way away from the Hook forging inevitably deeper into trouble, always heading toward that Climax? When our reader remembers this story, what will they remember?

A fascinating, uncontrollable couple love and need each other so deeply that they destroy their lives fighting against the pressures keeping them separated until death brings them together forever.
— *Wuthering Heights*, Emily Brontë

A solitary seeker fascinated by an unfamiliar world traverses it until he learns what he needs to know.
— *Stranger in a Strange Land*, Robert A. Heinlein

The members of a family torn apart by unexpected catastrophe reveal in their search for an explanation the terrible chasms between them all.
— pretty much anything by Ivy Compton-Burnett

Addiction in tension.
Fulfillment in resonance.

. . .(although the gloves have wonderful highlighted wrinkles in the soft leather). . .

This is where we choose our subplots. We know that not everything can go in. But because we're writing a story and not designing a half-inch logo, we have room to layer in wonderful highlighted wrinkles, secondary issues, complications feeding always like the threads of a braid back into the main fuel driving our story through conflict.

85

. . .and exaggerated her features

The protagonist *must* be the fullest, most powerful, most complex character. If we have a powerful secondary character, their relationship to the protagonist must take on a character of its own. We must always remember that, as soon as we let a secondary character become more powerful and complex than our protagonist, our reader will jump ship for them. We *must* keep the basic needs that drive our protagonist palpitating.

We erased all of her from chin to gloves. . .

We lose a lot of our first draft when we tighten for structure and character development, especially if we pants. It's just the way it is. We set that stuff aside in its own folders and save it for another day.

. . .and then went back, meticulously re-creating only those lines absolutely necessary to give her definition

And we will have pieces to add in revision, things we forgot to say or skipped over leaving only placeholders to remind ourselves that something goes there. It's fine. Stories are long. Novels—when we're writing them—are all but interminable. We won't force ourselves to slog through from beginning to end, all in elaborate detail, if it burns us out. We'll write it the way we want to, then go back and identify the holes and write those pieces. We'll meticulously re-create only those lines that are absolutely necessary.

She has a lot of ruffles around her face, which looked weird when they disappeared

This kind of thing happens in revision. We delete things that aren't necessary, and it shows up other holes we hadn't seen before. Now we're making decisions about what goes into those holes. A tension-filled subplot? Some brilliant, subtle illumination? Better, more vivid, more telling scenes that are always forcing the main plot forward?

We had to get just enough of them in to remove the weird without competing with her more important elements

So we stay focused on where we're going and how we're going to get there. If some secondary character absolutely insists on being big, bright, and fascinating we can always set them aside for their own story. Nobody's limiting us to only this one.

The *pièce de résistance* turned out to be not even a part of her, but the shadow her cardboard cut-out cast on the wall when she was photographed

And during the writing and revising and pondering and shaping of this story, we find those elements that keep cropping up, the beautiful images and paradoxical character traits and significant telling details that make this story unique. They become symbolic. They turn into that subterranean layer of story running silent and deep beneath the plotline. They are the fuel for the final epiphany.

Then we looked at her other arm, which has no such line. We paused. . .

And when we get to the end of our Climax, we pause.

We were going to flip the line and use its opposite on the other side

We re-think our notes on the Resolution, almost none of which we'll have taken before we started writing and most of which we'll have taken after we finished our early drafts.

. . .I remembered a fascinating fact about stylized images: what the eye knows should be there it will see *even when it's not there*

We ask ourselves how much faith we have in the relationship between a writer and their reader — the magic of fiction, the power of epiphany — how much faith in this art and craft we love.

And then we deliberately leave off the other arm.

Character is *Content*

Chapter 11

Being Mesmerized
with Louisa May Alcott

Write what you love, not what you should

I think we're all agreed that Laurie belonged with Jo.

I mean, why would an author *do* that? Marry Jo off to an elderly schoolteacher while sending her best friend into the arms of her preening, self-absorbed little sister? Laurie, the boy who accepts Jo as she is without preaching and loves her for her wit and strength and sense of adventure instead of in spite of them? Married off to the sister who's burned her *manuscripts*?

As it happens, Louisa May Alcott hated the preachiness of *Little Women* and her other popular novels. She wrote them for the money because, as she admitted, preaching does sell.

Her father, Bronson Alcott, was one of the Transcendentalists, the crowd to which Ralph Waldo Emerson and Henry David Thoreau belonged. It was only when her father gave talks on moral philosophy or taught in his revolutionary Temple School (where he raised a furor by teaching that procreation is linked to adults' inability to restrain themselves and which collapsed after white parents withdrew their children to protest the acceptance of a black child) that he ever made any money.

Alcott was raised in poverty not because her father — a highly-educated intellectual — was unable to support his family, but because work clashed with his philosophical doubts. Her mother, along with Louisa and her sisters, maintained them all on the communes to which Bronson took them, working incessantly to keep the family alive while Bronson met with his Transcendental pals to hash over the meaning of living.

For a few weeks in the fall of 1843 they even lived in a state of acute terror while Bronson actually pondered whether or not to abandon his wife and children to the poorhouse in order to pursue his philosophical destiny. The horror of that childhood experience must have stuck with Louisa for the rest of her life.

I mean, how would you get over such a trauma? What kind of *savoir faire* would you have to *have*?

What this experience did, I believe, was split Louisa in half.

One half was still and would always be firmly in the grip of the social principles her parents and her father's friends expounded: the principles of self-sacrifice and living for what we owe humanity rather than what we deserve. It was adherence to these principles that led to both Alcott's fame as the author of some of the most heavily-peddled children's morality tales in the history of English literature and — unfortunately — her early death.

Alcott died of mercury poisoning from the medication she was given to cure the typhoid she contracted nursing casualties of the Civil War. She also, most likely, died of a combination of exhaustion and guilt, having throughout her final illness nursed her father in his own, while simultaneously raising her sister's orphaned daughter. When her father died only two days before Alcott, he said to her, "Come with me."

Shades of Emily Brontë, who came down with a cold the day of her brother Branwell's funeral and died of the ensuing tuberculosis three months later.

However, the other half of Alcott was not the worshipful daughter of her father, the self-sacrificing child of her mother (her sister, Beth, died of the scarlet fever their mother brought home from her charitable works), the dutiful purveyor of morality to the young and impressionable. Before *Little Women* ever landed on a publisher's doorstep or fell into the hands of high-minded parents, Alcott had published a handful of stories in the pulp rags, the stories she herself loved, Jo's infamous "blood-and-thunder" tales.

I was given *Modern Magic: Five Stories* by Louisa May Alcott for my birthday one year and *A Modern Mephistopheles, and A Whisper in the Dark* the next.

Hot *dog*.

Here are stories worth reading! Magic shows, deception, opiates, hypnotism (known as mesmerism in Alcott's day). Friends venture unknowingly into danger under the influence of drugs, strangers lead each other astray, characters disappear and reappear under impossible circumstances. The dark, disturbing underbelly of human character blossoms with an unearthly light in Alcott's hands.

And the split between her two bodies of work — the harrowing self-sacrifice of the March sisters and the rambunctious exploration of the devil's domain — brought us both Laurie and his author's betrayal of him, both Amy's appalling vandalism and her saccharine reward.

Why did Alcott give Laurie to Amy? Because she thought she had to.

Why did she invent Laurie in the first place?

Because she *could*.

So don't waste your time trying to force your work into some popular fad. Alcott's done enough of that for all of us. If there's anything that we can learn from her tortured boomerang between duty and passion it's that ulterior motive poisoned the well of genius from which Laurie and Jo were drawn.

Keep your well clean.

Chapter 12

Hunting the Ghost Tiger

Cause-&-effect

Taking the Tiger by the Tail

Let's talk about **premise**.

A friend and I decided one winter that I should write a ghost story for the holiday season, a sort of *Christmas Carol* where Scrooge turns out to be right.

We were whining on and on about how much we hate converting our living rooms into moldy indoor forests every year, with all the attendant branches poking us in the eye and greasy puddles and mountains of composting needles being ground into carpets with other things we don't normally leave underfoot. How frustrating it is to try to thread electric cords with little light bulbs through all of that, especially when we spend half an hour getting poked and prodded by the needles and branches and risking breaking the fragile little bulbs into a thousand cutting shards in the carpet, and then we're done and it turns out that none of the bulbs work.

And hanging breakables from the wayward branches. Either climbing on teetering chairs to get a star on top of the tree and falling into the branches or putting a child up on our shoulders so *they* can fall into them. Our kids getting wound up on sugar from all the extra cookies and candy-canes, so that even if they don't fall into the tree we can enjoy the piercing, hysterical shrieks as they imagine they're just about to. The pointless fights among adults engendered by the raw nerves from listening to all the piercing shrieks. And getting to listen to nothing but Christmas carols for eight solid weeks.

Oh, yes. A ghost story.

So I thought right away, *What will be my Climax? My Development? My Hook?* And I had some ideas, which I had not yet written down, when I got deeply embroiled in sorting out the logic behind the story. Because ghost stories, being fantasy, need rules made up for them, and this involves a lot of **logic**.

It's bad enough to write a realistic story and let illogical things happen, but we simply can't get away with being illogical about fantasy. This is *deus ex machina* in the worst way, and as soon as the reader stops believing in our logic they stop caring about our story.

The real beauty of all stories is the logic behind them. Not only do we put our characters through hell, but we make sure the reader can't see *any way* to avoid it.

So I got involved in who the ghosts would be (I decided there'd be more than one), and why they were scroogey, and where, and when, and how. I sort of knew who the protagonist would be and how they'd get entangled with these ghosts, but then I had to get into the logic of how they'd get back *out* again. And that gave me a great Resolution. But it also gave me some problems with logic because, after all, if the Resolution is right there, why doesn't the protagonist just find it in the first place? I had good reasons for that, and they worked fabulously, but there were other loose threads in the logic, and this involved figuring out the logic behind *them*, and then making sure *this* didn't have loose threads, as well.

Guess what I was dealing with?

That's right. *Cause-&-effect.*

Someone does something. A full cause-&-effect action with a point. This is a story.

Hook: Why? What's the cause of this whole thing? This is known as the inciting incident—so named, I believe, by the screenwriting guru Robert McKee—and it's the first piece of the logic, the first *effect*, to sort out. When does this mess start? Why does it all happen? Why do these characters *do* this? Characters always have reasons for the things they do.

Backstory: And does that initial thing they do work out? Of course not. When it works out, the story ends. But why *doesn't* it work out? What's the logic behind the failure? The original reason this mess starts? The *cause* of that inciting incident? What logic can neither the characters nor the reader see?

Note that I did not say, "What information can neither the characters nor the reader see?" This is a *vital* distinction. We are not hiding things from the reader. That's trying to trick them, and 1) it very often doesn't work (don't aim for stupid readers), and 2) even when it does work, it's not fun for them.

We are *playing with logic.*

If I want ghosts in my story, naturally I must figure out why they're ghosts. What's my logic? They're ghosts for a reason. That reason is intricately tied to what's going to happen to my protagonist.

My premise—my logic—is the point of my whole story.

The three ghosts of Christmas exist for the purpose of teaching a grouchy old fart why kindness matters.

—*A Christmas Carol,* Charles Dickens

The ghosts of the governess and her paramour exist to illuminate what's happened to the two children.

— "The Turn of the Screw," Henry James

The poltergeist exists to frighten the girl and her mother for the entertainment of her dreadful father.

— *The Fountain Overflows*, Rebecca West

effect: ghosts

cause: logic

Now we can see that the original logic, which I've come up with after I decided what I want in my story, actually begins *before* my story. That makes it (I know you know this) Backstory. How my characters got into this mess has everything to do with what the mess is and how it's going to blow up in their faces. It's all tied together.

So once I'm at the root of the Backstory (who are these ghosts and why?), I have the tiger by the tail, and I can work my way forward through my story hand-over-hand, following the cause-&-effect:

If these characters became ghosts for this original reason

And if this protagonist gets entangled with them for that Hook reason

Then what happens?

That 'then what' is the effect of the Backstory mixed with the inciting incident: my Hook.

And how does the protagonist react to that effect? How do the ghosts react? The other characters? That's what the reader wants to know.

And what does that reaction cause? Another effect. The characters have made decisions, taken action, tried to extricate themselves from their problem—and failed. To which, again, everyone must react.

And what does that reaction cause that?

And that? And that? And that?

Hand-over-hand, up the tiger's body from the tip of the tail all the way to the other end, where my protagonist must, with impeccable logic, stick their head into the tiger's mouth.

What's going to make them do that?

The accumulation of logic all the way.

Now, granted, by the time they've worked their way hand-over-hand all the way up a tiger's body, my protagonist should reasonably know better than to stick their head into its mouth. So there must be something way, way back there on the tip of the tiger's tail that makes this inevitable. I might not know what it is before I get to the tiger's head the first time. That's okay. This is the glory and wonder of fiction—I get to go back and add things later, and the reader never finds out.

From the tiger's head, I look back over the entire chain of events I've followed, and the logic is perfect, the cause-&-effect is unbeatable. It's all set.

Now I look at that lolling tongue and those Bowie-knife teeth, and I need a *really good reason* for my protagonist to go for it.

I review my logic. What's been driving these characters this whole way? It doesn't matter if I didn't plan it out in detail. Now that I've gotten them here, I can stretch and yawn and scratch my belly and just generally take my time figuring it out. *No one will ever know.*

I notice something running like a thread through the story, and it has to do with my protagonist's character, their one driving need, how they're forced to react to things in one way and one way only. It's just who they are. It's their reason for being.

What can this golden, essential reason for being possibly have to do with sticking their head in the tiger's mouth? There must be oodles of logical possibilities. The important thing is that this protagonist is *driven*. Something has made them do the things they've done. That same something is going to make them take this one, last, gigantically disastrous step.

What's the logic? I must have *some* reason for telling this story. And it's my job to discover what it is.

Then I go back to the beginning of my story and *plant a clue* to that reason in the inciting incident.

So we can see how this particular Hook, following the unshakeable logic of the Backstory, leads my protagonist by the logic of cause-&-effect all the way through the Development *inevitably* to the Climax, the whole reason I'm telling this story. The illumination of my original premise.

Where I let the tiger eat them.

And they turn into a ghost!

Focusing the Tiger

I've dumped things quite unceremoniously on the casual question, "What's the logic?"

As in, "It's lying right there! Come on — pick it *up!*"

But what if it's not lying right there in front of me? What if I've looked everywhere, gotten down and crawled around on my hands and knees searching with a magnifying glass, looked under every rock and in every cranny, and still not found it? What if I am, in fact, sitting at my desk this very minute contemplating a premise, a series of Conflicts, and a tiger's mouth, and my characters are standing back shaking their heads solemnly and pointing in my general direction: "*You* do it"?

My characters are too smart for me.

So let's talk about endings. Lolling tongues and Bowie-knife teeth. Prying open those jaws and inserting the cranium.

I tell writers: identify your protagonist and their greatest need, then from that identify their worst nightmare, which always involves *not being able to meet* of their greatest need.

That's the Climax.

But there's a little more to it than that, because the *reason* a protagonist can't meet their greatest need is that they have a *second equally-great* need, and the two needs are in mutually-exclusive conflict with each other. (This should be sounding very familiar!)

The need to obey his great-uncle's deathbed command to carry religion to the secular conflicts with the need to escape his great-uncle's religious fanaticism.

—Francis Tarwater in *The Violent Bear It Away*, Flannery O'Connor

The need to find spiritual fulfillment in a small African tribe conflicts with the need to save his skin from the tribal leaders.

—Eugene Henderson in *Henderson the Rain King*, Saul Bellow

The need to hold onto their family traditions and live their daily lives conflicts with the need to cope with Ireland's violent attempts to overthrow British dominance.

—the Naylor family in *The Last September*, Elizabeth Bowen

And there of course is Henry James' narrator's need to acquire the precious "Aspern Papers," which conflicts with his need to avoid marrying a woman he does not love.

My characters have a very good reason to explore this particular tiger. They *need to.*

They also have a very good reason to *fight against* this tiger. The tiger does not come to them easily at all!

And the conflict between these two needs both blinds them and drives them relentlessly forward.

So by the time they get to the tiger's head, they've spent the entire story besting the odds in order to *hang onto* this darn tiger, blind to the inherent danger of such a plan. They've put their identity, their welfare, their very lives on the line for the sake of it. This tiger has become everything they want out of living. So sticking their heads in its mouth is the only logical (get that — logical!) culmination of this devotion.

It is the actual process of going hand-over-hand up the tiger's body that ingrains the need for this culmination in them so powerfully.

This is why I tell writers not to write the Climax until they've written the entire novel. Because the tiger's mouth is created out of the tiger's body. As we write chapters, episodes, scenes about these characters — moving them inexorably from their Hook to their dreadful Climax — we are creating the pressures that force the characters eventually to stick their heads in that tiger's mouth.

What happens to the protagonist in the Hook? Something impacts on them. Just as in life, what happens to someone changes them in some way — it either counters or reinforces a previous disposition, it creates a little bit more extremity in an already-weakened area, it heightens the contrast between their highs and lows. It, in fact, adds tension.

Now we figure out how the Hook leads to the first Conflict. How can this and the succeeding Conflicts continue to deepen the grooves, intensify the peaks, of the character's experience? How does the protagonist's overwhelming need for first one thing and then the other force them again and again into situations — Conflicts — in which those grooves and peaks become worse and worse?

How does the geography of the tiger's body eventually create the shape of the mouth that the protagonist *can no longer get out of?*

It is the conflict between a protagonist's two needs that creates their experience of the tiger's body.

And the body of the tiger is our story.

Chapter 13

Developing Character

A multi-chambered heart

Differentiating Yourself from Your Reader

We already know that we, as human beings, love stories because they teach us how to live. In particular, they teach us how to cope with the inevitable 'slings and arrows of outrageous fortune,' how to duck when we've got to duck, how to take it when we're not quick enough to duck, and what to do after we have failed to duck.

What's the point of learning how to live easy? We're pretty sure we can fly *that* one by the seat of our pants.

So one of the biggest problems facing aspiring writers is differentiating between themselves and their creations.

The thing is that we *love* these characters. This is why we create them. We thrill to their insights, we're heartbroken over their problems, we laugh our heads off at their jokes. We cherish them, we admire them, we identify with them.

How many first-person novels have we ever read in critique workshops where the protagonist has a blank personality? This is because the writer's not writing about a character, they're writing about themself. And, in their mind, they're not just another human personality—they're *the* human personality. Beyond characterization.

It is so easy to assume that everyone lives in our heads with us.

When I was a teenager, my father announced over dinner one night he'd just read *Alice Through the Looking-Glass* and realized he might be the Red King.

"Maybe I'm dreaming all of you," he said. "How would you know?"

"Maybe *I'm* dreaming *you*." I was fifteen years old, a master of logic, and I didn't care who knew it. "How would *you* know?"

However, we don't dream our readers. Not the ones we hope will read us, anyway. We do have to differentiate between ourselves, our readers, and our characters, and we have to differentiate between the individual characters, as well. *And* we have to differentiate between how our characters act when they're taking a breather and how they act when they're cowering under a hailstorm of dreadful, stinking, atrocious bad luck.

But here's the good news! We don't have to put our characters through a James Bondish ticking-bomb moment to give them conflict. What readers like more than anything else is when the conflict is *internal*.

Why?

What could readers possibly get out of seeing other people—even imaginary people—go through awful internal turmoil, fighting themselves, losing to themselves, defeating themselves, triumphing over themselves, transcending the reality of *being* themselves? Just like we do ourselves?

Fiction is revealing the unknowable, saying the unsayable. And the unsayable we all live with is: *it hurts to be us*.

Buddha knew this. He lived a cushy life for a long time, wandered off one day to sit under a tree and not eat until he figured out the meaning of it all, and came back saying, "Life is suffering. Knock off the funny stuff, you guys."

Great philosopher though he was, he was no fiction writer. He would never have put characters into trouble on purpose. But he understood something we all need to understand: characters are born to suffer.

When we look for ways to give our characters conflict, we must not be inhibited by our Buddha nature. Our characters are not us. They're not even *real*.

At the same time, we must not forget our Buddha nature. Our *readers* are real. And they desperately need to learn how to suffer with grace.

One night over the dinner table my father joked to my mother, "I've got you trained."

She laughed. "I've got *you* trained."

I looked at my little sister. "We've got them trained."

Everybody thinks they're the Red King.

But *really*? None of us is.

Seeing What Your Reader Sees in Character

We can't write publishable books solely for ourselves. This is the bedrock of what I know about fiction: "It's not about the writer's experience, it's about the *reader's*."

If it was only about the writer's experience, we'd just write it and then keep it around for the rest of our lives, re-reading it whenever we got the wind up, wouldn't we? And that's not what some of us have in mind, is it?

Okay, I actually *do* do this. However, the writing we want to be read by *other people* — by readers — we must write for them. We don't buy our kids clothes to fit ourselves.

And what the reader wants is to read about people like them. They want to be able to identify with our characters, to feel in their bones, *This character is* me. *Oh, this is the story of my life!*

So we must be able to create characters that speak for the reader. And to do this, we must understand how the reader experiences life.

1. Our reader's internal world is confusing

We're all masses of seething anguish and obfuscation. Being a storyteller means having empathy for the human condition.

Giving our reader tangible, identifiable guideposts to what's going on inside our characters helps the reader sort out their own internal world. A *lot*. It helps them get into our story, and it helps them to stay there.

Help the reader simplify themself.

What kinds of tangible guideposts can we give a reader?

- The poles of our character's extremes: how are our characters fun to be around? How are they not so fun? What are they like when they're happy? What about when they're not so happy? What are they like when they get what they want? And what about when they don't?

- A set number of challenges our characters must face: what annoys them? What hurts them? What breaks their hearts? And then, just when they think they've survived the worst, what totally wrecks their lives?

- An alternating pattern between types of event: when are they fired up? When are they relieved? When do they gird their loins? When are they hoisted on their own petard? How can we keep yanking their nose rings back and forth, right and left, up and down, through every single page?

2. Our reader's external world is also confusing

Stuff is always coming at them they don't expect or, if they do, they dread. Friends get snippy, co-workers cheat on workloads, relatives lay guilt trips, children and partners are yoked to the eyeballs on seriously important needs.

Give the reader ways to categorize the insanity.

How can we do this?

- Simplify our characters' dilemmas. Don't send them bumbling aimlessly through the world exactly the way real people do, meeting infinite strangers and keeping track of numerous almost-identical friends and remembering who went where with whom that time they didn't accomplish whatever. Condense multiple characters into one whenever possible. Shape their conflicts toward the obvious high points. Don't make pointless detours. Don't try to trick.

- Focus our characters' progress. We all take two steps forward and one step back. But we also take about a zillion steps sideways, this way and that, for no particular reason at all. We must give our characters at least two conflicting needs that cause certain behaviors that have effects and make our characters follow those conflicting needs through those effects into further causes and further effects. It's not the way we live, but

109

it helps life make sense to portray it that way. Just two conflicting needs are plenty. Three if we're real wild things.

3. Our reader's life is boring

They work for a living. They have responsibilities. Even when they're lying on a beach in Bali listening to the soft *shoof* of the waves on sand and the papery rustle of palm leaves in a salty breeze, they're wondering how they're going to get through another Thanksgiving with their closest kin, sitting around burping and farting and watching reality TV. They're cringing at the thought of getting on that plane and winding up, this exact time two weeks from today, in the same ole squeaky chair in the same ole veal-fattening pen. The endless drudgery is always in the back of their mind.

Relieve the reader's suffering.

What can we do to liven things up for them?

- Give our characters fascinating personality traits. Don't make them happy to sit around the kitchen stuffing envelopes for a hundred pages. Don't put them on the phone talking in whiny voices about the same uninteresting thing over and over again. Don't make them *dull*. We may not be the most charismatic thing coming down the pike—but we must make every protagonist one.
- Let exciting things happen to our characters. Don't write about the boring parts of their lives. They brush their teeth, wash the dishes, yell at their kids to clean their rooms. Yeah, yeah, our reader knows. They do that too. You know what? They're largely on autopilot while they're doing it for *real people* they *really love*. They won't

bother wading through it for imaginary people nobody actually loves but us. Stick to the scenes, the very moments, when Important Things Happen.

- Give our reader room to have thoughts of their own. Don't explain every single thing that passes through our characters' brains. Don't point out foreshadowing or get melodramatic over what happens to our characters or — god forbid — put information into their mouths the reader *already knows*. Have a sense of personal space.

Finally —

4. Our reader looks up to us

They really do. If they didn't, they wouldn't be reading our stories. Strive to create realistic, breathing, complex, believable characters for them to meet and be fascinated by and devote hard-won hours of their precious time to.

We have a professional responsibility to our reader.

Live up to it.

Understanding Sympathetic Character

The most important thing we need to do when we create a protagonist is make them someone the reader absolutely *loves* traveling all the way up the tiger alongside. This is not an easy trip, it's not always a pleasant trip, and it can at times be quite a harrowing trip (if we do it right). So this protagonist must be *intensely sympathetic* to our reader.

But what does this really mean to storytelling, 'sympathetic' and 'unsympathetic' characters?

Unsympathetic characters can be summed up in one word: boring.

Boring?

Boring.

But what about the evil arch-nemesis of the wonderful heroine? What about the wicked wizard/psychopathic stalker/heartless boss/reckless abuser/cruel shoe-seller who forces the struggling hero to run a mile in tight shoes? What about the monster the protagonist has to defeat in the spectacular, death-defying Climax, which monster must be described in only the most horrific and disgusting terms so that the reader will cheer when the protagonist finally makes it *pay*?

Boring. One-dimensional characters having nothing to say, nothing to show the reader, no reason for the reader to read the words of which they consist.

Ultimate fictional evil? No. Real evil happens in the real world. It is rooted in humanity, and because it is rooted in humanity it is complex. One-dimensional bogeys aren't evil. Why would we waste our precious moments on this planet trying to determine, "I wonder what I can write to make my reader vomit all over my book"? We don't know. Do you know why? Because we're not evil.

Never put anything in your fiction that is not true to you.

Two-dimensional characters are almost as bad. The staid, ignorant, housewife-slash-unpleasant mother. The plodding workaholic father. The girlfriend who suckers the hero into bed and turns into a gold-digging shrew. The boyfriend who lies about love and laughs cruelly when the heroine cries. The bullying authority figure. The cringing wimp. The featureless, characterless, mindless wives and husbands and children and siblings and neighbors (especially neighbors, for some reason) populating the worlds through which protagonists only marginally less white-washed make their hapless ways. Even the anti-hero who's just so troubled and jaded and tough that they *have* to hide their third dimension under an impenetrable exterior of ignorance & apathy. ("I don't know, and I don't care.")

Hear the clunk? This is the reader's head hitting the desk.

But what about one- and two-dimensional *sympathetic* characters?

They don't exist.

Not even the muscle-bound hunk who sweeps the heroine off her feet? The good-hearted best friend? The wise elderly teacher/smart-alec sidekick/sweet sibling/breathless admirer? The people who surround the protagonist demonstrating for the reader exactly how they're supposed to see them?

I'm afraid that's not sympathetic. That's transparent machination. Readers don't like machination, they like characters who are honestly intriguing.

Sympathetic characters are *always* three-dimensional characters. Characters with *internal conflict*.

But how can we lump all three-dimensional characters together under the heading 'sympathetic'? This can't be true. Heathcliff and Catherine aren't 'sympathetic.'

Oh, but they are! Torn between their passion for each other, for their beloved moors, for the wild animals with which they identify, and their uncontrollable fury and fascination with the financial and social constraints of human society? Readers *love* those two, best-selling and going strong even after a hundred and fifty years.

Or Kurtz—with his anguished, "the horror! the horror!" — what about him?

Intensely sympathetic! Not only has he created his own nightmare, he's human enough to discover what he's done and react to the knowledge, in the final hour, in all his soul-wracking turmoil.

113

Fyodor Pavlovich Karamazov, the drunken, abusive father of the brothers who struggle so desperately, in their separate ways, to come to terms with his death?

Dostoevsky was a master. He couldn't write a less-than-three-dimensional character to save his *life*.

A sympathetic character, by definition, is one with whom the reader feels some level of sympathy. One with whom the reader, in some way, identifies.

You know that old saw about villains who steal the show?

Those are sympathetic characters.

So now we see something mesmerizing, and this is that a sympathetic character is *always* a three-dimensional character and a three-dimensional character is *always* one with powerfully conflicting facets to their personality. A sympathetic character is both an angel and a devil. A sympathetic character is one whom the reader both loves and hates, both admires and yells, "Oh, no!" over, a character who — here it comes — both pushes the reader away and pulls them back again.

Push/pull. Push/pull.

Heathcliff, when he's young, is a teased and tormented young hothead who takes his lumps with grace (he lets Hindley hit him in the chest with a *metal weight* in exchange for Hindley's pony — *ow!*) and — unlike the spoiled children around him — never once complains when they all come down with a deadly childhood disease. Even as a bitter, vindictive man, the last illness of his one beloved can bring him to stand under a tree outside her window all night while she raves with brain fever, oblivious to his presence, oblivious to him bashing his head against the tree trunk in agony until he bleeds. When he gets the chance to see her, does he play the cold, vicious bastard he's so famous for? No — he grasps her in his arms and kisses her frantically all over her face and hands. He begs her to live. He breaks down in tears.

He becomes *human.*

Once on Twitter I had a brief but spirited disagreement with someone in which they informed me that Indiana Jones would kick Han Solo's butt.

"So not possible," I said.

"Sorry to be the one to tell you," they said.

"Han's younger," I said.

Why do we even *care?*

Because Harrison Ford has that lovable jerk persona down to a science: a character who's both callous and tender, both vulnerable and tough as nails, both commando and confused. ("It was nothing. Everything's fine. We're all fine here, don't come check — ah — how are *you?*")

A sympathetic character has all those types of wonderful characteristics that we hope we have when we're on top of the world, the strength and charm and wit and charisma, completely mixed in with all those dreadful characteristics that we actually know we have when the chips are down, the fear and self-doubt and terrible propensity to make really, incredibly wrong mistakes.

Do you know why they're sympathetic?

Because they're *us.*

We must use this to our advantage. Don't waste time trying to create The Most Dreadful Dastardly Criminal Ever or The Greatest Hero/Lover/Genius.

Nobody caaaaaaaaares.

Create sympathetic characters. Create real people.

Chapter 14

Condensing & Contrasting Characters

Two sides to a single coin

Condensing Multiple Characters into One

Is your manuscript crawling with miscellaneous people?

Marcel Proust supposedly put over 2,000 characters into *Remembrance of Things Past*. And even for seven volumes — *that's a lot of characters.*

Don't do this. Proust was creating characters out of people he'd presumably known, rambling on rather indiscriminately about moments, impressions, passing ideas as if he had all the time in the world — which, in fact, he did. He was bed-ridden at the end of his life with debilitating asthma, and writing his single, unending novel was the only thing going on with him. He was a brilliant, detail-obsessed author simply *overloaded* with free time.

However, our readers don't have the attention span to keep track of over 2,000 characters. In fact, they prefer less than twenty. In fact, they're most riveted if we can keep it down to a half-dozen. Or two. Maybe one.

Can we write an entire novel about only one person? Hey, we can try!

I recommend less than ten. One or two protagonists. (Ensemble casts work better on the screen than they do in novels, although if we're really talented and really dedicated and really determined, we could probably do something powerful.) Two to six secondary characters.

That's all the significant figures.

And a handful of minor supporting characters. Don't litter the place up with miscellaneous co-workers and police officers and almost-identical family members. Even our minor supporting characters must have *character*.

Do we have three characters when two or even one would do? We must explore the possibilities of condensing their personalities down into one. Then consider what happens when we lump three people's problems onto one person's head. Then spend some time doodling links between the characters on a sheet of paper.

We tap our chins and ask ourselves, "If I make Melvin the detective instead of Howie, how does that affect his love affair with Edna Jean, the State Senator? If I give Melvin his friend Lawrence's bad divorce and custody problems, what kind of pressure will that put on him to follow up clues even faster and more effectively? And when the gun-runner's plane crashes on take-off from Edna Jean's country estate, doesn't that eliminate the whole business about Melvin getting the message to Howie, while forcing him to deal with his kids in the process of dashing to the crash site before the gun-runner gets into her disguise as Edna Jean's mute cousin Natasha?"

See how condensing characters ratchets the tension, while upping the ante on whoever's left?

Simplify, simplify, simplify.

This is how we create layers: by accordioning the surface into deeper and vastly more tightly-knitted complexity.

Condensing Characters for Internal Conflict

Now let's talk about what effect condensing multiple characters has on a protagonist.

I once wrote a novel based loosely on the coffee shop where I worked. We poor misfits of a staff comprised a truly stunning spectrum of the socially-impaired, and the coffee shop was run—for a time at least—on the principles of the manager's therapy. She thought that maybe if we just asked nicely enough the clientele might be prevailed upon to handle the business of buying from us without our intervention. At this point it seemed like only a short step from reality to fantasy, so I took it.

And it was *fabulous*.

There I was, pantsing merrily along. (We didn't have the word pantsing in those days. We called it writing "off the top of your head." It was probably only a lucky glitch in the matrix that we don't all call it now "heading" or, even worse, "topping.")

Here came a character, a big, loud, domineering guy based more or less on a beloved uncle and more or less on the grouch in management at the coffee shop. And here came another character, a gentle, sensitive guy based more or less on my college mentor and more or less on the peacemaker in management. I thought it would be lovely if these guys were close friends, although in real life they weren't.

And it was.

So I kept writing, throwing in characters wherever they seemed appropriate and watching what happened when they interacted. All such glorious fun!

But then I took my fledgling novel to the Community of Writers at Squaw Valley, and one of the things critiquers said was, "You know, you've got a *lot* of characters."

And it was true. You couldn't even tell whom the story was about. (I *still* have trouble keeping it straight whom that story is about.)

Anne Lamott told me, in all patience, "You have written this wonderful story, this Michelangelo's David, kind of buried behind all its hair. You need to decide who it's about and gently clear the hair from its face."

So I went home, armed with the patience of the author of a great (then-new) book on writing, and began thinking about how to clear the hair from its face. And, as I did, I began condensing characters.

Did those two friends — true-to-life as it was to give that dinky café more managers than the Ritz — absolutely *have* to be two different people? Could this place have only one manager, the man who loves, cares for, rails against, and survives the plot alongside the one main tragic character, the café's lesbian owner?

What would this do to the story?

Well, it would focus it more on the relationship between the manager and owner. By removing the relationship between the two managers and letting the relationship between the manager and owner stand alone, it clarified the major theme of the novel, which is what happens to a lifelong love at the end of that life. (My grandmother had just died and left my grandfather completely bereft, and I had promised her on her deathbed to watch over him, so I was spending a lot of my weekends with him and witnessing the indescribable heartache that waits at the end of a long and happy marriage.)

It would streamline the Backstory from a trivial secondary plotline between these two managers — who, in the first version, apparently have met thirty years earlier in passing and only come together later through a second fortuitous accidental meeting — into the essential information about how this manager and owner came to be in this café going through their drama now.

And even more than all that, it would multiply the facets of this manager's personality, so that he'd become not only loud and domineering but also sensitive and caring, not only overbearing and with a voice to wake the dead, but profoundly wounded, lost and afraid among his own demons, fighting tooth-&-nail his own imminent collapse.

It would give him enormous *internal conflict*.

And through his enormous internal conflict, I found what holds him and the café owner together, the deeper layers between them, the unspoken ties that have given them this lifelong unfulfilled love — the fact that she's lesbian is the fuel for the entire plot — as well as the tragedy they're facing in this particular story.

Condensing him made both him and their story *real*.

And I'll tell you who pointed me into the wind with this: Lucia Orth, author of the critically-acclaimed debut novel *Baby Jesus Pawn Shop*. She was working on an early draft of her novel at the time, so we were critiquing each other's manuscripts, and she said, "Is he in love with her?"

"Oh, no," I said. "She's gay. They're just friends."

"Because *that* I would find riveting," Lucia said. "*Unrequited love*."

Of course! She was absolutely right.

Condensing Characters for Contrast

One of the most important things about character is opposition. They must be in opposition to each other, they must be in opposition to their story, they must be in opposition to themself.

I'm one of three sisters very close in age. We have a lot of *similarities*. So if I were writing a novel in which the interplay between us was only a minor element, I'd shrink us down to one. We don't have enough contrast in our basic personalities.

Of course, I'd shrink us down to *me*.

Even worse were my grandmother's parents, one from a family of twelve and the other from a family of fourteen. Between them they had *twenty-four siblings*. You should see the family photos.

If we wanted to put a family that size into a novel, we'd have no choice but to make it about *being* a family of that size. We couldn't possibly create twenty-four people of sufficient contrast. And we couldn't have all those extras wandering around without a compelling reason.

Contrast: the basic quality that makes characters visible to the reader.

Say we've got a couple of nice, normal people for our heroine and hero. A pair of charming ducks. But we can't just *leave* them a pair of charming ducks. They've got to contrast to each other. They've got to exemplify, somehow, the basic, fundamental differences between all individual human beings.

This is why readers like heroes and villains. It's easy math.

So we want to set up a dichotomy between these two characters, which of course turns out to be the root of all their ills.

They're super-compatible. They both love art and basketball and city life and role-playing bizarre games in front of other people. They love their life. They love each other. All's well in their world.

But there's an abyss between them, and it's the abyss that's going to eventually tear them apart.

Say when she was young she accidentally shot her brother while hunting and now has terrible recurring dreams about it. At the same time, he's a Licensed Practical Nurse and works in the ER. This contrast between their characters is going to bring about their worst nightmare, because when he's in charge of the ER the night a gunshot victim is brought in who rises unexpectedly from the gurney and pulls a pistol from the back of their belt and begins picking off staff, she's the only person who can drag him to safety and follow his gasped instructions on digging out the bullet so that she can save his life. . .

Or.

He's secretly gay. And she's secretly lesbian. But they need a child. (Why? Who knows? Maybe they're aristocrats of the Edwardian era and need an heir, like Vita Sackville-West and Harold Nicholson.) And the fact that they're terrified of revealing their secrets to anyone — especially each other — increases the tension in their contrast sky-high and means that their efforts to live up to the pressures upon them result in either great comedy or great tragedy, depending upon the tone we want to take. . .

Or.

They're not really a couple. But they must *pretend* to be a couple for very urgent reasons. Maybe they're in a Witness Protection Program. And their lives depend upon them maintaining the illusion of their cover. And during the course of the story it turns out that one of them isn't really a witness, which is, naturally, the contrast between them. And this means that the other *isn't really protected. . .*

Do you see how the contrast between characters is the tension that makes our story a great, big paintball aimed right at the reader's head?

Now let's try condensing some of these characters.

Say the woman who accidentally shot her brother originally had two sisters. They aren't identical—no two of us are identical—but the sisters don't really have a good reason to be there besides the fact that we have a lot of characteristics we want to use. We want a social climber, a tomboy, a Mommy's Little Girl. We want someone who'll knock others down to get her way, a black sheep, and someone with a (slightly-strained) smile for every season. We have all of this stuff going on, and we need someone to paste it onto.

But what if we eliminate the sisters? (They aren't any use, anyway—it's not as though she has more than surface conversations with them and those not essential to the plot.) What if we give *all those characteristics* to the same character?

Or maybe the homosexual man originally had a straight best friend with all the qualities that we didn't know how to give to our effeminate gay blade. The best friend is big, muscular, athletic, and has a way with the ladies. We've made our gay blade thin, willowy, soft-voiced, and limp-wristed.

What happens if we combine the two? Make the gay man big, willowy, muscular, soft-voiced, supremely athletic, with a charming way with the ladies to hide his passion for their boyfriends and brothers? The ladies don't mind his limp wrist. They think he's being sophisticated.

And the lesbian woman—maybe she originally was bluff and hearty, with a fondness for fresh air and dogs and comfortable shoes. And maybe the social-climber sister was

124

intensely competitive, while the smiley sister was a fainting lily who spent a lot of time on her chaise longue sipping absinthe and reading Lord Byron and fluttering her eyelashes at the big charming dude with muscles.

What if we made the lesbian a delicate flower with a fondness for fresh air and dogs and comfortable shoes, whose intense competitiveness makes her constantly over-do the bluff and hearty and have to retreat to her chaise longue with Lord Byron, while her husband brings her absinthe with a limp wrist and she flutters her eyelashes at him hoping against hope that he hasn't seen her rolling in the hay with the neighbor's governess?

And after they've survived the shoot-out in ER, he has to testify against the perpetrator, who can identify him. So he's put into a Witness Protection Program and given a fake wife, with whom our heroine falls in love. . .

Do you see how giving our characters powerful internal conflict brings them vividly alive? It forces us to climb over the obstacle course of our unconscious assumptions and clichés and create unique people with real needs and desires, real gestures and mannerisms, even while keeping them focused on their conflicted driving needs that get them (you saw this coming) from Hook, through Development, all the way to the Climax.

Which is now about a zillion times more interesting and compelling, since we've given ourselves so much richer and more *substantial* material to work with.

Chapter 15

Using Character

The jaws of life

Using Character to Create Plot

Has anyone ever told you, "plot grows out of character"? Well, I happen to know they have. *I've* said it.

But what do we *mean*?

We mean: character is the alpha and omega of fiction. And characters are only important to readers insofar as they *need* things. Things that contrast. Things that conflict. When someone seriously, desperately, aggressively *needs* two mutually-exclusive things, well, stuff tends to happen to them. Big, exciting stuff! That's the fabulous stuff of fiction.

One afternoon on Twitter I started a conversation I called, for no particular reason, #editingchat. A few readers and I conducted a little experiment in which we demonstrated Developmental Editing on an unwritten story.

I said, "Someone give me a story in a sentence," and someone gave us three aspects of a story: a death, a birth, and a mission, the protagonist a woman.

So I said, "What does this woman *need*?" And I opened it up to everyone — we were just horsing around.

It turned out that what this woman needs is forgiveness for a death due to the mission, specifically the death of the father of her baby. Somehow, she's done something that makes her think she's guilty, that she needs to stick with the mission in order to redeem his death, to prove to herself and others he has not died in vain. To earn forgiveness.

Then I said, "What *else* does she need? What *prevents her* from completely fulfilling her original need right now?"

And it turned out that she also needs to survive—in particular she needs her baby to survive.

So we talked for a long time about what kinds of situation could force this woman to choose between earning forgiveness and protecting her baby. We got a lot of ideas about what choice she should make—to give up seeking forgiveness outside herself, to realize that her beloved died for her sake, to learn that she can only get true forgiveness from herself.

"You are some optimistic little chipmunks, aren't you?" I said. "You really want to skip the Climax and get straight to that Resolution, don't you?"

In this way we learned what motivates a reader to read an entire story: *wanting to know the Resolution.*

But we don't know the Resolution before we finish writing our story. What we need to discover first is the Climax.

So we went back to it: what situation could force this woman to choose between her loyalty to her dead beloved—that fierce need to redeem his death, to earn forgiveness for what she cannot undo—and her instinct to protect her baby.

"What if the baby were in danger?" the writer suggested.

Well, that's a pretty good headlock to get that protagonist into! She's working on this mission that means everything in the world to her, but suddenly her baby's in danger and she has to choose between continuing her mission and saving her baby's life.

And this is when we learned that needs must reside not only in the protagonist (and their writer), but, most essentially, inside *the reader*.

Because we all know that we must save babies' lives! This is a top priority instilled in nearly all of us at a very early age. Those of us who don't have it. . .well, they're not generally interested in fiction. They can't empathize with humanity in general, and empathy is one of those things that fiction is about *in spades*.

So if we simply make this protagonist choose between saving her baby and continuing her so-far hopeless pursuit of forgiveness through a mission that may or may not mean much to the reader, the reader's going to close the book with a satisfying snap.

"All done! Conflict resolved."

This is the great, vast luxury of fiction. Because creating a *need for forgiveness* in our reader as powerful as their *need to save babies' lives* is what this story is all about.

Write it — the story of how this one character, this realistic, three-dimensional, internally-conflicted woman, becomes more and more deeply enmeshed in this mission, with her dreadful, transcendental need to prove that her beloved did not die in vain. Give her a series of catastrophes as the mission progresses, earthshaking developments to put the reader on the edge of their seat. Make her engagement with this mission, her pursuit of forgiveness, as detailed and real and vivid as humanly possible.

At the same time, bring in the baby, but keep it secondary to the main plot (undercut the reader's natural investment in saving babies). Let her pregnancy be a subplot running through

129

the story of the mission. Let her become pregnant (or discover her pregnancy), let her suffer a major setback in her pregnancy, let her give birth under terrible, almost deadly circumstances, and then, for a short time at least, let her believe that everything's finally going to be all right.

She made it. She's almost there, with both forgiveness and child safe. That's the Faux Resolution.

Then when we put the baby in danger and bring the woman all the way to the brink of her nightmare, where she must choose between forgiveness and child, we've got our reader exactly where our protagonist is: trapped between inescapable choices, forced to face themselves in their darkest and, maybe, brightest hour, tormented by the sheer reality of existence.

Which is where epiphany lies.

Using Character to Fuel Momentum

Every day, in every way, I am always telling aspiring writers, "Whatever you do, *never* interfere with the forward motion of your plot."

Life is short, and stories are legion. We haven't got that kind of time.

But even better than simply not interfering, we must know how to *increase* that forward motion.

Momentum: from snowball to avalanche.

We've been talking about how to use character to create plot, how our protagonist's two conflicting *needs* create the nightmare collision that is their inevitable Climax. But, while we're exploring this plot, how do we go beyond the admonishment not to interfere with our plot's momentum and actually increase the momentum, exaggerate, *fuel* it? Through character?

By taking every opportunity to conflict those two needs. And, at carefully timed intervals, *increase them*.

This technique is rooted in the character's freedom of choice. Because every time we set up a decision for them — **A** or **B** — whatever they choose leads to **C**, which we must arrange to be even worse than whatever they *didn't* choose.

Say a man *needs* to be safely on the right side of the law, even to believe in justice, or at least not make things any worse for himself. He's in prison for a crime he didn't commit, and he has a health problem that the prison environment is exacerbating badly. Staying and sticking out his term keeps him safe from further prosecution. But he also *needs* to survive.

He needs:

1) to be safe from the law (which he knows now he won't necessarily be even if he avoids breaking it)
2) to live

His choices are:

A: *obediently stick out his term and hope prison doesn't kill him*, or

B: *break out of prison and safeguard his health*

He chooses a need, and he breaks out of San Quentin.

Now, the movie version of David Goodis' *noir* classic, *Dark Passage*, made film history for the most inadvertently hilarious introductory scenes ever: the camera acting as the eyes of the protagonist, Humphrey Bogart, who must, upon his escape from prison, have plastic surgery to make his face unrecognizable. (They pulled this camera stunt so that they wouldn't have to either use another actor or attempt to alter beyond recognition Bogey himself.)

Anyway, as soon as Vincent Parry breaks out of San Quentin, he's in trouble. What has he done? He has chosen **A** over **B** and wound up with **C**. Now he must avoid getting caught, which would not only endanger his life but also lengthen his prison sentence.

His choices are:

C: *stick around where he is*, or

D: *get the heck out of there*

So he starts getting the heck out of there. He gets an offer of a ride. Should he take it?

E: *take the ride and risk being identified*, or

F: *keep walking and make slower progress*

He decides yes. He's taking **E**. He hops in, and in short order it turns out that this driver is quite a Nosy Parker and is about to identify him according to police reports now being broadcast over the car radio.

Parry must choose to:

E: *keep riding and take whatever comes of being identified*, or

F: *get the heck out of that ride*

He decides on **F**, to get the heck out of the ride, but when he asks the driver to pull over, the man makes it clear that he knows Parry is the recent escapee and, what's more, intends to turn him in.

Parry can:

E: *keep riding*, or

G: *hurt the driver to get the heck out of that ride*

He hurts the driver. (As well as being a necessary education on the mistake he made back with **E** and **F**—raising the tension on his *next* choice—this is also a fuse laid waiting to flare up again later when he can least afford it. One event playing more than one role in the story: that's layering.)

132

Then he's back on the road, this time disguised in the driver's clothes. He gets *another* offer of a ride. Should he take it?

The most important thing about making mistakes is the opportunity that we have to learn from them. Has Parry learned from the last mistake? Does he now know better than to take a ride? Yes, he does. But does he also now know that the police are announcing his break-out on the radio and asking local drivers to report him if they see him on the road? Yes, indeed.

What's he going to choose?

H: *refuse the ride and take his chances on the road*, or

I: *accept this second ride*

He's in a *really* bad bind now. This is worse than just sitting around waiting to die in prison! Making an impossible choice is so agonizing to the human animal that we often choose not to choose, even if this means staying put and suffering the torments of hell.

Then the second character throws a twist into it — she not only insists he get in, *she calls him by name*.

His option paralysis has been too great, and when she tips the scales for him, he accepts her decision. He dives in.

And here Goodis gives him a little break. She's kind! She tells him how to hide in the back of her car — very convenient, that tarp back there — and she smuggles him past the police guarding the entrance to San Francisco at the Golden Gate Bridge. She even takes him home with her, slips him into her building, and loans him her shower. She's like his *guardian angel*.

So now he has another choice to make:

J: *Take her at face value*, or

K: *find out what's going on — who is this woman, why is she treating him this way?*

Remember that characters always have powerful motivation for the things they do. They can't just be kind to our protagonists because *we* want to be nice to them. Our characters are not us.

Parry chooses **K** and asks her, and lo-&-behold she's got a clipping of a letter to the editor in his own defense, written at the time of his trial. It's signed Irene Janney. She says she's Irene Janney. Irene likes Vincent, and apparently she *has* liked him for a long time without his knowledge.

But *why*?

Again: every character in fiction has enormous, overpowering reasons for doing the things they do.

None of this is coincidence.

So he has another choice to make:

L: *believe whatever she tells him*, or

M: *find out for himself*

He chooses **M**. After he showers, he searches her room, and — what do you know? — there's a whole scrapbook of clippings of the news reports of his arrest, trial, and imprisonment.

What's going *on* here?

And so it goes.

We have two essential points to learn from Goodis:

1) Everything our protagonist does causes the next effect. That's right — even in fueling momentum, it's always cause-&-effect. While Parry doesn't know it, he has not only caused Janney to stop for him on the road, but even caused her to be out on that road at the same time as him in the first place,

conveniently beladen with a tarp under which a man could hide. How has he caused this? *Oooh,* that's the Backstory! And it's coming up next. It turns out that she has *extremely powerful reasons* for being interested in his welfare, reasons rooted, it so happens, in her very natural love for her own father.

2) The more difficult we make our protagonist's choices, the more complex the reasoning they must navigate in order to make the right choice, and the bigger the sword we hang over their head. And the more intensely the reader is invested in reading all the way to the end to find out how our protagonist finally rids themself of this excruciating sequence of cause-&-effect.

As soon as Vincent Parry learns why Irene Janney is helping him, he realizes that he has to find out who framed him, because this involves not only **protecting himself from the law** but also **protecting his guardian angel's father**. He's basically honorable, and he has a *need* to believe in the justice behind laws, even more so now for the sake of this woman who's done so much for him.

Increase his need.

Also now that he's spent some time with this adoring babe, he and Janney have begun falling in love, so he no longer just wants **to live** he wants **to live for love**.

Again — *increase his need.*

But he can't find out who framed him so long as his face is on Wanted posters all over San Francisco. Unless, perhaps, he can choose to lose his face.

And the next thing we know, our protagonist is walking around San Francisco looking like Humphrey Bogart!

Using Character to Addict Your Reader

Now we know how to both discover plot and fuel momentum with character. Is this everything? Must we turn to other aspects of fiction for the addictive quality that we know our story needs?

Not yet. Because character is not only the source of all plot and the fuel for all forward motion, it contains the most *fundamental addictive quality* that exists.

Readers read to learn how to survive. And our characters know how to do this. (If they don't, they'd sure better learn.) This is plot.

Meanwhile, constantly increasing the momentum keeps the reader in a state of intense belief that the next page is going to teach them even more about survival than they've already learned. They can't wait!

But readers also read to learn that life is *worth* surviving. And this reassurance is inherent in the very act of creating art — the deep, abiding, even paradoxical belief that the experience of living is worth preserving. It's worth the trouble of understanding. It's even worth the work of sharing. (And creating art others want to share is a *whole* lot of work.)

It was all worth it, after all.

We create this reassurance with rhythm, the push-pull rhythm at the core of all human experience.

There's a reason we crave this rhythm. It's the involuntary motion of breathing, the constant beat of pulse. It's the reverberation that made up our days and nights, our very instants, of the entire first nine months of life as we traveled hither and thither with our mothers listening to their hearts beat. This regular rhythm creates for us the moment-by-moment experience of being alive.

Mother in our senses! No, she's not there. Yes, she is! No, she's not. Yes! No. Yes! No. Yes! No. Yes!

So passes all eternity.

Here's a protagonist with a need — something so true to their way of being that they couldn't be themself without it. Maybe a woman needs freedom from fear of the occupying army that has taken over her rural village. She's a French woman, the conquerors are German, and aside from the long-standing animosity between the French and Germans for as long as either side can remember, the soldiers occupying her village don't just live here, *they own it*. They move into the houses, they patrol the streets, they monitor twenty-four hours a day the behavior and conversations of the locals whose land they have overrun.

Not only the woman but everyone she has ever known lives with the constant, inescapable adrenaline of fear. Fear of their lifelong enemy, the Germans. Fear for their lives. So whenever we show scenes of the woman under power of her need to survive — under power of this fear — we push the reader a little bit away.

Be afraid, we say to them. *Be very afraid.*

At the same time, this woman is young and strong and healthy. She's married, so she's already an active sexual being. Her husband is gone — a prisoner of war, a philanderer with whom she has actually been quite unhappy — and she lives with his mother, who doesn't particularly like her. The young German soldier billeted in their home is intelligent, gentle, a musician. . .and *he likes her*.

Not only the woman, now, but everyone in the village is making allowances for the fact that these Germans, far from being simple monsters, are complex humans just as they are themselves. They have their strengths and weaknesses, their petty irritabilities and surprising moments of spontaneous generosity. So whenever we show scenes of the woman under power of her need to be liked, her need for intelligence, gentleness, and music, her need for the tenderness that grows up between herself and the German soldier. . .we pull the reader deeply in.

There is love, we are saying. *Even in the darkest night, love can still find us.*

The struggle for survival.

The reassurance that survival is worth it.

Irene Némirovsky's heart-breakingly beautiful novella *Dolce* uses her first-hand knowledge of life under the German occupation of France during WW II to inspire in us first the fear and then the love. It's hypnotic, the way she creates in the reader a *need* to be *reading this story.*

Over and over again, scene after scene. Fear, then love. Fear, then love. Fear. Love. *Fear. Love.*

Tension, then fulfillment.

Addiction. And resonance.

This is the paradoxical truth buried under everything we ever experience, in fiction and in life, from conception to death — this back-&-forth rhythm. It's the very rhythm of what it means to us to live.

Chapter 16

Layering Character

Believable fiction I

And so we come to the deepest, richest, most *compelling* aspect of character: **layering**.

Layering is bringing together all of these approaches to character — developing, condensing, contrasting, motivation — to create levels within our protagonist that illuminate their internal conflict, those overwhelming conflicting needs that pit them against themself as they make their way through their adventures by the very skin of their teeth. All layering is based in the character's values, those things they *need*.

There is an infinite number of ways to layer character, just as there is an infinite number of characters to be created, with an infinite number of qualities on which to base their conflicting needs.

I'm going to talk about only three of the basics here, layering techniques so fundamental that they account for a ridiculously disproportionate amount of the fiction in the world today.

Layering Character with Behavior

Louisa May Alcott created layers to Jo March, but because she was writing about herself (and parts of herself she didn't fully understand) she didn't quite succeed the way she intended. We all believe that Jo is gutsy, tough, smart, creative, and adventurous. Heck, yes. She put the "Oh, boy!" into tomboy. It's much harder to believe, though, that Jo is sincere in her protestations of devotion to the altruistic hogwash that Alcott pasted over her character.

And yet, we *do* believe in Jo. We believe she's real. Why? What gives Jo her layering?

Her *tenderness*.

Sometimes Jo is running around the neighborhood wreaking havoc with Laurie, and sometimes she's sassing Marmee, and sometimes she's swashbuckling through the house pretending to take off pirate heads in the most dastardly unladylike way.

However, when Beth is dying Jo drops everything to be by her side — reading to her, caring for her, holding her hand and watching her slip away with tears in her eyes (tears that Jo feels compelled to hide behind gruffness).

The ways in which Jo acts are always true to herself, true to her own values. And this means that when the chips are down and her beloved sister needs her, Jo is there.

This is the layering that makes Jo a three-dimensional character and allows her to step off the page into the lives of her readers: her behavior.

We humans really *do* vacillate between our tough outer shells and the things that move our hearts. We do both flout authority and spontaneously give of ourselves. We do both make stupid mistakes and accidentally create flashes of light in another's darkness. The specific, detailed ways in which we do these things grow out of the specific values by which we live. These details — the ways in which we act out our values — are the stuff of fiction.

Everything Jo does has its roots in the fundamental, conflicting values of her character. And because this makes her behavior real, she is believable.

Layering Character with Confusion

Eugene Henderson is an extraordinarily *ordinary* person. He's a bluff, hearty American businessman with a simple-minded socialite for a wife. He goes on business trips. In fact, he goes on a business trip to Africa. He knows he's ordinary. What are you going to do? It's just who he is.

So when Saul Bellow sent him, in *Henderson the Rain King*, on a bizarre pilgrimage to the heart of the African foothills in search of an elusive, little-known tribe, he had to give him good reasons. Bellow wanted Henderson blind to himself because he knew that confusion often leads to epiphany, and Bellow had specific things he wanted to explore within this particular epiphany.

So he gave Henderson a surface motivation to venture into that African wilderness. But at the same time, he gave him *hidden* motivation, reasons for going on this pilgrimage and sticking with it that an ordinary man like Henderson wouldn't normally have. And because those hidden reasons are rooted firmly in the values of Henderson the ordinary man, the fact that Henderson is oblivious to them doesn't keep them from being perfectly plausible motivation.

Eventually, the confusion Henderson has about his own hidden side leads him not only to the obscure tribe but to the tribe's inexplicable ritual for calling rain, a ritual in which Henderson — precisely because of his size and the very qualities of bluffness and innocent heartiness that make a person an ordinary   American   businessman — becomes   inevitably entangled.

And the next thing Henderson knows, he's facing himself within the context of an experience that would be strange as hell even for the most *conscientiously* bizarre among us. Henderson has accidentally and through no fault of his own become the tribe's new Rain King.

Henderson's transformation from ordinary businessman to African Rain King is so implausible that it would be simply impossible if it weren't for Bellows' meticulous, matter-of-fact record of significant details, which allows the reader to experience the transformation with exactly the same level of oblivion and insight as Henderson. So by the time Bellows is done with us, we *are* Henderson the Rain King, trapped in an inexplicable reality from which we have no escape.

This innocent confusion is intensely real to the experience of being a human animal. And this makes Henderson — however unbelievable his story might be on the face of it — intensely believable.

Layering Character with Two Classical Needs

Vincent Parry is a canonical protagonist, caught between his need to live and his need to love. And I can't begin to tell you how much fiction — great literature, pulp, and everything in between — has been created through this straight-forward, eternal layering of these two most classical needs: **survival** and **love**.

Parry is simply an archetype.

David Goodis sent him into his story of *Dark Passage*, as so many protagonists are sent, running for his life from very real danger on page one. Violence! Injustice! Death! Oh, *no*!

We all believe enthusiastically in a character's need to survive.

At the same time, almost the first person he meets is a *babe*. Flirtation! Sex! Passion!

We also believe with all our hearts in a character's need to love.

So Parry's two conflicting needs are not unique to him at all. They're common to every human animal.

In fact, they're common to mammals in general. Everyone needs to live. And while we know only a little about how mammals aside from ourselves feel about each other, we do have evidence of powerful affection in their little mammalian hearts, and we honestly can't miss the proof of their overwhelming desire to copulate.

Back and forth, throughout the story, Goodis tosses Parry between these two most classical needs: survival, love — survival, love.

Every time Parry thinks he's on top of survival, something crops up in his need for love: his best friend dies mysteriously shortly after Parry visits him, then his nemesis surfaces, a woman he once rejected.

And every time Parry thinks he's on top of the love question, his life is threatened again: the Nosy Parker turns up, someone begins stalking Parry and Janney.

Until eventually Parry must choose between his safety and his passion for Janney — a nightmare choice, and the only possible Climax for his story, forcing him as it does to choose between his two overwhelming needs.

We recognize this, don't we? Of course we do. Némirovsky used exactly the same needs — survival, love — for her gorgeous story, *Dolce*, although otherwise the two stories couldn't be more different.

James M. Cain used them for *The Postman Always Rings Twice*.

Emily Brontë twisted the daylights out of them for *Wuthering Heights*.

A protagonist trapped between their need for survival and their need for love: one of those few plots we have. Brought to life through all the myriad significant details of existence and humanity: *an infinity of stories.*

Plot is *Context*

Chapter 17

Designing an Impossible Plot with Maria Dermout

Once upon a time

There was once a time when we could structure a novel like Maria Dermout's *The Ten Thousand Things* and get away with it.

I picked up *The Ten Thousand Things* in my local thrift shop because it was a 1950s hardback with nothing but the author's initials embossed in the center of the cover, and someday *I* intend to write a '50s hardback with nothing but *my* initials embossed in the center of the cover. There's something about them — the elegance. The restraint. The sheer courtesy to the author.

"This is, after all, your book."

Then I started reading it and thought, *That's why I've never heard of Dermout. Because she didn't know how to plot.*

The first half of the book is a lush, multifaceted, fascinating portrait of an obscure garden estate — a 'spice park' — on some island somewhere in the ocean (at a rather random point near page 100 we learn we're in Java) in the early twentieth century. It seems longer ago because the story dates back six generations from there, and even in the present the styles are quite old-fashioned — the characters wear batik sarongs with little jackets over them, the women carry burdens on their heads, the little girls playing in the garden wear pinafores.

The only thing that looks even remotely like a plot is the fact that the little girls playing in the garden happen to be *dead*.

So we read along, and we're waiting for the dead little girls to do something interesting. But they don't. In fact, everyone eventually admits that they've never actually seen them, just had them pointed out by others who claim *they* have. The girls were poisoned long ago, it seems. People think.

A child grows up in her grandmother's house on the obscure garden estate, goes to Europe with her parents, comes back as an adult with her baby son, and raises her son in her grandmother's house. The dead little girls remain just that— dead.

Around the middle of the book the grown son goes on an expedition to a local island as an officer and is killed by head-hunters.

End of that story.

Then we're in the second half of the book, which is a series of short stories: one story about the other ghost on the island, a man who has drowned on a beach near his creepy house, rumored to have been killed by his young wife and her three ancient aunts whom he kept locked behind a high thorn fence; one story about the cook of the woman on the obscure garden estate, rumored to have stabbed an ex-lover to death until she is, herself, stabbed to death with his knife; and one story about a foolish European professor of botany who wanders willy-nilly through the islands, giving out polished coins to children in exchange for orchids and other rare flowers, until he is killed by four young men with machetes for his father's gold watch and his polished coins.

I'm thinking, *She just fell in love with this imaginary world of the islands and couldn't stop writing stories about it.* Because, to her credit, it really is a rich, vibrant, detailed imaginary world. And each individual story has a good, solid plot.

But this is not really a novel.

Finally, in the last story we're back with the woman on the obscure garden estate, and it is the night of the anniversary of her son's murder by the head-hunters, and the servants have gone to town, as they do every year, leaving her alone to mourn. Only instead of mourning, she's sitting in a rattan chair on the beach waiting for her annual visitors to arrive: the man who drowned, the cook and her ex-lover, the professor of botany, and — usually, but not always — her son.

The three little girls are there, too. They like the professor of botany. He's nice.

The woman has an argument with her son about death. She's adamant that the murdered are wholly different from those who die by other means, and she's quite annoyed that the man who drowned doesn't know whether he was pushed or fell and doesn't seem to care.

Her son says, no, that's right, it doesn't really matter.

He says that it isn't easy to die, whether you're killed or not, and his mother is furious with him for pretending. She says that the murdered just don't want to admit the truth.

And this makes him laugh, which he has never done for her before.

Shortly after that they're all gone, and she is still sitting quietly in her rattan chair on the beach, and she whispers, frightened, for them to stay with her, but she's not sure now whether they were ever even there at all.

While she sits in the dark staring out at the moon path across the bay she sees coming toward her a *proa* — a boat — carrying the

149

mystical symbols of her life: a purple Palm of the Sea, a plate from Ceram, snails she calls the Sentinels of Good Fortune, a Crab for controlling the tide, and the nest of a holy Bird in the top of the Palm. There's a long list of magical talismans, and everyone she has ever known and loved is there. And all the murderers are there, too, because they belong there.

She wonders if she's dying, if these are her 'hundred things' that supposedly appear at the moment of death. But there are more than a hundred, there are a hundred hundred, and she can see no link between them except the spectacle of all of them together on this extraordinary *proa* coming toward her under the moonlight.

And then for just a split second. . .she sees the link. One moment of utter, focused brilliance flashing at the reader out of the depths of this gorgeous, seemingly-unfocused narrative.

And this is the Climax. The whole point of this story.

Later the woman's cook comes to fetch her to bed, a simple Resolution of two paragraphs. She will go on living.

Sigh.

I want to tell you that there was a time when we could write beautiful, ephemeral novels like this, when the reader didn't need to be dragged along by the hair but was willing to walk quite companionably by our side of their own free will. Because in those days we were reading for pleasure as much as escape, we had fewer things clamoring incessantly for our attention (less marketing by a zillion miles), we had — for lack of a better term — more peace of mind.

So while we're wondering about plots and sales and agents calling for fresh ideas and how to come up with some story that's never been told before, we must remember. . .

There once was a time.

Chapter 18

Beating Your Drum

Introduction to holographic structure

It's incredibly difficult to get proper structure from the sheer feel of creating a work, and yet it's how so many of us approach writing.

Do you know the longest it can possibly take to write a novel by feel rather than plan? Neither do I. But I can tell you that I once spent fourteen years on a novel without ever figuring it out. I finally sat myself down and analyzed *other people's* plots — great novels and stories — and read a book on screenwriting: *Screenplay* by Syd Field. So now I know how to do it. That part took about two months.

And I'm going to teach it to you.

Here's what we want out of plot structure:

We want to spark our reader's interest. Make them look up. Make them do a double-take in our direction. Make them say, *"What the heck?"*

Then we want to build on our reader's interest by showing them lots of interesting things happening to our protagonist. But we can't just pile a bunch of stuff together randomly, with no sense of order or chronology and without letting the reader know which things are more important than others and which things are *the most important things* of all. Because this just takes them to a flat plateau, and when we're standing on one, a flat plateau is indistinguishable from a flat plane. Boring.

So we organize the most important events that we want to show our reader in increasing order of tension, from least to most. And for every one of those events:

We want to spark our reader's interest in this *one* event. Make them jerk their head around. "Who did *what*?"

We want to build on our reader's interest by showing them a variety of interesting things related to this *one* event. But we can't just create a smaller plateau. So we organize all the interesting parts of this *one* event in increasing order of tension, from least to most. And for each *one* part of this *one* event:

We want to spark our reader's interest in this part. Make them snap their mouth open. "Did it *how*?"

We want to build on our reader's interest by showing them new and complex and intriguing bits about this *one* part of the *one* event. We organize these bits in increasing order of tension, from least to most. And we show them to the reader.

We give our reader a second to integrate it all. That's our beat.

Then we reward our reader for their interest in this *one* part of the *one* event by showing them *the coolest bit there is to this one part*.

Then we go on to the *next* part of the *one* event and repeat that whole step, a spark followed by organized bits with a beat and reward.

We keep doing this until we run out of interesting parts to this *one* event.

We give our reader a minute to integrate the *last* part of this *one* event. That's our beat.

Then we reward our reader for their interest in this entire *one* event by showing them *the most exciting part there is to the one event.*

Then we go on to the *next* event we're going to throw at our protagonist. And do the whole thing over again.

We keep doing this until we run out of events for this story.

We give our reader some time to integrate the last event. That's our big beat with a backbeat.

Then we reward our reader for their interest in every single event in this entire story, all of the anguish and chaos and recovery we've forced on our protagonist. We show the reader *the most important event of all.*

Total meltdown! This event is the reason we're telling this story.

And if we're really, really concerned about the reader, we throw in a Resolution on the final page for good measure, one last beat.

The End.

You can see, when we do this, that we wind up with a pattern, in which the very first part is gripping:

HOOK
"What the *heck*?"
"Who did *what*?"
"Did it *how*?"
And it settles into a rhythm:
"And *how*?"
"And *how*?"
Beat.
"Oh! *That's* how!"

CONFLICT #1

Which blows up in their faces:

"Whoa! They did *what* then?"

"Did it *how?*"

And it goes back to the rhythm:

"And *how?*"

"And *how?*"

Beat.

First Plot Point, end of Act I: "Oh! *That's* how!"

CONFLICT #2

And it blows up even worse, in what now turns to be a major rhythm:

"Whoa! They did *what* then?"

"Did it *how?*"

And there's the minor rhythm again:

"And *how?*"

"And *how?*"

Beat.

Fulcrum, midpoint of Act II: "Oh! *That's* how!"

CONFLICT #3

And it blows up again, a real crisis:

"Whoa! They did *what* then?"

"Did it *how?*"

And there's the minor rhythm again:

"And *how?*"

"And *how?*"

Beat.

And this time the big beat's got a little backbeat: Backbeat.

Because this time the major rhythm kicks someone's butt:

Second Plot Point, end of Act II: *"Ow! That's* how!"

FAUX RESOLUTION

And this time the beat is a major beat:

Beat.

Beat.

Beat.

Startle your reader for a second with a little poke:

"*Wowza!*"

Go back to the beat:

Biggest backbeat of all.

CLIMAX

And now it's going to blow up irrevocably, once and for all, and our reader can feel the tingling in their bones:

"Whoa! They did *what* then?"

"Did it *how*?"

And there's the minor rhythm for the last time, quicker and more powerful than ever:

"And *how*?"

"And *how*?"

Beat.

Until finally the reader unexpectedly learns the answer to the question they asked way, way back in the very beginning, "*What the heck?*" Which answer makes their hair stand on end.

It's the whole point of our story, the end of Act III: "*Aghghghgh!* That's *what the heck!*"

Then we either provide the very, very final beat in the last moments of Act III, or we leave the reader flying through the air, forced to provide that beat for themself.

Keep them baffled, clinging to the chandelier.

And *coming back for more.*

Chapter 19

Designing a Crescendo

Explication of holographic structure

We talked about Hook, Development, and Climax in *Art & Craft of Writing Fiction: 1st Practitioner's Manual,* so we should all be familiar with these terms. A computer professor once told me that studies show it takes fourteen iterations to work an idea into the human brain, so assuming that you've read and re-read *Art & Craft of Writing Fiction* — which I am *certain* that you have — poring over it through the long, winter's night, hunched by candlelight in your garret under the cold, rainy eaves. . .we'll call this iteration #7.

As playwrights and screenwriters have known for eons, all stories are constructed chronologically from a basic set of building blocks. Because fiction is so dense and novels are so long, I break them down into six parts: Hook, Conflict #1, Conflict #2, Conflict #3, Faux Resolution, Climax.

But these can also be understood under a larger umbrella known as *three-act structure:*

Act I: Hook
Act II: Development
Act III: Climax

I lump them together roughly this way:

Act I: Hook
HOOK
CONFLICT #1

Act II: Development
CONFLICT #2
CONFLICT #3

Act III: Climax
FAUX RESOLUTION
CLIMAX

The thing to remember about the three acts of three-act structure is that each episode can be constructed, internally, exactly the same way the story is constructed as a whole, that is—hook, development, and climax. And *that* means:

Act I: Hook

HOOK
- Hook
- Conflict (1-3)
- Faux Resolution
- Climax

CONFLICT#1
- Hook
- Conflict (1-3)
- Faux Resolution
- Climax

Act II: Development

CONFLICT #2
- Hook
- Conflict (1-3)
- Faux Resolution
- Climax

CONFLICT #3
- Hook
- Conflict (1-3)
- Faux Resolution
- Climax

Act III: Climax

FAUX RESOLUTION
- Hook
- Conflict (1-3)
- Anti-Faux Resolution
- Climax

CLIMAX
- Hook
- Conflict (1-3)
- Faux Resolution
- Climax

I know it looks like formula. But it's not. This is primal rhythm, the one we just bongo'd out in the last chapter.

Yank! Boom, boom, boom. A beat. *Boom!*

Sit with it for a minute. Mess around with it a little — two or four booms, multiple or no beats, multiple or no yanks, multiple final *booms!* or none at all. Push the rhythm to the limit of as much build-up as humanly possible without going overboard. Balance the elements against each other. Notice what feels most like riding a falling avalanche on a toboggan.

Feel it in your bones.

Now, take a good, hard gander at that list. Notice that if we include the full three conflicts in each episode (we don't have to, but we shouldn't do more than three, or our build-up will become long-winded), we wind up with — thirty-six pieces. Which is a rather convenient divisor of the 72,000 words that are these days commonly considered minimum for a novel. Particularly if we make a point of averaging either 1,000 or 2,000 words per scene, depending upon our own internal rhythms.

Do the math. Take your time. Because this piece of information is absolutely *incredible*.

It means that it's perfectly possible to plan an entire novel *scene-by-scene*. Either thirty-six scenes of approximately 2,000 words apiece. Or thirty-six episodes each containing two scenes of approximately 1,000 words apiece. Or some combination of the two.

Not only *that* — it means when all those scenes are written the whole thing not only hangs together with unshakable cohesion, but it builds in tension, modulates pacing with breathtaking accuracy, and reaches the best and brightest, most spectacular catastrophe at exactly the right instant to blow the reader right out of their chair.

Haven't you ever wondered how pulp writers of the Golden Age of vintage fiction did it?

This is how.

Aspiring pantsers have *no idea.* Yes, Stephen King and Flannery O'Connor could feel their way through this blindfolded. Raymond Chandler and Agatha Christie did it, too. But nobody has to. And it's far, far easier to take off the blindfold and just watch where we step.

Chandler wrote only seven literary novels in his entire lifetime. His close friend Erle Stanley Gardner cranked out so many genre novels that he had to use half-a-dozen pseudonyms to deal with them, the Perry Mason mysteries alone numbering over seventy.

Structure.

Vintage pulp's gift to us all.

Fatal Ignition

What the authors of vintage pulp knew that literary artists were assumed not to know is that readers read for thrills. They want to see the characters dynamited, they want to see it big, and they want to see it *now.*

Although there was period in literary history in which great artists like Dermout could assemble their fuses, explosives, and igniting sparks at their leisure, these days the necessity for a quick *bang!* is taken as a given by almost everyone in the publishing industry. This is what agents look for in manuscripts, it's what publishers' acquisitions editors look for, it's what the marketers and bookseller reps who sit in on publishers' acquisitions meetings look for. And it's what readers look for.

Thrills.

Occasionally we'll hear someone who doesn't understand the industry very well bewailing this situation. "All you slummers want is sensationalist low-brow genre!" Or the other side of the coin, "All you stuffed shirts want is dry, high-brow literary gobbledygook!"

But thrill is what readers of all types of fiction have *always* wanted, as Edward Anderson showed us at the beginning of his beautiful Dustbowl novel *Thieves Like Us, a romance,* when Bowie, his insides twisting, watches a car come bumping slowly down the old dirt road toward him where he waits in his convict's clothing under the shadow of a prison wall.

Anyone who's ever watched a movie that begins with a release from prison (and they are legion) knows that they don't release you in your convict's clothing. And so we understand that this is a story about an escaped con—about *thieves*, we are told, *like us.*

And this does indeed turn out at the Climax to be exactly what this story is about.

The Hook scene, although not the most important moment in our novel, is the most important moment in the *career* of our novel.

Especially in today's publishing climate, when tens of thousands of newly-hatched aspiring writers are being urged and exhorted every day to query agents and publishers' acquisitions editors with the first-draft fruits of their uncoordinated infant efforts at fiction, nobody in the industry has more than a few seconds to glance at any particular manuscript and decide then-&-there whether or not they want to see the rest.

"Am I piqued? And I intrigued? Am I *thrilled*?"

First scene. Character, plot, and prose must all combine in a primeval quark of almost unimaginable mass right there on the first page. We must ignite that fuse, make it short, dynamite our reader out of their chair.

We'll have time later to pick up all the pieces and assemble the puzzle.

Backstory

What is this? Why is it important? And what on earth are we supposed to *do* with the stuff?

As little as humanly possible.

It's true that Backstory plays a part in proper plot structure. Sometimes we need a little illumination from behind the curtain. A little light filtering through the lace, highlighting the pattern as it begins to move. However, extra information is awkward, it requires its own special techniques, and the reader prefers to get this information the way they get almost everything else these days — on the fly.

So before we start throwing on the flood lamps and ripping holes in the fabric of our story, we must spend a good long time spelling out all that information in great detail in our notes and identifying ways to layer it into our characters' interactions and adventures.

The reason Backstory is so often confused with exposition is that they share a lot in common:

- lack of momentum
- lack of in-the-moment excitement
- lack of mystery

You see? All lacks. *Not* a good quality in storytelling.

Everything that we put into a story must add to the forward momentum of our plot. It must be about getting our characters from point $(x1,y1,z1)$ to point (xn,yn,zn) with as much velocity as humanly possible. We are here to make our characters' lives a hellbent-for-leather ride. When we stop the action in order to explain what's gone before or what's going on now — to point at the curtains — we throw our reader right into the dashboard.

They don't like this. They like their hair flying straight back off their heads.

So our job with Backstory is to make sure that it does not throw our reader into the dashboard.

At the same time, everything we put into a story must serve the purposes of pacing. Most of what readers want out of pacing is increasing tension in order to make previous excitement look like the slow part laying the groundwork for what's *really* electrifying.

Now, there are subtle undulations that we, the writers, know that we've layered into this increasing tension. But the reader is feeling the pulsing increase in pressure of Gs that — if all goes well — will eventually implode on them, blasting them into a parallel universe. When we stop adding significant description, action, and dialog to keep that pressure stimulating, soothing, stimulating in carefully-modulated doses — when we lift the Gs to pause and discourse on general stuff — it feels weak. And our reader is likely to lurch out of our grip and fall like a lump back to earth while they're still under the sway of gravity.

Our job with Backstory is to make sure that it keeps our reader forever entirely engaged in the thrilling experience of the story, heading into orbit.

Finally, our story must always be about launching our reader out of our imagination and into their own, the curiosity that impels them out into the ether. When we drag the story backward with Backstory or exposition, we're dragging the reader's attention back to ourselves. And they don't want to pay attention to us. Then want to pay attention to themself, to their own experience of this mysterious, rocketing ride through the wilds of the imagination.

Our job with Backstory is to make sure that our reader is *always* wholly engaged in exploring our fictional landscape, completely forgetting that there's a human being behind it all typing frantically away.

Ray Bradbury helped bring dark literary (pre-'edgy' 'edgy') fantasy and sci-fi to the forefront of modern fiction through his meticulous, unerring instinct for pure scene without a speck of exposition. In "The Dwarf," the first story in his literary masterpiece collection *The October Country*, Bradbury teaches us *exactly* how to handle Backstory.

Instead of telling us in exposition what the Dwarf has done before the hook scene of his story's Hook, Bradbury shows the owner of the carnival Mirror Maze telling the protagonist, innocent Aimee, how the Dwarf has come to him more than once in the past asking about the price of his funhouse mirrors.

Bradbury places this Backstory exactly right, directly between the Hook and Conflict #1, and he ties it back into the Hook by introducing the conversation through Aimee's observation that the Dwarf almost came up to them after he'd been inside the Mirror Maze, almost asked something he just couldn't bring himself to ask.

This gives the owner of the Mirror Maze the opportunity to tell the story of the other times the Dwarf has come to him and almost asked where he could buy such a mirror, something he couldn't quite, in the end, bring himself to ask.

This is Backstory with forward momentum, ominous tingling, and ever deeper curiosity about Bradbury's special melancholy country of inner torment.

And it's only what's *absolutely* necessary.

We must winnow our Backstory down to only that most essential information the reader simply *must* have as they venture into our story, layering as much of this as possible into the process of our characters getting to know each other, and casting what's left (if anything) into either very brief exposition or — better yet — thoroughly vivid flashback scenes.

We put these flashback scenes into Chapter Two or Three, after the Hook, before we get too deep into Conflict #1.

But only what's *absolutely* necessary.

Three Acts

And now we've launched our reader into the first of our three acts: Hook, Development, Climax.

So let's talk about the purposes of these three acts, since they serve as the building blocks of pretty much *all* storytelling, in one form or another. Yes — they're that powerful.

Act I is the set-up: we're setting our protagonist up like a bowling pin. What the reader really wants out of a good story is to see the protagonist knocked down so hard they bring the bowling alley down on their heads. This doesn't happen in Act I, though. Act I is the set-up. Set your protagonist up *really well*.

Act II is the big game: the reason we don't leap straight from Act I to Act III is that stories are *fun*. Especially really long stories like novels. They're full, complicated, devilishly entertaining. A good story chases the reader around the corral with the lasso swinging — *thwip thwip thwip* — over its head until it's thrown it and got the reader by one hind leg, and then it drags them in circles through the dust and mud and cow-pies while they shriek with glee.

Does the lasso matter to how the story ends?

It's *essential*.

Finally, Act III is the pay-off: the catastrophe our reader has come here to witness. There's some fancy footwork we do, some classic shuffling we employ to make the final *whallop* as vast and deep and supremely satisfying as humanly possible.

But this is where the bowling alley collapses. Breaks the water main. Bursts the gas lines. And the next thing you know, our reader is staggering out of a cloud of smoke like 1906 San Francisco, coughing and squinting, with singed hair and a staggered gait, their hands groping blindly in front of them.

Utterly *thrilled*.

In 1934 James M. Cain blew the lid off genre thriller with his classic novella *The Postman Always Rings Twice*, not-quite 120 pages. It's written with such gorgeous, dark *noir* detail that no one's ever cared that there's no obvious postman in it and, in fact, no one to ring the doorbell twice. . .or even once.

In perfect three-act structure.

Act I

On the first page, the protagonist, Frank Chambers, turns up at the roadside diner at which he will eventually rob, kidnap, and finally kill. In fact, in the first sentence he gets thrown off a hay truck right in front of it. Now, *that's* a Hook!

Cain needed Frank to commit the pivotal crime around which he intended to structure his story, so that's Act I—setting Frank up.

Frank meets the Greek who owns the diner and, in short order, the Greek's wife, Cora, for whom he develops an instantaneous hot flash that takes over his entire awareness and rides him from that moment to the very end. It turns out that Cora's got the same hot flash for Frank, and between them they're in the sack quicker than you can say cat-on-a-ladder.

Frank doesn't want to kill the Greek. Frank's not the killing type. Neither, really, is Cora. But she's trapped in this marriage, as so many young women of her era were trapped. Even more, this diner is all she's ever earned through her own hard labor and common sense, and it's in the Greek's name. She needs to get out, to be with Frank. And she also needs to keep the one valuable thing she owns (conflicting *needs*!).

At the same time, Frank, who needs not to get entangled in nefarious illegal stuff, realizes that he also needs Cora (conflicting *needs*!). And he finds himself, in the throes of sexual passion, agreeing to help her.

So Frank and Cora go through with their plan to kill the Greek, which involves conking him unconscious in the bathtub. However, while Cora is upstairs in the act, Frank and a passing cop watch a cat climb the stepladder Cora's supposed to use to escape, and as soon as the cop pulls out of the driveway there's a flash and all the power goes out. Cora botches the job in the dark, and she and Frank wind up having to save the Greek so that the botched attempt won't be obvious. It turns out that at just the wrong instant the cat stepped off the ladder onto the fuse box and electrocuted itself.

These guys are *born losers*.

Now they need a *second* plan. Which is twice as hard to plan and carry out, now that they've got that close call on their consciences. (And on the reader's.) But this one works! Against all odds — truthfully, both Frank and Cora are kind of surprised. The Greek is dead, and their lives have suddenly altered forever.

Page forty, $^1/_3$ of the way in. End of Act I.

Act II

Because Frank and Cora are present when the Greek dies, they're investigated, and Cora winds up on trial. Frank's involved. There's a DA who forces Frank to point the finger at Cora in order to be cleared of suspicion himself. Then Frank's lawyer arranges for Cora to confess the truth to a private detective she believes is a cop, so she won't blurt it out in court. It's all quite complex, but again, weirdly enough, it works. They planned it carefully, and even when their plans backfire the lawyer saves them in the eleventh hour through fancy machinations with the insurance companies who have insured the life of the Greek. Forty of the most hair-raising pages in the literary canon, and suddenly Frank and Cora are going home to the roadside diner, not only free of suspicion, but with ten thousand dollars of the Greek's insurance money in their pockets.

Page eighty, $^2/_3$ of the way in. End of Act II.

Act III

And after drama and mayhem and terror. . .this is where things get *bad*.

Because the lawyer's detective goes renegade, he has Cora's confession, and he's a blackmailer. But even more than this, Frank has gone a little renegade himself, done a little philandering behind Cora's back, and now the whole business about Frank having sold Cora out comes back to haunt them.

This is cause-&-effect. This is plot grown straight out of character. And it's handled simply brilliantly.

The purpose of three-act structure is to set the protagonist up, knock them down, set them up, knock them down, and then set them up *really big* while the reader's heart is still trying to get out their throat. It's the quintessential Third Time's a Charm.

By the end of his novel, Cain has Frank and Cora exactly where he wants them, in the core of their very worst nightmare, on the bullseye he aimed them toward way, way back in the beginning, when he gave Frank that shove off the hay truck in the very first sentence on page one. And he has the reader clinging to the chandelier.

If you were an unskilled blue-collar drifter type during the Depression Era,

And you got away with murder to the tune of $10,000,

But you put yourself in a position to lose trust in the one person you absolutely needed to trust in order to stay clear of the electric chair. . .

What would you do?

Exactly what Frank and Cora do in the Climax of *The Postman Always Rings Twice.*

Two Plot Points

'Spin.' Those two structural supports at the ends of Acts I and II that fling our characters willy-nilly off one trajectory and onto another. Again, we borrow this term from scriptwriting: Robert McKee and Sydney Field.

These are the climaxes of Conflict #1 and Conflict #3. (There's also a climax to Conflict #2, of course, which we'll get to later.)

We've seen how James M. Cain spun his characters with a vengeance when he constructed the three acts of his canonical spine-tingler. First he gave them what they wanted. Then he gave it to them *again*. Wow — we'd better all be careful what we wish for!

But can it be done with a more sedate story, a longer plot structure, a less deadly premise?

Zane Grey's classic Western, *Riders of the Purple Sage,* tells two intertwined stories:

1) That of the young cowpoke Venters, nearly flogged to death in Chapter One by the Mormon Elder of a little Utah town, Tull, for being too close to the woman who owns the town, the unmarried and independent Jane Withersteen. In his constant struggle to keep from being killed by either Tull or the bandits known to hide out in the local canyons, Venters shoots a masked rider who turns out to be a young woman held captive by the local bandit king, Oldring, and whom Venters must hide in the wild and beautiful Utah canyons until he can nurse her back to health.

2) That of the Gentile outlaw Lassiter. Too smart for Tull, too tough for Oldring, only Lassiter can save Withersteen from Tull's heartless efforts to acquire her as one of his Mormon wives and the ownership of the entire town along with her.

So what spins their stories?

First of all, 280 pages of novel means the $1/4$-point arrives on page 70 and the $1/3$-point around page 93, the $2/3$-point around page 187 and the $3/4$-point on page 210. These are the approximate ends of Acts I and II.

This is important. We don't know yet whether Grey likes to put the end of Act I closer to $1/4$ or $1/3$ or the end of Act II closer to $2/3$ or $3/4$. (We've seen that Cain slammed them down right on the $1/3$ and $2/3$ marks.)

However, with this heavily layered a story, Grey's given himself some room to maneuver. How does he do it?

Act I end, first Plot Point, pages 70–93

On page 70, Lassiter is stumbling at the end of a chapter up a long slope toward Withersteen, having just saved an entire herd of her cattle that's been maliciously stampeded by Tull's men in order to terrify Withersteen, cost her thousands of costly head of cattle, and humble her into submission—the first dreadful showdown between Tull and Withersteen.

This is the **first climax of Act I**.

Withersteen owns the fastest and most beautiful horses in the region, and when Lassiter arrives at her feet and pants out that his horse is dead, she offers him not only one of her prize horses but also the position of main rider on her ranch. Although up until now she's hoped she could call a truce between Tull, the leader of the Mormon Church in which she fervently believes, and Lassiter, the maverick Gentile she trusts—Tull has just forced her down off the fence between them and drawn the battle line.

This is the **first resolution of Act I**, which 'spins' their story in a new direction.

And so sides are chosen.

Meanwhile, Venters, feeling simply terrible about having nearly killed the innocent Masked Rider, is carrying her in his arms deeper and deeper into the canyons where the bandits she's escaped can't find them. He's discovered a wonderful valley high in the hills beyond nearly impassible crags, and this is where he carries the wounded young woman, at great physical cost to himself. On page 89, he's actually climbing his lasso up a sheer cliff face with the woman's limp body in his arms.

This is the **second climax of Act I**.

And on page 91, the end of a chapter, they have arrived at a cave at the mouth of the valley, where he informs her under the night sky that she's finally safe from the bandits she so fiercely hates.

This is the **second resolution of Act I**, and it 'spins' *their* story in a new direction.

The new chapter on page 92 begins with Venters' exploration of the magical valley where he's going to spend the bulk of the book. And so his current goal—saving the life of the young woman he's shot—becomes another goal—making a home for them both here in the wilderness.

End of Conflict #1 and Act I.

Spin!

Act II end, second Plot Point, pages 187–210

Now, Venters has been busy for the past 94 pages, ever since we left Act I. He's been up and down the canyons, back to Withersteen's ranch and up to the valley again, working secretly to feed and support the young woman while hiding her existence from everyone, including his employer. He's gotten to know Lassiter pretty well, but he hasn't even told *him*.

And on page 187 the young woman, still recovering, gives an almighty scream that brings Venters running like a madman, in terror that Oldring has discovered them at last.

This is the **first climax of Act II.**

When he arrives he finds—what do you know?—Lassiter standing bemusedly over their campfire. He doesn't mean them any harm. He's just finally followed Venters back up the torturous canyon paths to find out what the heck is going on out in them thar hills.

This is the **first resolution of Act II,** and again it 'spins' the story of Venters and the woman in a new direction.

From here on out, Venters is no longer a man with a secret. He is a man *revealing* his secret and struggling to resolve it safely within the context of his world.

This sets him up for the big showdown at the novel's Climax with Oldring himself.

173

Meanwhile, just like the chapter about the stampeded cattle at the first climax of Act I, the chapter at the second climax of Act II is an all-out hellbent-for-leather race across the chaparral. Tull's right-hand man Jerry Card has killed one of Withersteen's hired hands and stolen her prize horses — including one belonging to Venters called Wrangle, who's always been a bit unpredictable although he's fast as the dickens. Venters is hot on Card's heels, knowing that if Card succeeds at stealing the horses Tull has won the battle against Lassiter and Withersteen.

This chapter has the reader hanging onto their hat with both hands from the first page. And it's only at the very end of the chapter that Venters finally catches up with Card, after Card has ridden to the brink of death and abandoned Withersteen's number one prize horse and transferred in mid-flight to the hot-tempered but fresher Wrangle.

This is the **second climax of Act II**. And it's a *humdinger*.

On page 208, Venters has reached the cliff edge upon which Wrangle is — bizarrely — dancing with Card clinging to his neck. Venters realizes that this is what's been odd about Wrangle all along: he's simply not right in the head. And now he's lost it completely. The horse has gone mad.

At the end of page 208, Venters is wasting bullets trying to shoot the horse before Card gets control of him and escapes.

Venters fires his last shot. The horse, still carrying Card, cartwheels off the cliff.

On page 209, in the final short paragraph, Venters hears the rumble of the avalanche that the falling horse has triggered.

Boy, *howdy*.

Second resolution of Act II.

Truly, there's no way around it now. Lassiter and Withersteen are heading into the novel's Climax, facing Tull down in person, loaded for bear.

End of Conflict #3 and Act II.

Super-duper spin!

Now pay close attention: the law of cause-&-effect means that every one of those spins was *earned* by the preceding actions of the characters.

Earned.

Of course, we don't need both first *and* second *anything* at the ends of our Acts. Grey did this because his two nearly-parallel plotlines (remember that all novels have two nearly-parallel plotlines) are so far apart they don't actually merge until the novel's Climax. And this means they give good examples of different ways to design those 'spins.'

In most novels, the climaxes and resolutions that spin the stories are just single events in which the two plotlines crash into each other and bounce off again. (Frank and Cora kill the Greek. Frank and Cora are almost taken down by the investigation.)

But you see how Grey with his distinctly separate plotlines kept them detailed and varied all the way through, so that when they each reach the ends of his Acts he could spin his characters' stories, once and then once again, to keep the reader guessing every step of the way where this is all headed.

And in this manner, he managed to give hundreds of thousands of readers throughout the ages *the ride of their lives.*

One Fulcrum

Although we get those all-important two Plot Points from three-act structure, there's yet a third leg to this extraordinary storytelling stool: the *mid-point.*

I call it the Fulcrum: where everything pivots from light to dark.

175

Halfway to $^2/_3$ of the way through our novel—just about halfway through Act II, as a matter of fact—something simple and yet earthshaking happens to our characters: they stop moving away from their Hook and begin moving toward their Climax.

In a mystery, this is when the second poor sap dies.

While the first Plot Point (the climax of Act I) is the climax of Conflict #1, and the second Plot Point (the climax of Act II) is the climax of Conflict #3, this Fulcrum is the climax of Conflict #2, right in the middle.

At this point, we have laid all our fuses. We've introduced the protagonist and any other characters essential to the Climax. We've created and arranged the separate tracks convening upon inevitable catastrophe, the whole reason we're telling this story. We've given our protagonist the two loggerhead needs that are driving them relentlessly toward that catastrophe, and we've raised the pressure on those needs, exaggerating and enhancing them until our reader can't distinguish anymore between the protagonist and themself. Now we need to give the hourglass a good, solid shake. Settle the sand before we flip the whole thing over and let time begin to run out. . .

In 1764, Horace Walpole launched not one but several of today's healthiest genres with his wonderful black comedy, *The Castle of Otranto*. Although at not-quite 100 pages too short for the delicate sensibilities of most of today's agents and publishers, *Otranto* is the original gothic novel (gothic 'romance,' in the terms of Walpole's day, meaning a story for entertainment rather than a moral lecture), the root of both gothic fiction of the nineteenth century and today's popular horror/thriller/paranormal genres. Although in the nineteenth century Mrs. Radcliffe took the ball and ran with it right through the goalposts—wow, did she—it was Walpole's rascally little handbook on how to tweak the noses of the literati that first kicked the whole thing off.

And, sure enough, right there on page 50 of *Otranto*, something enormous happens. The one character standing in the way of the villain's agenda *dies*. Sadly, he's squished by a ghost's giant helmet.

Up until that moment, the villain Manfred, Prince of Otranto, has been struggling to free himself of both his lawful and rather dizzyingly submissive wife Hippolita and his son Conrad, the betrothed of young Isabella for whom Manfred has suddenly developed a terrible case of the racing hots. Someone (not Manfred) has dropped a giant marble helmet on young Conrad—bummer about that. There goes Manfred's competition. Unfortunately, Isabella has recently had the unmitigated gall to not only repulse Manfred's advances but take shelter under the protection of her father's knights.

What's a Prince got to do to get a *little service* around here?

But now, just halfway through the novel, Manfred has an unexpected stroke of luck. His son dies of the terrible squishing. Poor Conrad! His pride and joy! Child and heir! Bootjack over which he's tripped incessantly since he first got a load of young Isabella in her nightie!

And this heartens Manfred so much that he is struck again, this time by divine inspiration. He rushes to give the news of Conrad's death to Isabella's father's knights, along with the information—*oh, heartbreak!*—that as much as he loves his dear wife to whom he would fain cleave in conjugal bliss. . .they've discovered they're too-close kin. Their marriage cannot produce a legal heir.

Given these two circumstances, Manfred explains in all heartfelt guilelessness, it really would be best for everyone involved if Isabella were surrendered up to him for immediate conjugation.

Now, we won't examine too carefully the claim that in Walpole's day it was quite possible to *accidentally* marry too-close kin. Even as recently as the early 1900s, my own great-grandparents were free to marry their second cousins (which they promptly did), and a generation before that my great-great-grandparents were free to marry their *first* cousins (each other). Even granting enormous families — and my German ancestors produced nothing if not enormous families — it seems a bit far-fetched to think that in 1764 you could marry someone even closer than this and not even notice.

Who would that have to be? Your *brother*?

But let's take very good note of when this amazing switch in Manfred's fortunes occurs: exactly halfway through his story.

Because up until this point Isabella, Conrad, Hippolita, and the mysterious stranger lurking in the castle's subterranean catacombs, as well as the friar of the local monastery and Bianca the faithful maid (*nobody* wants Manfred to wind up with Isabella), have all had a chance. Isabella was betrothed to Conrad. Sure, he wasn't exactly her idea of a hot night in Rio. But he was okay. He'd do. At least he wasn't a lecher, like his father.

And after the Fulcrum, everything's changed. Manfred's not going to have any trouble shucking Hippolita, we already know, because as much as she wrings her hands and dribbles tears down the front of her embroidered shift, she's too much of a doormat to put up a fight.

Now it's up to Isabella and her defenders, of whom the most powerful — her father — isn't even present. The friar can shield her to some extent. Bianca is willing to stand up for her. But, truly, Isabella's best bet lies in casting herself upon the mercy of the mysterious stranger, the charming young buck of the catacombs for whom she's already feeling more than a peck of pheromonal interest: that swashbuckling tasty treat, Theo.

(I know—Theo's actually in love with Conrad's sister and the friend of Isabella's bosom, Matilda, but she conveniently dies in time for Isabella to get her man in the end. It's just too bad that he feels compelled to live out his life of conjugal bliss sunk in melancholy over the loss of the toothsome Mattie. Walpole had a *very dark* sense of humor.)

And we can see how this change of fortunes throws the burden of the story firmly onto the shoulders of the protagonists—far more so than ever before—as they cease to run higgledy-piggledy in all directions, searching for an escape route, and begin to thunder with concerted deafening tread in the direction of their—supposed—saving grace.

Feinting

So let's talk a little about that fascinating element directly *before* the Climax of a novel: the Faux Resolution.

I named it.

Yay me.

But I didn't invent it. No, the Faux Resolution has been around forever, generally thought of (if it's thought of at all) as the denouement to Conflict #3, the beginning of Act III right before the Climax.

It's something more than this, though. Something much, much more.

Isak Dinesen was an absolute fiend with plot. She didn't study plot structure, but she did have a fabulous innate sense of it. (Geniuses get to have such things.) Of course, since she *didn't* study it her plots wouldn't really stand up to today's rigorous genre-dominated standards — they're almost jazz riffs. But her innate sense led her true.

Dinesen knew pacing like the back of her hand, and she used it to keep her reader hooked throughout endless permutations that morph almost compulsively from one chronological layer to another, as her characters discourse on religion, society, history, gender roles, even the ultimate definition of truth.

She built and built and built her stories in tension, as they morphed through their multiple layers, until she had her characters hanging from a cliff by their fingernails.

Then she did something diabolical.

She threw them a rope.

Unfortunately, she didn't *tie* it to anything. So when her characters let go of the cliff to reach for it. . .

In the first and most canonical of her *Seven Gothic Tales*, "The Deluge at Norderney," Dinesen takes the reader through the life stories of four unusual, complex souls trapped together overnight during a rising flood, fully aware that they are all on the brink of death, only to finally marry off one young couple (strangers to each other) and force the others (an elderly Cardinal and even more elderly, virtuous madwoman) to confess to each other their darkest secrets.

Just before the Climax, after the married young couple has fallen asleep holding hands and after the dreadful, profound confessions of the elders, the elderly madwoman insists that the elderly Cardinal kiss her so she will not die unkissed. Although he's just confessed to assault and impersonation, he realizes that she's right — their confessions have, in a strange way, been as much a wedding ceremony as the one they've so recently performed for the young couple.

So he kisses her.

Her life is vindicated.

This is why it's such a shock when she lifts the hem of her skirt in the next sentence, the beginning of the Climax, and hands it to him to show him that their high, dry loft has begun filling with water.

The flood has caught up with them.

When we talk about plotting a novel, we must by definition talk about pacing. I like to think of this as the Great Fictional Rollercoaster, which we induce our reader to ride by luring them into the cars with the bright, shiny carrot of our novel's Hook.

"Come along, little one," we say. "Step right in. Settle down. Fasten your seat belt. Why a seat belt? *Nice* shiny carrot. See the pretty carrot? Keep your eyes on the shiny, dangly carrot. All comfy? That's right. . .*take 'em, Joe —*"

And they're off.

Down, down, down we drop them into the depths of the Hook, gasping and clutching the rail with wide, popping eyes. Up, up, up they go to the lead-in to Conflict #1, where first they take in the view ("Wow! Cool view!") and then leave their lunch behind when they go plummeting straight down into the bowels of Conflict #1, flying off the end of Act I shrieking at the top of their lungs.

Up, up, up we bring them, climbing into Conflict #2. "Hey! There's that great view again! It's even *better* from here —" Down, down, down they plummet, shrieking even louder to the depths of Conflict #2. Up, up, up into Conflict #3, so high that they're standing up on the seat when we drop them like a rock back down again at the end of Act II.

Up and down, up and down, all the way through our novel. And all along we're also bouncing them like yo-yos holographically, in telescoping replicas of the overall Rollercoaster.

Ka-boing. Ka-boing, Ka-boing. Ka-boing.

They're a puppet in our hands. The Master.

Until we've finally dropped them off the end of Act II so long and so fast and so hard that they've left not only their lunch, but their teeth, eyeballs, and most of their internal organs back at that last view and are now not much more than a trembling skeleton, a shadow of their former self, a complete minion to our every whim.

Power. You bet. This is why people write.

And now we take a little pity. Not too much. Nobody wants too much pity. But just the tiniest smidgen, a gentle, kindly hand smoothing their fevered brow.

"Mommy," our reader whimpers. "Big freaky plotline go *boom bang boom!*"

This is the Faux Resolution. It's the point at which we finally give our reader a break. Have we shaken them to the core? Made their hair stand trembling on end? Yanked them right out of their shoes?

We rock them in our arms. Stroke their hair. Give them a little smooch. "I was only kidding," we tell them. "I don't really hate you. All in the service of the story, you know."

And they buy it. "We know. We weren't really scared. Just a little. Startled, really. Caught off-guard, that's all. We're fine now."

"Of course you are." Rock, rock. Stroke, stroke. Smooch, smooch. "All better? Aren't you glad you went for that ride? Wasn't it the most exciting thing ever?"

"*Unbelievable,*" they're saying. "We are so coming back again, the instant we are fully recovered —"

"Did you really love it?"

"We loved it. We *loved* it. You are the Fiction Goddess."

We sigh. "I'm so glad you feel that way. . ."

Yank goes the cord. *Bam* goes Joe.

"*Aaaaaghghgh!*" goes our reader, as we shoot them point-blank, top speed at the Climax, which they hit with such force that it smacks an epiphany out of the deepest reaches of their raw subconscious soul.

The Whole Point

What's the Climax of a novel?

We must understand, for now, only this one, fundamental thing: the Climax is the *real reason we write our stories.*

Once upon a time, two teenagers became so distraught over their passion for each other that they committed suicide — this is the premise. Cause? Their parents wouldn't let them marry or even date — this is the story. Cause of that? Their families hated each other — this is the backstory.

— *Romeo & Juliet*, William Shakespeare

Once upon a time, a man succumbed to idiocy over the death of the woman he loved — this is the premise. Cause? His rival for her love stole her from him and then killed her in anguish over the betrayal he'd committed against a saintly man — this is the story. Cause of that? His rival was an old and close friend of his — this is the backstory.

— *The Idiot*, Fyodor Dostoevsky

Once upon a time, a woman nearly lost the man she loved through her own machinations — this is the premise. Cause? She was an inveterate social meddler — this is the story. Cause of

that? Although good-hearted, she had always been spoiled —
this is the backstory.

 — *Emma*, Jane Austen

Once upon a time, a woman became so distraught over her
adulterous affair that she committed suicide — this is the
premise. Cause? Society ostracized her for her affair, while at the
same time her lover made her intensely jealous — this is the
story. Cause of that? She was a married female aristocrat of
nineteenth-century Russia with an intensely passionate
nature — this is the backstory.

 — *Anna Karenina*, Leo Tolstoy

Once upon a time, a man encountered a ghoul and
disappeared — this is the premise. Cause? He was out at night
after spending the evening competing with another man for the
love of a young woman — this is the story. Cause of that? He was
an unattractive schoolteacher, with a ruthless and
contemptuous rival — this is the backstory.

 — "The Legend Sleepy Hollow," Washington Irving

Do you see how the Climax is, bizarrely enough, the
premise?

We must dwell on this in the depths of our souls until it
makes total and complete sense. Mull it over. Meditate upon it.
Make it a part of our writing identity. We cannot take this fact
too seriously.

The Climax is the whole point.

Otherwise, we have no reason for writing any of this.

Chapter 20

Hook

Holographic structure, Act I

Now we're going to do something long and slow and meticulous.

We're going to walk step-by-step through the six stories I've used to demonstrate the different parts of structure: Edward Anderson's historical novel, *Thieves Like Us, a romance*; Ray Bradbury's brooding 'edgy' story, "The Dwarf"; James M. Cain's *noir* thriller, *The Postman Always Rings Twice*; Zane Grey's Western adventure, *Riders of the Purple Sage*; Horace Walpole's black comedy, the gothic/horror/thriller/ paranormal romance, *The Castle of Otranto*; and Isak Dinesen's mystical literary fable, "The Deluge at Norderney."

These are classics of their genres, the roots from which all such stories today have sprung (although some modern genres appear on the surface to be quite different from their roots, as is the case with Western adventure and post-apocalyptic adventure).

We're going to uncover, piece-by-piece, all the parts in all the stories to learn — once and for all, down to our bones — how *all* great stories, of *all* genres, use the same building blocks to create the imaginary worlds in which we love to dwell.

Act I: Hook

The first thing a reader reads when they open a novel or short story is the Hook — that first most exciting episode that occurs to start these characters down the path trying to resolve the conflict between their two intense needs.

And the first part of *that* is the hook of the Hook (because of course each of the six basic elements has its own basic elements — lending the entire discussion its quintessential Dr. Seuss air).

And the first bit of *that* is the *hook scene*. (The hook of the Hook is often just that one scene. But not always.)

And the very first words — those few precious, optimally-powerfully words that pull the reader in and make them want to read the next words — that's the *hook sentence*.

Hook

Hook sentence

In *Thieves Like Us*, Anderson shows us a car trundling with difficulty down a rutted road off the highway toward someone waiting.

In "The Dwarf," Bradbury shows us his protagonist, Aimee, quietly and with implied expectation gazing around.

In *The Postman Always Rings Twice*, Cain shows us his protagonist, Frank, being hucked off a hay truck in front of a diner.

In *Riders of the Purple Sage*, Grey shows us a messenger leaving one of his three protagonists, Jane Withersteen. (A *rider*. Across the *purple sage*.)

In *The Castle of Otranto*, Walpole shows us wealthy Prince Manfred and his children, Conrad and Matilda. (This expository type of introduction wasn't common even in Walpole's day, but it certainly was for the era in which he was *pretending* to write, the twelfth century.)

And in "The Deluge at Norderney" Dinesen shows us a Danish seaside resort of the early 1800s at a time, she says, when the people of Northern Europe still regarded the ocean as their age-old 'demonic' enemy.

Hook scene

In *Thieves*, the protagonist Bowie waits with his friend Chicamaw under the prison wall in their convicts' clothing for the car to reach them, and Bowie asks Chicamaw if he's really committed to their plan.

In "Dwarf," Aimee meets up with her friend Ralph, the owner of the Mirror Maze, and he tells her carnivals are the easiest places to die if that's what you want, bringing up as an example a dwarf regular of his.

In *Postman*, Frank wanders into the diner and begins to pull his standard con on the Greek who owns it.

In *Riders*, Withersteen reflects upon the message she's just received, which demands she hand over her Gentile hired help, Venters, to the local Mormon leader, Tull. Withersteen, who is a faithful Mormon woman, tries to shield Venters when Tull arrives, even as Tull prepares to whip Venters for being too friendly with Withersteen, until a stranger on horseback unexpectedly interrupts — the infamous maverick Gentile outlaw, Lassiter.

In *Otranto*, Manfred's subjects raise their eyebrows over his plans to marry off his sickly son Conrad to his daughter Matilda's best friend, the delectable Isabella, gossiping that his haste is based on a prophecy of doom to his sovereignty over the Castle of Otranto.

And in "Norderney," fashionable ladies and gentlemen brave proximity to the sea for the sake of rubbing elbows with dukes, princes, and merchant aristocracy, even as the local peasants remember the monstrous hidden danger.

Spend some time studying these six beginnings. Notice what goes into the *hook sentence* and what can wait to be illuminated in the full *hook scene*. Pay particular attention to the clues to fundamental, inherent conflict in the hook scenes: the convicts' dependence upon each other, death at a carnival, a drifter's con, violence based upon religious conflict, a prophecy of doom, and high society under the shadow of mortality.

These are all clues to these stories' Climaxes. Right there— *on the first page.*

Development

So, after they're initially hooked, the reader reads the Hook development, how that first hook scene builds upon itself (always aiming toward the whole point of the Hook). This occurs in a series of one to three conflicts, which may be longer or shorter, depending upon the length of the story and intentions of the writer.

In *Thieves*, Bowie hops out of the car in which their third partner, T-Dub, has picked up Bowie and Chicamaw. Bowie waits by the side of the road while Chicamaw and T-Dub head off to look for the friend who's going to hide them out, and when they don't return for Bowie he watches for them all night in the rain.

In "Dwarf," Ralph shows Aimee, who doesn't really want to know, how to spy on the Dwarf in the Mirror Maze.

In *Postman*, Frank establishes rapport with the Greek and meets his wife Cora, to whom Frank is instantly intensely attracted, although he admits she's more disturbingly unhappy than lovely.

In *Riders*, the backstory of the Hook is cast in a scene in which Lassiter tells Withersteen he's come to town to find the grave of a Milly Erne, who, it turns out, was once Withersteen's closest friend who died of a broken heart years ago when the Mormons kidnapped her little girl because she refused to raise her Mormon. Lassiter and Venters make friends, both of them loyal to Withersteen.

In *Otranto*, Manfred's plans for the wedding of Isabella and Conrad are interrupted when the servants rush in in hysterics to inform everyone that Conrad has been squashed underneath a giant marble helmet and is now dying. The helmet turns up missing from the enormous marble statue of the original owner of the Castle of Otranto, Alfonso, from whom Manfred's ancestor inherited it when Alfonso died during the Crusades.

And in "Norderney" a dreadful storm create enormous sea pressure, which, after the end of the storm, breaks the dikes and floods the lowland where the resort lies. The four main characters are the last of those being rescued by boat when they come across a barn loft containing a woman and her children.

Again, mull all this over. Take notes. Examine how the Hook is being built upon, bringing in complications, forcing the characters to cope, *immediately* and *without mercy*. The writer puts their characters in the soup and makes them struggle — when they're struggling, that's when they show what they're made of, and *what they're made of* is exactly what the reader's reading for.

You see how this is all heats up within the *first five pages*?(Although we're not going to reach the climax of the Hook until either $1/8$ or $1/6$ of the way into the entire story, leaving room yet for plenty of Hook development between page five and that climax.)

And now we know how agents and publishers can make decisions on whether or not we've got a good, gripping story so early in the manuscript.

Act I: Hook climax— *Fatal Ignition*

Now we're reaching the whole point of this Hook, which I like to consider the story's *Fatal Ignition*.

The reader has become intrigued by the build-up of this Hook and deeply curious about where it's all going.

Well, *we* know where it's going! It's going toward the whole point of the Hook, that first most exciting episode, the Fatal Ignition that sets these characters struggling valiantly against themselves.

But first. . .

Faux Resolution

That build-up takes an unexpected detour at the last minute and culminates in the faux resolution of the Hook. *Yippee!* Disaster averted!

In *Thieves*, morning brings dry weather, Bowie feels better, and he gets a ride on a passing wagon into town.

In "Dwarf," the Dwarf goes straight to a room that makes him look tall and dances beatifically in front of the mirror.

In *Postman*, Frank establishes himself over the ensuing weeks as the Greek's right-hand help around the diner, even while he also shares a brief, passionate grope with Cora.

In *Riders*, Withersteen takes Lassiter and Venters to see Milly's grave, where they all bond.

In *Otranto,* Isabella, fighting off the advances of Manfred, descends to the castle dungeons, where she stumbles upon a gracious and very good-looking young scamp willing to help her escape.

And in "Norderney," a Cardinal and an elderly madwoman volunteer to trade places with the woman and her children trapped by the flood in the loft, followed quickly by the madwoman's fierce young companion and an unknown young man, all of them anxious to be a part of this rescue operation. They each have their reasons for this—all character behavior is based upon authentic motivation—although the reader doesn't know yet what they are.

This faux resolution creates a beat in the storytelling rhythm, a significant pause to bring out the full resonance of the climax. Fiction is about contrast, so watch carefully how the contrast between the faux resolution and the climax of the Hook creates a visceral vibration *inside the reader.*

Climax

Finally the reader reaches the whole point of the Hook, which is that first exciting catastrophe that starts the story's entire avalanche—whatever event the writer has designed to illuminate for the characters (for the very first time) exactly what they're up against—the climax of the Hook.

In *Thieves,* Bowie arrives in town and has to guess that a stranger he meets is the man in charge of their hide-out, taking a gamble on revealing himself without knowing for sure, even as the young woman he's going to fall in love with watches— suddenly he's risking his very neck just when he thinks he's finally escaped.

In "The Dwarf," as the Dwarf dances with joy at his reflection, Ralph sniggers contemptuously at him — suddenly Aimee realizes her friend is hostile to the Dwarf.

In *Postman*, Frank's passion for Cora leads him, in a moment of sexual light-headedness, to agree to help her kill the Greek — suddenly he's committed himself to this crime for the sake of passion.

In *Riders*, Withersteen realizes Lassiter might be Milly's long-lost husband come to avenge her death against Tull and the Mormon Bishop Dyer — suddenly Withersteen is trapped between loyalty to the man who's come here for the sake of her dead best friend (and who saved Venters when she couldn't) and loyalty to her religion.

In *Otranto*, Isabella just barely escapes as Manfred appears, accidentally leaving the adorable stranger to Manfred's vicious clutches — suddenly the three of them are caught up together in the story's deadly *ménage a trois*.

And in "Norderney" the Cardinal and elderly madwoman admit to the others they have almost no chance of surviving the night, as the flood waters are deep and moving and the building beneath them will probably collapse out from underneath them before sunrise — suddenly they all face the fact that they're going to die.

So you see how the writer has lead the reader skillfully from a single *hook sentence*, through illumination of that sentence in a *hook scene*, into tension and conflict built upon that hook scene, with a subtle little dodge at the last minute to make the impact of the climax truly unexpected. . .and then sprung the hidden purpose of the Hook on the reader without warning while they're looking the other way?

Wow, there's a leap in the gut for the reader! Reader involvement — reader *investment.*

Now we're approximately $^1/_8$-$^1/_6$ of the way into this, and the reader's full, undivided, viscerally-stimulated attention is Hooked.

So the writer can begin to tell their story.

Act I: Backstory

But first the writer slips in whatever Backstory they need. Remember: only what's *absolutely* necessary. And, if at all possible, layered into the characters getting to know each other.

In *Thieves*, the owner of the hide-out, Dee Mowbley, fills them in on the law enforcement in the local town and explains just enough about his daughter Keechie for the reader to understand she's a pivotal character.

In "Dwarf," Ralph tells Aimee a brief story about the Dwarf wanting very badly to buy one of the mirrors that make him look tall.

In *Postman*, there's no full Backstory, just a leap straight into the hook to Conflict #1.

In *Riders*, there's no full Backstory, as it's all been told already in that scene in the backstory of the Hook.

In *Otranto*, yet again, there's no full Backstory.

And in "Norderney," the narrator gives the Backstory of the elderly madwoman in exposition. (Dinesen's narrative voice is intensely old-fashioned, so although she wrote lovely scenes she also knew how to write marvelous exposition — as was common two hundred years ago, the era in which most of her stories are set.)

Act I: Conflict #1

Whew! Hooked by the gills! Thrown up in the air and just about to be caught deftly again in the writer's brilliant web.

Once again, we're at a hook, this time the hook of Conflict #1, which is going to culminate eventually in the whole point of Conflict #1, its climax: the story's *first Plot Point*.

And the first bit of *that* hook is the *hook scene*.

And the very first words — those few essential words that pull the reader in and make them want to read the next words — that's the *hook sentence*.

Hook

Hook sentence

In *Thieves*, T-Dub says Keechie gave him the evil eye when she first saw him.

In "Dwarf," Aimee addresses Ralph urgently to get his attention — she has something important to ask.

In *Postman*, what appears to be a trivial piece of dialog is illuminated a few lines later as a staged scene meant to lead into murder.

In *Riders*, one of Withersteen's riders appears, his horse in a lather.

In *Otranto*, Manfred hears the trap door close after the escaping Isabella.

And in "Norderney," the Cardinal begins to tell his life story describing how, as a boy, he knew a famous Danish painter who claimed a washed face is the only truthful face.

Hook scene

In *Thieves*, After Dee assures Bowie, Chicamaw, and T-Dub that Keechie will take care of them while he's working, the others talk over their new life—how to avoid the Laws when you travel, who's most likely to snitch on you (a sore woman), and, most important for justifying their lives as armed bank robbers, how politicians prove they're "thieves," too, "just like us."

In "Dwarf," Aimee asks Ralph why he doesn't sell one of his old mirrors to the Dwarf.

In *Postman*, Frank goes downstairs as look-out while Cora approaches the Greek in his bath to murder him, and a cop stops by to see what Frank's doing. The cop has just left when the lights blow out.

In *Riders*, Withersteen's rider tells her one of her herds of cattle has been stampeded by rustlers.

In *Otranto*, Manfred, incensed, squares off against the young stranger, Theodore, who misleads him so he won't catch Isabella.

And in "Norderney," the madwoman laughs at the Cardinal's idea that God wants the truth from humans.

Again, be aware of what goes into the *hook sentence* and what waits to be illuminated in the full *hook scene*. You'll see now how the clues to conflict in these hook scenes of Conflict #1 relate to the climaxes of Conflict #1 (not necessarily the stories' Climaxes, but one step removed): the convicts' relationship to the Laws and political collusion with lawbreaking, the *ménage a trois* of Aimee, Ralph, and the Dwarf, the murder of the Greek, the stampede of Withersteen's cattle, Manfred's pursuit of Isabella, and the difficulty of meeting a moral goal in this material world.

The climax of Conflict #1 is going to crystallize the extremes of the characters' dilemmas, the poles between which they ricochet—creating another visceral vibration in the reader.

Development

Now, after they're hooked on Conflict #1, the reader reads the Conflict development, how that hook scene builds upon itself, revealing new aspects of the story never seen before while elaborating upon elements first introduced in the Hook (and always aiming toward the whole point of Conflict #1). Just as in the Hook, this occurs in Conflict #1 in a series of one to three conflicts, which may be longer or shorter, depending upon the length of the story and intentions of the writer.

In *Thieves*, Keechie turns up, and she and Bowie start falling for each other. Bowie, Chicamaw, and T-Dub read about their prison break in the newspaper and make plans to move on. Bowie learns more about Keechie's life and confides in her that he plans to quit bank robbery and go straight. However, first he and the others head for a new hide-out, planning one last job.

In "Dwarf," Ralph admits he could get a second-hand mirror for thirty-five dollars but refuses to help the Dwarf buy one, explaining to Aimee the Dwarf wouldn't take it, and even if he would he couldn't afford it, because, after all, where can a Dwarf earn money outside circus freak shows?

In *Postman*, Frank rushes upstairs, and Cora tells him she fumbled it in the dark, only stunning the Greek and not killing him. They call an ambulance, and the Greek goes to the hospital and is saved.

In *Riders*, Venters rides out to save Withersteen's cattle herd, and in a shoot-out with the head rustler, Oldring, shoots Oldring's legendary Masked Rider. Venters is appalled to learn, when he stops to help him, that the legendary Masked Rider is actually a young woman trying to escape the rustlers.

In *Otranto*, Manfred's servants, again hysterical, inform him they've come across a giant lying full-length in the castle gallery and blocking the door with his foot.

196

And in "Norderney," the young man tells the story of how he was raised the son of a skipper and then favored as a teen by a rich Baron who turned out to be his real father, so that in his despair over losing the father he loves for a rich man who has deceived him, he has run away.

Now the characters are struggling harder and harder all the time. And as their struggles become more protracted, they're forced to reach deeper into their souls for the resources with which to cope. And that's when they show what they're made of, because, as we remember, *what they're made of* is what the reader's reading to find out.

Act I: Conflict #1 climax— *First Plot Point*

So we're reaching the whole point of Conflict #1, which is the story's *first Plot Point*.

The reader has been drawn in by the build-up of this Conflict and is anxious to learn where it's all going.

Of course, *we* know where it's going. It's going toward the whole point of Conflict #1, that first Plot Point, which is going to turn the characters on their heads and completely bamboozle them, sending them off in a new direction they simply do *not* expect.

But first. . .

Faux Resolution

That build-up takes a quick detour at the last minute and results in the faux resolution of Conflict #1. *Thank goodness! Things are looking up!*

In *Thieves*, Bowie and Chicamaw settle down for a few days in their new hide-out and tell stories, laughing over Chicamaw having been thanked once by a cop for not killing him when he could.

In "Dwarf," Aimee says facetiously she's in love with the Dwarf, trying to lighten the tone of the conversation while pushing Ralph away a little.

In *Postman*, on their way home from the hospital, Frank guides Cora through dismantling the 'slungshot' they made out of ball bearings in a sack, so no one will ever know what they almost did.

In *Riders*, Venters carries the young woman he shot high into the canyons until he discovers a hidden valley with an entrance guarded by an enormous Balancing Rock, where they can hide from Oldring.

In *Otranto*, Hippolita is the only one who can soothe Manfred.

And in "Norderney," in the young man's story, his father, the skipper, finds him and comforts him with the information that he has gold buried in Haiti the young man can have.

Again—there's that beat. The characters take a breath. The reader looks the other way. . .

Climax

And finally the reader reaches that whole point of Conflict #1, which is that first Plot Point—the first huge event that spins the characters' story and sends them whirling off in an unexpected direction, still madly fleeing their Hook—the climax of Conflict #1.

In *Thieves*, Chicamaw tells Bowie about the Laws shooting men they don't like in front of banks in order to collect huge rewards for dead bank robbers, "thieves" of the public coffers, "just like us," explains what it's like to live in the lap of luxury in Mexico, and finally describes a deadly Texas prison farm where inmates are deliberately worked to death and sometimes killed outright—suddenly they have both an exotic, hopeful goal and terrible, deadly danger to avoid.

In "Dwarf," Ralph, who is in love with Aimee, pretends to be amused by Aimee saying she's in love with the Dwarf, although he's not amused at all—suddenly he's intensely jealous, which makes him a secret threat to the Dwarf.

In *Postman*, the cop comes back, suspicious of Frank, and insists on looking at the fuse box. That's when they find the dead cat, and there's a brief, exhilarating resolution when the cop concludes the cat stepped off the ladder onto the fuse box and blew the fuse—suddenly Frank is both terrified of the cop's suspicions and impossibly relieved there's no proof to support them.

In *Riders*, in a hellbent-for-leather, rip-snorting chase scene across the sage, Lassiter saves Withersteen's cattle herd, which has been deliberately stampeded, and she asks him to be her rider, offering him one of her prize horses. Meanwhile, Venters carries the wounded young woman, Bess, through the steep entrance to the hidden valley—suddenly both pairs of characters are allied for the long-term against their two enemies, Tull and Oldring (who, the characters don't yet realize, are in cahoots).

In *Otranto*, Manfred, all but rubbing his hands in evil glee, plots to use Hippolita's blind loyalty to gain her cooperation in acquiring Isabella—suddenly his power to destroy Isabella's life takes on real credibility.

And in "Norderney," the young man refuses his father's gold, but accepts his advice to take to the sea—and suddenly he is, like the others in the loft, loose in the dangerous world all on his own.

Again, spend some long, deep, thoughtful hours with all this. Take your time. Take your notes. Examine how the Hook has roped the characters in and Conflict #1 thrown them a live coal, so that Act I becomes a whole, blistering, brilliant flash of lightning upon a situation for which these characters are not prepared and to which they're only now being fully, painfully awakened.

They're threatened! They have a glimpse of hope! The poles of their dilemmas are crystallized!

Now we're approximately $^1/_4$-$^1/_3$ of the way into this story, and the reader's *invested*.

So the writer can turn up the heat.

Chapter 21

Development

Holographic structure, Act II

Act II: Conflict #2

Deep in drama! We're done with Act I and forging into Act II.

We've passed the first Plot Point, the characters' trajectories have shifted significantly, and the ends of the spectrum upon which they struggle are beginning to come into focus. Things are more intriguing than ever.

And, yet again, we're at a hook, this time the hook of Conflict #2, which is going to culminate eventually in the whole point of Conflict #2, its climax: the story's *Fulcrum*.

And the first bit of *that* hook is the *hook scene*.

And the very first words — those few gripping words that pull the reader in and make them need to read the next words — that's the *hook sentence*.

Hook

Hook sentence

In *Thieves*, Bowie, Chicamaw, and T-Dub rent a furnished house where they can stay awhile.

In "Dwarf," we feel the warmth of a summer night turning through morning to the heat of afternoon. (Bradbury tosses in a wonderful descriptive sentence after that first one in this brief hook paragraph — he's a whiz with wonderful description.)

In *Postman*, all Frank can say is that they didn't do anything about *anything*. Their relief over escaping a bungled murder of the Greek is too overpowering.

In *Riders*, Venters is lying in the starlight and then gloom of dawn in the hidden valley.

In *Otranto*, Manfred's daughter Matilda is restless.

And in "Norderney," the madwoman offers to tell the story of her young companion, Calypso, describing the uncle who raised the young woman as a man obsessed with spiritual matters.

Hook scene

In *Thieves*, Bowie, Chicamaw, and T-Dub admit they are low on money, so they plan a bank robbery.

In "Dwarf," Aimee tells Ralph she's discovered the Dwarf is a brilliant, tormented writer. She reads the Dwarf's writing aloud to Ralph, amazed that he's so much smarter and more talented than either of them. She says she can't stand the unfairness of life, that she and Ralph can choose between the carnival and normal life, while the Dwarf's body limits him to being a carny.

In *Postman*, Frank and Cora, in bed together for the first time while the Greek is in the hospital, swear they will never try anything so insane as murder again.

In *Riders*, Venters tends to the young woman's wounds and learns how much she hates herself and the life she's led with Oldring, so that he promises himself he'll take revenge upon Oldring for her.

In *Otranto*, Matilda is telling her maid Bianca she's in love with the portrait of her ancestor Alfonso when Bianca hears a ghostly voice, which turns out to be Theodore, the captivating young man of the catacombs, singing out the window of his cell in the dungeon in which Manfred has had him flung. Matilda flirts with Theodore, and Bianca informs Matilda that Isabella is hiding out at the local monastery.

And in "Norderney," the madwoman tells how Calypso's old uncle taught her to hate being a woman, until she saw her own naked body in a mirror and very nearly took a hatchet to herself in loathing, only to be saved by the sight of happy, naked nymphs in an ancient tapestry.

Once again, be aware of what goes into the *hook sentence* and what will wait to be illuminated in the full *hook scene*. The clues to conflict in these hook scenes of Conflict #2 relate to the climaxes of Conflict #2 (not necessarily the stories' Climaxes, but one step removed, just as in the climax of Conflict #1): the convicts' return to bank robbery that will narrow their hopes for the future down to simple escape from the Laws, the way in which the Dwarf illuminates Aimee's growing separation from Ralph, the bond between Frank and Cora that will narrow their prospects down to pulling off a murder, the uniting against opposition of Withersteen and Lassiter, of Venters and Bess, the squaring off of Manfred against Isabella and Theodore and Matilda, and a passion for embracing life while we still have it.

The climax of Conflict #2 is going to close the door on alternative futures and focus upon driving the characters relentlessly toward the story's Climax.

Development

Now, after they're hooked on Conflict #2, the reader reads the Conflict development, how that hook scene builds upon itself, revealing the last of the essential new aspects of the story, getting down to the real nitty-gritty here as we hone in on the Fulcrum that's going to flip this story on its back, tying everything together with elements already introduced in the Hook and Conflict #1 in Act I (and always aiming toward the whole point of Conflict #2). Just as in the Hook and Conflict #1, this occurs in a series of one to three conflicts, which may be longer or shorter, depending upon the length of the story and intentions of the writer.

In *Thieves*, Bowie, Chicamaw, and T-Dub pull first a small bank robbery and then a larger one and are in an accident during the second get-away, which brings the police. They get in a shoot-out with the police when they refuse to stick around to make a statement.

In "Dwarf," Aimee pulls thirty-five dollars out of her purse and tells Ralph she's going to buy the Dwarf that mirror he wants so badly. Ralph tries to dissuade her, but she's determined, until he slams out in anger.

In *Postman*, Frank and Cora have a happy week, then they begin fighting. They try to run away together, but Cora chickens out. Frank does run away, and when he comes back the Greek is home, thrilled to see him, and Cora is desperate to get rid of Frank before she falls in love with him again. She confesses to Frank that the Greek wants children now, and she's thought she could go through with it so long as she never saw Frank again.

In *Riders*, Lassiter settles down as Withersteen's right-hand man. Withersteen's friends among the Mormon women all urge her to marry Tull and get it over with, and only a dying Gentile woman, the mother of Withersteen's favorite little child, Faye, tells Withersteen she'll trust her to raise Faye so long as Withersteen promises not to raise her Mormon. Unexpectedly, Lassiter learns Withersteen has only been pretending to be fond of him in order to keep him from killing Tull and Dyer—she really doesn't know him well enough to feel true affection.

In *Otranto*, Manfred hot-foots it over to the monastery after Isabella, where he learns Theodore is the son of the friar, Jerome, and blackmails Jerome with Theodore's life.

And in "Norderney," the madwoman tells how, after her epiphany over her woman's body, Calypso went into her uncle's room with a hatchet while he was sleeping to take revenge upon him for teaching her his terrible misogyny, but instead she turned away at the last moment and escaped his house. The madwoman tells Calypso the young man now in the loft with them has sacrificed his life to be with her, and although the young man knows she is lying he is swept up in the thrill of her imagination and falls in love with Calypso.

Go ahead and once again study all this carefully. Make copious notes to yourself. Analyze how Act I is being built upon in Act II, complicated, illuminated, *developed*. The characters are handling a plethora of issues now that come at them from all sides—they're juggling, dancing, yodeling for all they're worth, constantly and with driving urgency. They're up to their necks in showing what they're made of. Because *what they're made of* is, of course, *what matters*.

Act II: Conflict #2 climax— *Fulcrum*

So we're reaching the whole point of Conflict #2, which I've described as the story's *Fulcrum*.

The reader is halfway through the story now, completely beguiled by the build-up of this Conflict and desperate to find out where it's all going.

As you remember, *we* know where it's going. It's going toward the whole point of Conflict #2, the Fulcrum of the story, which is going to throw those characters from a black-&-white world into full-color.

But first. . .

Faux Resolution

That build-up takes a much-needed detour at the last minute and turns into the faux resolution of Conflict #2. *Holy smokes!* A last-minute reprieve!

In *Thieves*, Keechie shows up to nurse Bowie of his injuries from the shoot-out, and they reach an understanding.

In "Dwarf," Aimee calls the man who sells mirrors to Ralph, imagining the Dwarf waking in the cold in the middle of the night to dance beatifically in front of his tall mirror.

In *Postman*, Frank and Cora are on the road taking a holiday with the Greek, Frank and the Greek drunk and singing in the back seat and Cora driving.

In *Riders*, Withersteen and Lassiter come clean with each other—she admits she's been snowing him to protect Dyer and Tull from him, and he admits he meant to kill whoever was responsible for the death of Milly, and they have their first passionate love scene.

In *Otranto*, the knights of Isabella's father, Frederic, arrive to verify that her marriage to Conrad is going through as planned.

And in "Norderney," the Cardinal, at the madwoman's behest, marries the young man and Calypso.

This is a little bit bigger of a beat than the last faux resolution. This is a lovely beat, the first moment in which the writer flashes a quick revelation of the intense hopes and dreams for which these characters struggle so hard. Love! Beauty! Bonding! Truth! This is the point at which the writer begins to promise the reader, "They're going to make it."

Climax

Finally the reader reaches the whole point of Conflict #2, which is that pivotal Fulcrum — the moment the scales shift and the characters stop fleeing their Hook and begin pursuing with every ounce of passion in their souls something they don't yet know is going to turn out to be their worst nightmare, the Climax. That Fulcrum is the climax of Conflict #2.

In *Thieves*, Chicamaw, drunk and broke, turns up saying he's lost all his bank robbery money gambling — gamblers are "thieves" — and admits to Bowie that he knows, although he's a loser, Bowie's the kind of guy who will go straight. The problem is there's a reward out for them now, and Chicamaw, worried, says they're terribly hot, in real danger of winding up at the deadly prison farm in Texas. He brings out their guns, and he and Bowie plan their escape to Mexico — suddenly they're no longer escaping jail and building their savings, they're plowing headfirst through danger toward their dreams of safety.

In "Dwarf," Aimee gets ahold of the man who sells mirrors and cries out to him, thinking of the Dwarf's anguish — suddenly she's no longer following Ralph's lead, she's forging ahead toward her own solution to circumstances.

In *Postman*, in a carefully-planned sequence, Frank waits until Cora has driven them to a cliff edge and then kills the Greek with a blow to the head with a wrench — suddenly they're no longer trying to escape the urge to eliminate the Greek, they've done it and must move forward with the consequences.

In *Riders*, Lassiter proves to Withersteen she couldn't escape Tull and Dyer now if she wanted to, as she's watched constantly by men hidden in the sage around her house and by the women who work for her. They share a moment of anguished soul-searching over their internal conflicts — suddenly Withersteen no longer believes she can be reconciled to Tull and Dyer, she's cut loose from her church and even her home, and she must cope with a future she can't possibly predict.

In *Otranto*, Manfred announces to Frederic's knights that Conrad has finally died and Hippolita has turned out to be too close a relation to bear him lawful children, so he's going to marry Isabella himself—suddenly the characters are no longer playing cat-&-mouse with Manfred, they're forced to face his determined machinations head-on.

And in "Norderney," the madwoman suggests to the Cardinal the definition of 'humbug' might be sinners in hell pretending they have not been living in hell from the day they were born—suddenly they're not talking about how they've made their deadly sacrifice during the flood to save their moral lives, they're talking about what happens to our souls after we die.

The doors onto alternative futures have slammed shut, and the characters know now what they need and what will happen to them if they don't get it.

We're approximately $1/2$-$2/3$ of the way into this story, and the reader is feeling the balance of it swing portentously inside them, carrying them right along with it.

So the writer can get crazy.

Act II: Conflict #3

We've passed the Fulcrum, and we're no longer laying fuses in all directions. We're beginning to blow things up.

And once again, we're at another hook, this time the hook of Conflict #3, which is going to culminate eventually in the whole point of Conflict #3, its climax: the story's second Plot Point.

And the first bit of *that* hook is the *hook scene*.

And the very first words — those few seductive words that pull the reader in and make them want to read the next words — that's the *hook sentence*.

Hook

Hook sentence

In *Thieves*, Bowie lies in bed worrying about everything that frightens him.

In "Dwarf," night arrives, and again Bradbury makes a transition, as he so often does, with a simple, classical declarative sentence marking the passage of time.

In *Postman*, again, all Frank can say is that he and Cora didn't say anything (their chronic inability to say what they need to say when they need to say it is key to their dreadful downhill slide).

In *Riders*, Venters wakes in the hidden valley.

In *Otranto*, Jerome arrives at the castle from the monastery.

And in "Norderney," the Cardinal compliments the elderly madwoman on her insight, making her blush.

Hook scene

In *Thieves*, Keechie returns to take care of Bowie, and when she soothes his fears they sleep together.

In "Dwarf," Aimee fights with Ralph over the Dwarf.

In *Postman*, Frank and Cora stage the 'accident' in which the Greek will appear to have died, including beating each other badly.

In *Riders*, Venters and Bess are falling in love, safe in their hidden valley, which he's named Surprise Valley. He tells her about his horse, Wrangle, the fastest horse on Withersteen's ranch, although just a trifle unpredictable.

In *Otranto*, before Manfred can shut Jerome up, he announces that Isabella has vanished from the monastery, so Frederic's knights are alerted to Isabella's objections to Manfred.

And in "Norderney," the Cardinal tells the madwoman there are worse things than eternal damnation.

Again, be aware of what goes into the *hook sentence* and what is illuminated in the full *hook scene*. You'll see now how the clues to conflict in these hook scenes of Conflict #3 relate to the climaxes of Conflict #3 (not necessarily the stories' Climaxes, but the final of this series of steps once-removed): the—eventually tragic—love between Bowie and Keechie, Aimee's revelation of Ralph's true self, the extraordinary murder plot that teaches Frank and Cora to trust *no one*, the brilliant but unstable horse Wrangle whose reckless pursuit of his own ends will determine all their fates (just as Dyer once did), the attempt and thwarting of a desperate bid for freedom, and the argument for free will in an uncontrollable universe.

The climax of Conflict #3 is going to throw back the veil and reveal in vivid, concrete terms the themes this writer has come here to explore.

Development

Now that they're hooked on Conflict #3, the reader reads the Conflict development, how that hook scene builds upon itself, continuing to reveal and intertwine hidden aspects of all the elements introduced in the Hook, Conflict #1, and Conflict #2 (and always aiming toward the whole point of Conflict #3, which is going to kick the characters right in the teeth). Just as in the earlier episodes, this occurs in a series of one to three conflicts, which may be longer or shorter, depending upon the length of the story and intentions of the writer.

In *Thieves*, Bowies admits to Keechie that two Laws were killed in the shoot-out at the accident after their last bank robbery, and she knows Chicamaw's the one who killed them. Keechie's father tells the newspapers Bowie's kidnapped her, and Bowie decides to send her home. However, before he does, he, Chicamaw, and T-Dub rob one last bank, where T-Dub is killed, Chicamaw injured, and T-Dub's new young wife arrested. Bowie is the only one who escapes, accused in the newspapers of being a dangerous outlaw aided and abetted by a mysterious woman. Bowie, terrified and humbled by his close brush with disaster, promises Keechie never to see Chicamaw again.

In "Dwarf," Ralph goes away for a minute and comes back looking pleased with himself. Through the intense loneliness of the carnival crowd, the Dwarf appears, heading toward the Mirror Maze.

In *Postman*, this is where it gets complicated. Frank and Cora are interrogated by the DA, who bullies Frank into signing a complaint against Cora for his injuries so it won't appear he killed the Greek for the insurance (which Frank has never even known the Greek has). Frank gets a lawyer then, who arranges for Cora to confess to his own assistant posing as a fake detective in order to get it off her chest so she won't panic in front of the judge, then pits the insurance companies against each other, forcing them to collude in self-protection because the Greek had three policies in effect at once — one almost expired and two new ones overlapping that particular week.

In *Riders*, Faye's mother dies, and Faye comes to live with Withersteen. Venters returns from Surprise Valley and confronts Tull over stealing Withersteen's cattle, and Tull, in revenge, sends his right-hand man, Jerry Card, to steal

Withersteen's prize horses, killing one of her riders in the process.

In *Otranto*, Matilda meets Theodore in person, they fall instantly in love, and she sends him to hide in the forest. There he stumbles across Isabella and valiantly hacks the daylights out of her father Frederic in her defense when Frederic appears in disguise to rescue her. Dangerously wounded, Frederic gasps out his identity and the prophecy against Manfred. Frederic is conveyed to the castle, where he recovers.

And in "Norderney," the Cardinal tells the story of "The Wine of the Tetrarch," in which St. Peter is so obsessed with his own reaction to the crucifixion he's unable to help a stranger with a mysterious spiritual burden.

Now the characters are showing things they're made of through aspects they never even knew about themselves, and that revelation of *what they're made of* is the heart of everything the writer has to say about being alive.

Act II: Conflict #3 climax— *Second Plot Point*

Now we're reaching the whole point of Conflict #3, which is the story's *second Plot Point.*

The reader has become addicted to this story through the build-up of Conflicts and is gradually succumbing to the complexities of the plotline. Up until now, they've thought they could keep things straight and even guess where it's all going. After this, they have no idea what the writer has in mind.

Yep, *we* know where it's going. It's going toward the whole point of Conflict #3, the climax, which is that second Plot Point that's going to spin them like whirligig bugs, completely altering all their preconceptions about what they want and how to get it.

But first. . .

Faux Resolution

That build-up takes a heart-moving detour at the last minute and the characters fall into the faux resolution of Conflict #3. *The saints have arrived!* It's a happy story, after all!

In *Thieves*, Bowie and Keechie are settled down in a sweet little cabin in a small town far from anywhere, finished with their lives as bank robbers. Keechie is relieved that they're not going to Mexico, and Bowie says he's decided to hire a lawyer to rescue Chicamaw from the death sentence, although he reassures Keechie he still won't see him. They'll stay quiet, straight, and safe.

In "Dwarf," Ralph waves the Dwarf into the Mirror Maze for free, assuring Aimee he's being benevolent, just as she's always wanted him to be.

In *Postman*, Frank is released without prosecution, and Cora is acquitted when the insurance companies refuse to testify against her. And just when Frank and Cora think it can't get any better, the lawyer hands them the insurance check from the insurance company that has agreed to act as figurehead — ten thousand dollars (in 1934!).

In *Riders*, Lassiter discovers Venters and Bess, happy and in love, in beautiful Surprise Valley.

In *Otranto*, Theodore reveals the story of how he came to Otranto, an honest man on a noble mission.

And in "Norderney," the mysterious stranger of the Cardinal's story reassures St. Peter he, too, will probably be crucified, if that's what he hopes for, his moral soul saved.

This faux resolution is more profound than the last, not just a quick glimpse of a dream but a three-dimensional revelation of what would make these characters truly happy. The reader identifies with these characters now, and this beat draws them fully in emotionally. Now the reader *longs* for these characters to find their happiness.

Climax

Finally the reader reaches the whole point of Conflict #3, which is that second Plot Point — the other huge event that spins the characters' story and sends them flying off in an even more unexpected direction, that deadly direction they didn't see coming but should have, their heads whirling until they just about snap off their necks — the climax of Conflict #3.

In *Thieves*, it's Christmas Eve morning when Bowie's and Keechie's pipes freeze and they have to call in a plumber. When the plumber behaves suspiciously, they realize he's going to turn them in to the police for the reward, and they leave their sweet little cabin without packing — suddenly they're on their way south in the direction of Mexico.

In "Dwarf," the Dwarf goes to his regular room in the Mirror Maze and begins to scream and scream, and when Aimee arrives she realizes the mirror has been altered to make him look even shorter than he really is — suddenly Aimee realizes, after he's already done his damage, that Ralph is heartless and cruel, and she has no hope of ever reconciling him with the Dwarf.

In *Postman*, the lawyer says he wants the ten grand. No, he only wants half. No — there's a brief resolution at the last second, when he laughs and says he won't take any of it, he's just tickled to death that he pulled such a good one over on the DA he hates — suddenly the seeds of doubt are sown in Frank's and Cora's minds and they know they have no hope of trusting *anyone*.

In *Riders*, Venters chases down Card in another hellbent-for-leather, rip-snorting chase scene, cornering him on the stolen Wrangle on the edge of a cliff. Wrangle, who's lost his mind in the intensity of the chase, must be shot. And when Venters finally succeeds, Wrangle falls over the cliff, taking Card with him — suddenly both Withersteen and Tull have lost something of huge importance, and they have no hope of avoiding a cataclysmic show-down.

In *Otranto*, Matilda and Isabella square off over Theodore, whom they both covet. Hippolita, attempting to reconcile them, advises Matilda to marry Frederic as Manfred desires, and Isabella, appalled at the idea, tells Hippolita Manfred intends to divorce *her* — suddenly they all become aware that they have no hope of escaping futures that have been decided for them by others in exactly the wrong way.

And in "Norderney," the Cardinal's story ends on the revelation of the mysterious stranger as Barabbas, who was crucified alongside Jesus — suddenly the characters realize nobody is what they seem and we have no hope of designing our fates for our own purposes, not even to save our souls.

Wow — Act II has brought us so much to *work with*. We must give it our undivided attention, perform our analysis upon it, take our long, involved notes. Examine exactly how Act II has turned into a revelation of the characters and their story. They've confronted their fears, the obstacles to their hopes and dreams, and revealed the deep significance of their themes.

But their stories *still* haven't been resolved.

We're approximately $^2/_3$-$^3/_4$ of the way into this story, and the reader's reeling.

So the writer can switch tactics.

Chapter 22

Climax

Holographic structure, Act III

Act III: Faux Resolution

Whee, doggies! We're done with Act II and suddenly, *unexpectedly* being slipped into Act III.

We've passed the second Plot Point, the characters' trajectories have shifted once again, even more significantly, and all our hair is standing on end. The reader doesn't know up from down anymore, and this new switch in tactics keeps them completely off-balance.

And (again, you say!) we're at a hook, this time the hook of the Faux Resolution, which is going to culminate eventually in the whole point of the Faux Resolution, its climax: the utter relief of everyone involved, that point in the story at which the characters (and reader) believe they've actually gotten out of facing their worst nightmare.

And the first bit of *that* hook is the *hook scene*.

And the very first words — those few reassuring words that pull the reader in and make them want to read the next words — that's the *hook sentence*.

Hook

Hook sentence

In *Thieves,* a lawyer's house is described as both straight and a little warped, next to a church (subtle irony).

In "Dwarf," Aimee turns on Ralph in tears.

In *Postman,* all in one sentence, Frank and Cora put the insurance money in the bank, buy lots of flowers, and go to the Greek's funeral (which just happens to be occurring that day — but the whole business with the complicated insurance maneuver has the reader's head buzzing so hard they never even notice this coincidence, which allows the writer to keep the tension at a singing peak).

In *Riders,* Venters rides defiantly through town leading Withersteen's recovered horses.

In *Otranto,* Jerome, reunited with his beloved son, interrogates Theodore about his escape from Otranto.

And in "Norderney," the young man gets up to change the tallow in the candle, as it goes into its death throes (again — subtle symbolism).

Hook scene

In *Thieves,* Bowie and Keechie meet with the lawyer, who says he can keep Chicamaw from getting the death sentence and also pass Bowie's money on to him so Bowie won't have to see him. The lawyer invites them to eat Christmas Eve dinner with him and talks through the whole meal with real insight about the economic conditions that create a climate of bank robbery, blaming the wealthy. Bowie agrees that capitalists are "thieves" just "like us."

In "Dwarf," Aimee asks Ralph what's wrong with him, how he could do such a thing to the Dwarf, and runs away from him without waiting for an answer.

In *Postman*, Frank and Cora attend the Greek's funeral, amid whispers of who they are and how the Greek died.

In *Riders*, Venters announces to everyone on the street that Card is dead, a message for Tull. One of Withersteen's riders tells Venters he's seen Lassiter in the bar with Oldring, so Venters — in a rage — goes into the bar, announces he's there for vengeance on behalf of Bess, and kills Oldring, only puzzled that the last look in Oldring's eyes is of love and his last words an unfinished sentence about Bess.

In *Otranto*, Theodore admits to Jerome that he lied to Manfred about how he escaped Otranto in order to protect Isabella.

And in "Norderney," the young married couple lies down in the hay together holding hands and falls asleep while the madwoman and Cardinal sit awake.

As always, we must be aware of what goes into the *hook sentence* and what illumination reveals in the full *hook scene*. You'll see how the clues to conflict in these hook scenes of the Faux Resolution relate to the climaxes of the Faux Resolution, now eerily like the stories' Climaxes, only their opposites: Bowie and Keechie agreeing on the necessity of springing Chicamaw from prison and escaping south, Aimee defending the Dwarf, Frank and Cora coping successfully with the aftermath of the Greek's murder, Venters and Lassiter gunning down their enemies, the thwarting of Manfred, and the uniting of the hearts of the Cardinal and the madwoman.

The climax of the Faux Resolution is going to resolve the characters' surface dilemmas, laying the groundwork for the contrast between that and their real, underlying nightmares, which brings all the viscerally vibrating threads of the story into the same frequency at the same moment.

Development

Now the reader is hooked on the Faux Resolution, and, full of relief and new-found confidence, they read the Faux Resolution development, luxuriating in how that hook scene builds upon itself and finds ways to *appear* to resolve all the aspects of the story and put out the burning fuses, subtly drawing the reader's attention away from the real danger ahead (and always aiming toward the whole point of the Faux Resolution, enticing the reader to look completely the other way). Just as in all the previous episodes, this occurs in a series of one to three conflicts, which may be longer or shorter, depending upon the length of the story and intentions of the writer.

In *Thieves*, Bowie and Keechie settle down in New Orleans, within a safe distance of the Mexican border, and Bowie reads in the paper that Chicamaw's trial is over and he's escaped the death sentence.

In "Dwarf," Aimee finds her way out of the Mirror Maze and begins searching the carnival for the Dwarf. She feels numb — not angry at Ralph anymore, not shocked or frightened — just numb.

In *Postman*, although they should now be happy, the tension of what they've been through is too much for Frank and Cora. Cora leaves town, and Frank's solution is to take up with another woman, who invites him to go with her to Nicaragua to catch pumas. He almost goes with her — but in a brilliant one-liner realizes Nicaragua won't be far enough away.

In *Riders*, Venters learns from Bess that she was not Oldring's involuntary wife but his daughter, whom he loved.

Meanwhile, Lassiter tells Withersteen Milly was not his wife but his sister, so Lassiter is free to love Withersteen. And Withersteen swears to Lassiter she loves him (although he doesn't believe her because she faked her fondness for him when she first knew him).

In *Otranto*, Hippolita fails to get permission from Jerome to divorce Manfred, as he desires, a solid win for Isabella and the others.

And in "Norderney," the madwoman and the Cardinal exchange profound insights as the young people sleep, realizing they understand each other in a way nobody has ever understood them before.

The characters are managing not to face their nightmares here. They don't believe they *can* face their nightmares. And *what they don't believe they're made of* is the other side of the portrait their writer is going to such long and meticulous and heartfelt lengths to draw.

Act III: Faux Resolution climax—*Feinting*

So we're reaching the whole point of this Faux Resolution, which I've described as the story's *Feint*.

The reader has been soothed by the build-up of this Faux Resolution and deeply reassured that *they know* where it's all going.

Oh, yes. *We* know where it's going. It's going toward the whole point of the Faux Resolution, which is suckering the reader into believing exactly what they now hope to believe. And that will set up the greatest possible contrast between that enormous relief and the knock-out blow of the Climax.

But first. . .

Anti-Faux Resolution

. . .something tricky. Instead of a faux resolution to give the reader a chance to take a breath between conflicts, as in all the previous faux resolutions, this time there's an *anti-faux resolution* — the opposite of a breather, a little poke with a sharp stick to make sure the reader's still awake. It ain't over 'til it's over. *You there!* Sit up!

In *Thieves*, Bowie learns from a newspaper that Chicamaw has been sent to the deadly prison farm in Texas.

In "Dwarf," The owner of the shooting gallery runs up and says the Dwarf has stolen one of his guns.

In *Postman*, after Cora gets home, the lawyer's fake detective/assistant tries to blackmail them with her confession.

In *Riders*, while Withersteen and Lassiter are arguing over whether or not she really loves him, little Faye is kidnapped.

In *Otranto*, Manfred convinces Frederic to agree to a double wedding between Frederic and Matilda, Manfred and Isabella, causing blood to drip from the marble nose of the statue of Alfonso at the mere thought.

And in "Norderney," the Cardinal admits to the madwoman that he is not the Cardinal at all, but the Cardinal's assistant, who killed the Cardinal so he could take his place.

This beat throws the reader for a loop, because the writer has conditioned them through the three-time repetition (remember that humans resonate deeply with threes) to expect relief at this point. But it's not relief! It's the opposite! *What?*

Suddenly, the reader doesn't know which way to turn.

Climax

And finally the reader reaches that whole point of the Faux Resolution, which is the point of total surrender — the opposite of the up-coming Climax, that point at which the characters (and reader) truly believe the nightmare has been avoided — that clever Feint, the climax of the Faux Resolution.

In *Thieves*, Bowie talks to Keechie, who hasn't been feeling good, about going to Mexico, finally convincing her it's the only place they'll be safe.

In "Dwarf," Ralph has cornered Aimee back in the Dwarf's room of the Mirror Maze. She realizes she has no feeling for Ralph anymore and turns to leave.

In *Postman*, Frank beats the lawyer's assistant to a pulp and gets the confession away from him.

In *Riders*, Lassiter goes to the Mormon church and shoots Bishop Dyer dead, telling him he knows Dyer is the one who ruined Lassiter's sister Milly, kidnapped her little girl, and has now kidnapped little Faye, and declaring Dyer won't destroy the lives of any more young girls.

Lassiter reveals to everyone that Bess is the little girl kidnapped long ago from his sister Milly and proves Oldring was not Bess's father but the man to whom Dyer gave the child. Dyer and Tull intended Oldring to raise Bess as a rustler and break the heart of Milly's husband — Tull's old antagonist back home, from whom Tull kidnapped Milly to bring her to Utah at Dyer's bidding. However, Oldring came to love Bess and raised her as his own daughter, educating and protecting her, foiling Tull's revenge — all of which Lassiter learned that day Withersteen's rider saw him with Oldring in the bar, right before Venters killed Oldring. Now Withersteen gives Venters and Bess her prize horses so they can escape Utah (and the Mormons) forever.

In *Otranto*, Hippolita shuts everyone up by docilely taking Manfred home with her.

And in "Norderney," the false Cardinal asks the madwoman if life has any more purpose than to smile at the Devil. She agrees that this is a great art and the purpose of life. Then she demands he kiss her so she will not die unkissed, and he kisses her.

Oooh, the Faux Resolution is a marvelous twist in the story. We must be sure we understand exactly what's going on here and why. Examine how Acts I and II have been brought to their culminations and then suddenly, adroitly, turned inside-out.

The Faux Resolution is the point at which so many aspiring writers think they've finished writing their stories. They think they're done.

They're not done.

Now is the moment for the characters to *stop* showing what they're made of, to take a break, to collapse and let their weakness and wounds and lack of capability be fully revealed. That lack of capability is what spells their downfall.

We're approximately $5/6$-$7/8$ of the way into this story, and the reader's a complete, unsuspecting innocent.

So the writer can sock it to them.

Act III: Climax

The stage is set. The characters are poised. All of this long, involved story, all of those complications, all of that deep, wonderful, rich development—and we're ready for the real reason we're all here.

So, of course, we're at a hook, this time the hook of the Climax, which is going to culminate eventually in *the whole point* of this *entire story*.

And the first bit of *that* hook is the *hook scene*.

And the very first words—those few electrifying words that pull the reader in and make them want to read the next words—that's the *hook sentence*.

Hook

Hook sentence

In *Thieves*, Bowie tests a pen in order to write a letter to the lawyer.

In "Dwarf," Aimee catches sight of Ralph in the Dwarf's mirror.

In *Postman*, Cora announces to Frank that she's going to turn her confession over to the police.

In *Riders*, Withersteen's prize horses carry Venters and Bess across the sage.

In *Otranto*, Manfred realizes Jerome knows Isabella loves Theodore.

And in "Norderney," the madwoman gracefully lifts the hem of her skirt and hands it to the Cardinal.

Hook scene

In *Thieves*, Bowie sends money to the lawyer to buy a faked bench warrant and sheriff's badge for Bowie, who feels obliged to break Chicamaw out of the Texas prison farm before he's killed there.

In "Dwarf," Aimee can't stop staring at Ralph in the mirror.

In *Postman*, Cora explains she's confessing to the police because she wants to see Frank hang, knowing she can't be found guilty of a crime for which she's already been acquitted. It turns out the woman with whom Frank almost went to Nicaragua has shown up looking for him.

In *Riders*, Tull and his men chase Venters and Bess, so Bess gives her horse its head and in another fabulous chase scene proves to Venters she's the best rider out there on the purple sage. Having outrun Tull, they pause together at the sound of bizarre thunder coming from the high canyons around Surprise Valley.

In *Otranto*, Manfred worries over Theodore's striking resemblance to the portrait of Alfonso.

And in "Norderney," the sopping hem of the madwoman's skirt proves the flood has reached them.

Now for the last time, we are aware of what goes into the *hook sentence* and what is illuminated in the full *hook scene*. The clues to conflict in these hook scenes of the Climax relate, finally, to the climaxes of Climax. Bowie struggles against all odds to satisfy both his loyalty to Chicamaw and his love for Keechie — resulting in the destruction of all three. Aimee and Ralph face the truth about who he is — a man with a stunted soul. Frank and Cora can never be together — although they truly love each other. Venters and Bess, Withersteen and Lassiter, must all escape Utah and the Mormons — before they are destroyed by Tull. Manfred faces his prophesied doom — and is undone by Theodore's rightful claim to the Castle of Otranto. And the Cardinal and the madwoman face the awful mystery and majesty of life and death simultaneously — both together and alone.

The climax of the Climax is going to *catapult the reader into epiphany*.

Development

So here the reader is, thoroughly hooked on the Climax, with the entire story dragging behind it like a burning fuse. The reader reads the Climax development — by now simply unable to stop — and discovers how that hook scene builds upon itself, revealing the story in ways the reader never expected, while scaring the pants off them and making it appear there is really, truly no way out of this utter catastrophe (and always aiming toward the whole point of the Climax, which is *proof* that there's no way out). Just as in all the other episodes, this occurs in a series of one to three conflicts, which may be longer or shorter, depending upon the length of the story and intentions of the writer.

In *Thieves*, Keechie learns she hasn't been feeling well because she's pregnant and finally agrees to go to Mexico with Bowie, and Bowie, in a harrowing scene, finally manages to free Chicamaw from the prison farm in Texas.

In "Dwarf," there's no room for development scenes — it's all fast as a sledgehammer at this point.

In *Postman*, Frank convinces Cora he loves her, and she breaks down and admits she loves him back. The two of them, crumbling under the pressure, lie awake nights wondering how Frank is now going to kill Cora so she won't turn him in. Eventually, they confess everything they've been through to each other, swear they love each other, and Cora tells him she's pregnant. She insists he *prove* he won't kill her by giving him a perfect chance.

In *Riders*, Withersteen and Lassiter ride into the high canyons in search of Surprise Valley. However, partway there Lassiter tells Withersteen he has to confront Tull and his men, who are now following them, and as she waits for him she hears a terrible shoot-out.

In *Otranto*, when Bianca screams that she's seen the giant's hand on the stairs, Frederic calls off the double wedding. Manfred, overhearing Theodore in a love tryst and believing Theodore's beloved to be Isabella, stabs the woman and manages to kill his own daughter, Matilda. Everyone stands around her shrieking and wailing as she dies.

And in "Norderney," the madwoman and the Cardinal gaze at the sleeping young couple on the brink of death.

Now the characters are beginning to face their nightmares. Not the full extent yet—the writer saves that for last—but a taunting, terrifying, foreshadowing of their nightmares in the final conflict of the Climax, which sets up one final, overwhelming visceral vibration inside the reader, who begins suffering bodily symptoms of stress and euphoria. The reader is no longer just hooked in the gut. They're not even emotionally invested.

They're *trapped.*

The characters (and their reader) are going into a state of literary psychosis in which they're no longer able to distinguish between reality and surreality. *They don't know what they're made of anymore.* And it is by detaching them from reality that the writer prepares the reader for epiphany.

Act III: Climax climax—*the Whole Point*

So we've reached the whole point of the Climax. This is the grand finale.

The reader has been shocked, startled, and eventually petrified by the build-up of this Climax, unable to live now without finally learning where this whole story's been going all along.

We know where it's been going all along. It's been going toward the whole point of the Climax, which is *the whole point of the entire story.*

But first. . .

Faux Resolution

That build-up takes one last detour that dupes the reader one last time into believing the Climax has come and gone, the nightmare has been averted, and the characters have survived unscathed. It's the faux resolution of the Climax. *Thank your lucky stars! We escaped just in time!*

In *Thieves*, Bowie anxiously but safely returns from breaking Chicamaw out of the prison camp before Keechie wakes from a nap, and Bowie promises he'll never leave her again. Chicamaw is free, and they're just across the border from Mexico. *They're going home.*

In "Dwarf," Ralph turns to see what Aimee's staring at. *They're about to be reconciled.*

In *Postman*, Frank and Cora get married, then swim far out into the ocean so he can kill her if that's what he intends, and Frank realizes how much he loves her. He dives deep and feels everything being cleaned from him, leaving only his love and their future. *Everything becomes clear and beautiful.*

In *Riders*, Lassiter returns to Withersteen, injured but safe, with little Faye, whom he has taken back from Tull. They arrive in Surprise Valley. *They've made it.*

In *Otranto*, Manfred at long last repents of his evil ways. *Evil is conquered.*

And in "Norderney," the madwoman stops the Cardinal from waking the young couple, telling him when she was young she aspired to live so that no birds were ever again confined in cages. *Life is a vision of freedom.*

This beat is the full development of the joyous face of the story's theme. Freedom! Reconciliation! Virtue! Beauty! The reader thinks they've finally found what they came for.

They haven't found it yet.

Climax

And here the reader is at whole point of the Climax, which is *the whole point of the entire story.*

In *Thieves*, Just as Bowie is getting up to fetch Keechie something to soothe her morning sickness, the two of them are shot down in a burst of gunfire. This is described immediately afterward in a newspaper articles as the righteous end of a manhunt for the dangerous bank robber, Bowie Bowers, and his armed girlfriend—thereby making society safe from "thieves" like them.

In "Dwarf," Ralph sees that he has turned into the Dwarf in the mirror—he has become what he has mocked.

In *Postman*, Cora thinks she might be miscarrying, so Frank in a panic rushes her toward a hospital, but in a single, brief scene he wrecks the car and kills her. He is convicted (in one sentence) of murdering both the Greek and Cora for the insurance money and given the death penalty—and in the very last sentence of the very last page he unexpectedly breaks the Fourth Wall and asks the reader to pray that he and the woman he loves wind up after death in the same place.

In *Riders*, Lassiter must roll Balancing Rock across the entrance to Surprise Valley in order to cut off Tull, but at the last minute he can't do it. He knows once he has there will be no way out and the three of them will be trapped forever. Only Withersteen's passionate declaration of love and insistence finally decide him at the very bottom of the very last page, and he rolls the rock, causing an enormous avalanche to rain down on Tull—the thunder Venters and Bess have paused for as they escaped Utah.

In *Otranto*, The ghost of Alfonso appears, finally freed of his marble statue. There is a long and involved Resolution, in which Alfonso names Theodore his heir, Manfred confesses that his grandfather poisoned Alfonso and faked his will so his own heirs could inherit the Castle of Otranto, and Jerome explains that before Alfonso died he married a young Sicilian woman, who gave birth to a daughter, who was Jerome's wife and Theodore's mother. Manfred, exposed, abdicates in humiliation, and Theodore marries Isabella, although he will always be in love with the dead Matilda — a black-humor, gothic resolution to a gothic comedy.

And in "Norderney," Dinesen reveals that dawn is breaking, throwing bars (subtly like a birdcage) across the loft, and — at this moment when the madwoman is about to tell whether or not her life has been worth living — Dinesen uses the cliffhanger technique of her idol Scheherazade to illuminate the inherent precariousness of human life, just as the false Cardinal and madwoman have spent all night illuminating it, by *refusing to tell.*

That epiphany belongs to the reader.

Chapter 23

More Climax

Confronting the pirate

Pin-Pointing Your Climax

Suppose we're working intensely on an *incredibly* deep and meaningful story.

We're not us, though. We're an eighteenth-century American writer, maybe, who's been to Europe and is now on the way home, so that we have to do this work on shipboard. But this is okay because we're so completely immersed that we could work on it anywhere. Or else we're a European who's been to America. Or an Asian who's been to South America. Or an Indian who's been to Asia. Or an African who's been to Antarctica—but anyway, we're on a ship, working, working, working away as towering waves crash over the prow and the tang of salt wafts to our nostrils.

News of our extraordinary story has leaked out into the general public. Since we have a huge international reputation as a storyteller, everyone knows that this story is worth a fortune. It's rumored to be the pinnacle of our career. It's the most amazing production of a genius brain, which has already produced stories more memorable than Cervantes's, plot twists more baffling than Shakespeare's, audience investment more powerful than Homer's. Anyone who possesses this story will be richer than Croesus.

It is — as Bertie Wooster would say — a real *pip*.

But of course we keep it top secret so that no one can steal it.

Then *disaster strikes*. Oh, no! Our ship is hailed and, in quick order, boarded by pirates. They hog-tie everyone on board and take command. We are hauled up in chains before the pirate captain, the notorious Assuipe, with his reputation for collecting strange and unusual treasures and selling them to buyers of enormous wealth known only to him.

And he wants our story.

"No!" we cry. "I won't tell you! I'd rather *die first*."

Unfortunately, he's okay with this.

In an instant, his minions have flung out a plank, and we are encouraged at sword point to climb up on it and begin our promenade. They're leaning over the side of the ship tossing edibles to attract sharks.

"Well?" he calls when we're a third of the way along.

"I won't!" we yell furiously over our shoulder, rattling our chains above our head.

Poke, poke go the points of the swords.

"What do you think?" he calls when we're two thirds of the way along.

"Never!" we bellow, yanking futilely against our chains. One foot slips, and we jerk it back with a private whimper.

Poke, poke go the points of the swords.

"It's time, matey. Will you tell me, or won't you?" he calls when we get to the end of the plank.

"No!" we cry passionately from the very depth of our soul.

The pirates lift, and the plank begins to tip. Below our feet, shark fins are circling. The tang of salt wafts to our nostrils.

We shriek. "It's —!"

What?

Making a Scene Out of Your Climax

So we're sitting at the table in the captain's cabin across from Assuipe, guzzling a flagon of wine and trying not to bang our elbows on the brass table rail that keeps stuff from flying off during storms. He's allowed us to change our britches, but we're still wondering whether or not our heart will ever stop pounding.

Probably not.

"Tell me again," Assuipe says, clutching his quill and preparing to write laboriously as we speak. He's not very literate.

"It's the story of a genius of a writer," we say wearily, "whose greatest idea, the most extraordinary premise, the pinnacle of a brilliant career, is stolen by a —a pirate."

"I like it!" Assuipe belches into his fist. "Go on."

"It starts in a little seaside village where the writer lives. She's down in the waterfront pub with her best friend, Panther Jack —"

"Screw that," says Assuipe. "Tell me about the pirate who steals the idea."

"No, that's at the *end*." It's obvious that Assuipe knows nothing about storytelling. What a cretin. "First I have to tell you the story. See, Panther Jack is a kind of maverick sailor. She could be a ship's captain, she's so experienced, but she's not into power or authority, so instead she roams the seas on whatever adventure strikes her fancy. She and the writer grew up together —"

"Screw Panther Jack," says Assuipe. "I want to hear about the pirate."

"Could you *stop* interrupting? I'm trying to tell you —"

"About a pirate."

"*No.* The pirate's not even *in* most of the story. He only comes in at the very end. And, anyway, he just wrecks everything. He's just part of the premise. He's not what the story's about —"

"I like him." Assuipe grins, and we immediately wish he hadn't, because his teeth are the worst. "Your premise is the whole point of your story. *Bozo.*"

"—so the writer goes overseas, and while she's there the pattern of everything she's been through crystallizes in her mind, and — *bingo!* — Panther Jack's story comes back to her, and she realizes that it's the kernel to the most brilliant premise —"

"—which *is* that a terrible and swashbuckling pirate king steals a stupid story so he can live happily ever after —" Assuipe is trying to massage the cramp out of his writing hand.

We shake our head. "Living happily ever after isn't part of the premise. It's the resolution to the Climax."

"Living happily ever after is the Resolution to the *story.*" Assuipe sighs and puts down his quill. "But before that, the resolution to the Climax is me letting you get down off that plank." He hawks and spits into his empty flagon. "You know, for a famous writer, you sure don't know squat about structure."

Romeo & Juliet, Climax

faux resolution scene

The star-crossed teenagers have planned to meet in secret immediately after they're married. The girl and the priest who married them have come up with an elaborate plot in which she fakes death to escape her family so that she and the boy can run away together. The only thing left to do is tell the boy.

The girl drinks the potion and falls into her drugged sleep. When she wakes, she and her young husband will be reunited, and they'll be free.

That's the *faux resolution* scene of the Climax.

climax scene

However, the boy arrives at the girl's tomb ahead of schedule and finds her apparently dead. In his horror and anguish, he drinks poison and dies. The girl comes to shortly after that, finds him draped dead over her, and in *her* horror and anguish pulls out his dagger and stabs *herself* to death.

That's the *climax* scene of the Climax.

After that, the priest rushes in just in time to not save anybody.

He's the *resolution* to the Climax (which is not the same as the Resolution to the story—you notice a minor *resolution* is so fleeting that it can be tacked onto the end of the climax scene).

Down curtain.

The Idiot, Climax

faux resolution scene

The man finds his rival, an old and close friend, with the woman they both love. The man's friend has become increasingly deranged throughout their mutual courtship of this woman, even to the extent of threatening to kill the man, who is an epileptic and a kind of saintly fool. He loves the woman partly because she's a fallen woman who needs his empathy. Now she has first agreed to marry him and then run off with his friend yet again, leaving him at the altar.

The man chases the woman and his friend and finally catches up at his friend's house, where he's sure that they can all be reconciled.

That's the *faux resolution* scene of the Climax.

climax scene

The friend shows the man the woman's dead body. In his anguish over breaking the heart of his best friend — the saintly fool — he has killed her.

That's the *climax* scene of the Climax.

They cower together in their mutual despair.

That's the *resolution* to the Climax.

Down curtain.

Emma, Climax

faux resolution scene

The meddling young woman has managed, through her incessant interference, to prevent a friend from marrying the man who loves her. She's also managed to get herself proposed to by the last man she would ever marry and to act the dupe for a couple hiding their engagement from their elders. She has, in her frustration over constantly screwing up, been inexcusably rude to a woman of much lesser advantages.

Now she is on her way to meet the man she loves, joyfully unaware that, through this final screw-up, she has alienated his affections.

That's the *faux resolution* scene of the Climax.

climax scene

The young woman's beloved scolds her roundly for her behavior throughout the story, and she realizes that she's been completely wrong about everything.

That's the *climax* scene of the Climax.

She has an epiphany about who she is and what her life is all about.

That's the *resolution* to the Climax.

Down curtain.

Anna Karenina, **Climax**

faux resolution scene

The Russian aristocrat who has left her husband and son for her lover looks one final time to her friends and lover to pull her out of the spiraling depression into which she has fallen after the birth of her illicit daughter. However, they can't save her from herself.

She realizes in a flash of epiphany that it's up to her to resolve her tragic life and goes alone to a train station to think.

That's the *faux resolution* scene of the Climax.

climax scene

The woman, distraught, listens to people talking around her and, little by little, comes to see her life as a complete sham. She decides quite rationally to kill herself, carefully times the passing of a train, and throws herself under its wheels.

That's the *climax* scene of the Climax.

All light goes out — she is dead.

That's the *resolution* to the Climax.

Down curtain.

"The Legend of Sleepy Hollow," Climax

faux resolution scene

A man competing with a more successful, more rakish, generally more likely suitor for the love of a young woman learns at a party that the woman appears to have chosen the other man. He leaves for home feeling rather downhearted but not defeated. He has faith in himself. And nobody's won the young woman's heart yet.

That's the *faux resolution* scene of the Climax.

climax scene

On the way home, the man sees the headless horseman of legend riding toward him. Panic-stricken, he tries to out-run the ghoul. He is heading for a bridge, thinking that if he can get across it he can make it home safely. He comes to the bridge, and the figure *throws its head at him.*

That's the *climax* scene of the Climax.

This Climax has no *resolution.* (It's a ghost story.)

Down curtain.

Identifying the Crux of Your Climax

The problem that most writers run into is that their best moment *isn't their Climax.*

Because what interests them most isn't what they thought would.

We *thought* we wanted to write a story about teenage love that proves youngsters must abide by the wisdom of older and cooler heads. But you know what really got us? The boy hiding in the girl's garden under her balcony. It was too much for us! And the girl leaning over the rail of her balcony under the stars to the sight of his beautiful face in the dusk below? We didn't plan on that. But, wow, does that scene throw off *sparks.*

So by the time we get to the premise, the reader's thinking, *Tell me more about that fascinating scene in which teenage love catches fire.*

This is probably the biggest reason people pants. Because they don't want to get to their planned Climax and discover that they've come all this way for nothing.

But it's not for nothing! Oh, *no*. It's all part of the work. We would never have figured out about the balcony and the garden if we hadn't gotten ourselves thoroughly involved in these characters' world, if we hadn't been in there wandering around, following them from place to place, spying, eavesdropping, taking notes as fast as we could.

If we hadn't been asking ourselves, "But what about this angle? What about that thread? Where is this going? Where has that been?"

We might have wandered right past the girl and boy flirting under cover of night and never given the import of that scene another thought.

"Minor scene. Useful only for moving characters from one point to another. Nothing to notice here. Carry on."

This is why I tell writers to identify first their protagonist's *needs*. Two mutually-incompatible needs. The needs that drag them into this story.

Because the *choice* between our protagonist's needs is the ultimate nightmare that they must eventually face.

Juliet needs to obey her parents. She's a young teen, docile, intelligent, *cultured*. Her parents' whims are her commands. And this is fine so long as she never needs anything else. But then one starry night hormones appear in her world in the figure of a beautiful, poetic young man her own age, and suddenly Juliet is trapped between her awakening passion and her painful denial, between obedience to and rebellion against those under whose authority she lives. In a story of *love*. And *survival*.

This makes the Climax of her story the moment in which she must choose between her beloved and her life.

Romeo also needs to obey his parents. He's also a teen, and although he longs to be level-headed in the heat of anger he is volatile enough to kill. And when he falls in love with Juliet and kills her cousin Tybalt in a fight over her, he too becomes trapped in this story of passion and denial, of obedience and rebellion. Of *love*. And *survival*.

This makes the Climax of his story, as well, the moment in which he must choose between his beloved and his life.

Which makes the two of them simply fabulous co-protagonists for this heart-wrenching drama.

So we work with our protagonists until we know — as deeply as we know ourselves — exactly what they need and how they manage to thwart that need. Then we imagine any number of situations that might force them to choose between those opposing needs, and we select the one that affects us most powerfully. Our Climax.

We won't write it yet.

Building Total, Complex, Shocking, & Inevitable Significance into Your Climax

We've got a Climax in mind. It's not our original idea. No. We just used that to point the cannon in a likely direction so that we could climb in and fire ourselves off. We went flying over the landscape, and the further into this fictional world we got the more of it we saw, the better we understood it, the clearer became the forces that make it what it is. And at some point we saw the apex of the whole thing.

There it is. This is what we were after all along.

It appears right after things seem to have finally all settled down.

And it's *fabulous*.

Oh, we want to write it. We're climbing over our own head to get at it. *Everything's there.*

But we wait.

Because a Climax needs to be the culmination of the entire story. And how do we know what that culmination is until we've written the entire thing?

Not only does the Climax hold our premise, it also holds everything most essential and fundamental to our protagonist and main characters. And not just what we assumed was most essential and fundamental to them when we first met them, either. Not even what we figured out it was after we'd spent a lot of time hanging around with them. Not even what they told us, secretly, deep in their hearts, when nobody else was listening, as we contemplated together the ruin of their lives.

Even more than that.

As we write a story — what pantsers love about it — things crop up. Things we never saw coming. And, as Flannery O'Connor pointed out so many years ago, certain of these things keep coming *back*. The more times they come back, the more varied the situations in which they appear, the more meaning they begin to acquire in and of themselves. They take on resonance. By the end of the novel, they have become symbolic.

These could be objects. Or images. Or sounds. Or mannerisms. They could be certain colors, certain environments, certain memories, certain conclusions that certain characters keep finding themselves drawing about different circumstances. They could be mysterious triggers. Mysterious people.

A carved button. A blood orange. The call of an osprey. A finger on a collarbone. Someone in a trenchcoat on a bicycle. Waves battering at the dark base of a cliff. *I turn inside-out all I love best.*

We won't know what these symbols are until we've worked ourselves deep into the heart and soul of every single scene, traveling alongside our characters through all of the trauma through which they must go. We can't see those symbols from up high. We have to get down inside the scenes and live them. Everything is there, and we're looking only for the most striking, pertinent, unique details out of everything, and when we've listed them, considered them, fingered them, and finally included them, they begin very. . .slowly. . .to accumulate.

So that when we write the climax scene to our Climax, the one big scene that it's all about, we need this accumulation of significant details at our elbow to go through for *only the most significant and telling.*

And we don't have the whole accumulation until we're done with every other scene.

Not only this, but out of that accumulation, chances are the details that are going to hit our reader the hardest in the Climax are the ones so subtle they haven't made hardly any appearances yet.

Oh! The secret fuse burning away underneath it all!

Yes.

So we save the Climax. We take notes on it. Add questions. Scrawl comments on the backs of envelopes. Fill page after page of ideas and thoughts and ruminations and meanderings. We interview our characters. Stage conversations between them that they could never hold in the course of the plot. Let the detective sit down with the murderer and share a flask of rotgut and hash out some of the more important details.

"You were there?"

"Behind the door. You never even knew."

"That's going to affect my investigation—"

"It's probably when I dropped that slip of paper."

"You think? But that would mean —"

"You had to get it before I threw the sailor out of the dinghy."

"And *that* didn't happen until after Mariah called the watchmaker."

"Of course! Which is why the watchmaker *already knew* about the *drop*."

Eureka!

I was working with a client one day on a Young Adult (YA) fantasy novel. We'd done great work on a scene the week before, in which one character charges to the rescue of a friend in a lake, throwing up a huge, dramatic splash of white water against the night. It was a great moment. A *great* effect.

My client came in the next week saying, "You know that scene we wrote last week? Yeah. *Huge hole.*" And he reminded me that the character who charges to his friend's rescue is deathly afraid of water.

Rats. So we sat down and talked about this. And we decided that it's perfectly possible to lose our head and charge straight into a phobia in the defense of someone we care about if our adrenaline gets up suddenly and we truly believe that our friend is in mortal danger. Sure, it is! But afterward?

Well, it just so happened we'd planned for a scene after this particular subplot in which the friends all have personal meltdowns and go their separate ways (setting them up for the Climax). And what plugs into the need for a meltdown better than having just gotten ourselves totally immersed in our worst phobia?

Accidental motivation — there it is!

We must let go the reins and let our subconscious work. There's so much in there that we can't pry out with a crowbar.

We must immerse ourselves in our fictional world, write scenes around and about our characters, see what floats to the surface.

When I was in high school, I had a teacher who loved the word 'serendipity.' She talked about it all the time for most of a year. She was obsessed with the concept of how things can just *happen* to occur and it turns out that they fit together like the pieces of a puzzle.

Those flashes of insight are the layering that makes a Climax shocking.

Shocking, as yet *inevitable.*

Chapter 24

Layering Plot

Believable fiction II

So now we come to the most complex, authentic, essential aspect of structure: **layering**.

Novels are long. Series are even longer. And in this day and age, when such gorgeous works as Jean Rhys' *Wide Sargasso Sea*, Joseph Conrad's *Heart of Darkness*, Virginia Woolf's *To the Lighthouse*, and John Steinbeck's *Tortilla Flat* simply aren't good enough for us, because they're — by golly — less than 70,000 words, even a short publishable novel is by definition longer than most of the great novels in our literary canon.

All of which means that now, more than ever, we need layering.

Plot layering is using one or more subplots and a whole handful of plot threads to string out the action and intensify the significance, dragging our reader along through hundreds of pages and tens of thousands of words by the very scruff of their neck, never once losing our grip on them or letting them glance — however momentarily — at the clock.

Without them, the reader is simply too likely to look up and realize that they have their own life to live.

We must prevent this from occurring to them.

Main plotline

All stories have a main plotline: the fundamental struggle inside the protagonist between their two conflicting needs. This is what we talk about when we talk about the basic progress of a story from Hook through Development to Climax. This is what our story *is*.

We've discussed the main plotlines of each of these stories in detail: the tragic love stories of *Romeo & Juliet*, *Wuthering Heights*, *Dolce*, and *Anna Karenina*; the tension-packed adventures of *Thieves Like Us*, *Dark Passage*, *The Postman Always Rings Twice*, *Heart of Darkness*, and *Riders of the Purple Sage*; the tragicomic escapades of *The Castle of Otranto*, *The Violent Bear It Away*, *Henderson the Rain King*, *Little Women*, and "The Aspern Papers"; the profound insight of "The Dwarf," *The Fountain Overflows*, *The Brothers Karamazov*, *The Idiot*, and "The Deluge at Norderney."

When we examine the ways in which plots are structured, paced, and interwoven, we must be aware of this. We must always be watching for hints to subplots and plot threads within them.

Everything swings from the main plotline like a braid depending luxuriously from one luxurious head of hair.

Subplots

Subplots come and go throughout a story. They interact with the main plotline. They help develop character traits, illuminate motivation, and focus the driving fuel of the main plotline. They even appear at crucial moments — such as the climaxes of each episode — to bolster and cast into relief the main plotline, adding to its power.

When we're designing a climax for an episode of our main plotline—the climax to a Hook, Conflict, Faux Resolution, or Climax—we need all the *oomph!* we can get. So we coordinate at least one subplot to reach a climax at the same time. We begin the climactic scene in the main plotline, do a quickstep into a subplot, maybe throw in a subtle plot thread, and end on the main plotline again.

This forces a single scene to serve more than one purpose at once.

And that's scene-level layering.

In this way the climactic scene is multiply gripping, the reader's visceral investment in the story stimulated by the depth of following more than one plotline at once, while also satisfied by the resonance of the main plotline within the scene itself.

The key to using subplots is to remember that they are *always* subservient to the main plotline.

When the beloved cousin Rosamund of Rebecca West's *The Fountain Overflows* is haunted by the poltergeists who apparently operate on her father's behalf, this isn't the main plotline. The main plotline has to do with the childhood of the protagonist, of which Rosamund is the pivotal secondary character.

West needed Rosamund and her mother to move in with the protagonist's family, and she needed them to have a tragic and even dangerous other life that would never allow a reconciliation with Rosamund's father, which might remove Rosamund from the protagonist's family circle. So at the climax of Conflict #1, West sent the protagonist and her mother to call on Rosamund and her mother and thereby witness the violence of the poltergeists in person. The next thing we know, Rosamund and her mother have moved in, and the story has gained its essential secondary character.

West could have used any number of pressures upon the characters to accomplish this goal, and she could have told her story without any such goals at all if she'd really wanted to. It would still have been the story of the protagonist and Rosamund. It would still have ended in their arrival at the threshold of adulthood, facing the inevitable Climax of the paths upon which they've walked throughout all their years together.

But the story would have been missing that layering, that complexity that contributes so much to the realism of what West wanted to explore.

It's *vital* to distinguish between the story we really mean to tell and the subplots that add and contrast to it but are not the story itself. Sometimes these things can become confusing, and the writer winds up writing a story quite different from the one that leads to the Climax inherent to the personality of their protagonist.

We know, of course, that we need more than one story: a main plotline and a secondary plotline running alongside it. That secondary plotline is our main subplot. But it's not the only subplot. And it is *not* the main plotline.

West constructed her story around the premise: what if an ordinary girl and an extraordinary girl grew up together? What would happen when they stood on the threshold of adulthood and the ordinary girl was forced to face the inexplicable extraordinariness of her dearest companion?

West's main plotline is the childhood story of the ordinary girl. Her main subplot is the childhood story of the extraordinary girl. And her minor subplots add to both.

Rosamund's story could not be told without the protagonist's. But the protagonist's could — if necessary — be told with some character other than Rosamund.

Any time that the minor subplot of Rosamund's dreadful father and the threat of paranormal tampering ceases to add to the main plotline, all of this sinks out of sight for awhile. Then when that minor subplot is needed again, the father reappears — until he eventually reveals himself as a musician so consummate that it brings tears to the eyes of the protagonist's concert pianist mother.

"Why?" She is devastated by the knowledge of his beautiful talent coupled with his cruelty.

He has no answer for her and in this way adds to the tragic undertone of the story, the sense of growing danger on all sides in this otherwise fairly ordinary and yet exquisitely-rendered childhood.

A subplot is *always* subservient. It must *always* serve the forward movement of the main plotline — as must even the main subplot, as it crashes against the main plotline over and over until it alters that story into something it has never been before.

Subplots are not the braid itself — they are the locks of hair from which the braid is woven.

Plot threads

And then there are plot threads, those zillions of minor moments that appear and disappear like fireflies in the night.

Plots threads are different from subplots in that they're not major storylines running along concurrent to the main plotline. But they're different from simple scenes in that they're capable of moving from scene to scene, appearing more than once as the story progresses.

Plot threads not only add to the significance and interest of each subplot, pacing themselves perfectly to lull whenever the subplot lulls, to build whenever the subplot builds, and to peak whenever the subplot adds its weight to a climax in the main plotline. They also create delicate rhythms of their own, so that plot threads are used by the most adept to toy with the reader's mind and develop complex beats and backbeats so minor that they can only be felt—like the high notes of a dog whistle—by the sensors of the subconscious mind.

When Francis Tarwater catches a ride to the city with the salesman Meeks in Flannery O'Connor's *The Violent Bear It Away*, it's a tragicomic episode in which Tarwater reveals for the first time in interaction with another character the many facets of his suspicious and ignorant mind in almost equal measures, to the accompaniment of Meeks' own questionable grasp on reality.

Yes, O'Connor needed to get Tarwater from his great-uncle's remote cabin (now a smoldering wreck) to the city where his only other relative lives. This is how this plot thread adds to the forward motion of the main plotline. But she didn't have to do it this way. She could have managed without this scene at all and still told her story just as well. And Meeks goes away after this. We never hear from him again. We do hear from other characters who play his role in Tarwater's life—strange and sinister characters without roots in the main plotline whose sole purpose is to drag Tarwater from pole to pole of his journey, until one of Meeks' prototypes finally leaves the young man passed out and robbed by the side of the road.

Riding with strangers is a plot thread—a vivid series of moments in the telling of this story that illuminates a plethora of miniscule shining details about the characters and their setting, giving the reader their money's worth as they ride the avalanche of this wonderful story.

As with subplots, the story could survive without these plot threads. But it wouldn't have the complex layering of a truly complete novel.

And as with subplots, plot threads accomplish all of their subtle purposes while *always* simultaneously forwarding the movement of the main plotline.

Plot threads are not the locks of hair — they are the shining individual hairs that make up each of the locks of the intricate braid we're weaving.

Without subplots and plot threads, we can still have a head of hair. But what we do with it. . .*aaah.*

That's storytelling.

Chapter 25

Epiphany

Beyond holography

You know what I love about the Internet? (Not everything, by any means.) I love that I can get nostalgic over a silly 1969 movie that thrilled my soul when I was a young teen, and look it up and — hey, presto! — there it is.

If It's Tuesday, This Must Be Belgium.

I saw this dippy movie in the early 1970s, probably the very summer that my family returned from an endless nine-month tour of South America and Europe in a modified Land Rover named after a dog. I was thirteen, romantic, anxious to finish growing up and become a cute hippie. *Seriously* out of touch with reality.

This movie could have been made just for me.

What I did not realize was that this movie *wasn't* aimed at young teen travelers abjectly grateful not to be stuck in a car with their siblings anymore. This honestly never even crossed my mind. It was aimed at *older* teen travelers who had — *en masse* — suddenly in the late 1960s 'discovered' Europe and European hostels (much the way Europe 'discovered' America a scant 475 years earlier), along with the idea that you could dash wildly around the planet on a schedule to make a double-booking dentist blush, trying to see the world without ever stopping long enough for the world to see you.

Well, we were young.

And the only reason I know all this as well as I do is that I eventually returned to Europe. Having had world travel, dim and smoky hostels full of *painfully* attractive older teens, and the sight of Europe passing through a car window in an unidentified blur all embedded in my developing adolescent DNA, I had no choice. I had to get back to my roots.

I was thirty by then—still too young to afford decent hotel rooms, but now too old to join those wonderful teens over whom I'd originally swooned. I had five weeks to see everything from England to Italy, three of which I spent in a youth hostel in London playing pool with Australians.

I'm telling you, I *was* that movie. When I got home, reeling and dizzy, exhausted and twenty pounds thinner and stone-cold broke, I was in love.

I went right back to Europe as soon as I could afford it and began interviewing for jobs. I actually had two job offers as a tech writer in London, but I got hung up in Immigrations. I toyed with the idea of joining the expatriate writers' community I heard was springing up in Prague the summer after Czechoslovakia split.

Instead I got laid off from my dreadful job tech writing at IBM and went to Australia to visit the Australians I'd met in London (a whole other kettle of fish).

But I left a part of me behind in Europe. That footloose, artistic expatriate life had been my *destiny*.

I'd known this since I was a young child. I have an aunt who had been a starving artist on Paris' Left Bank in the 1950s, running around the rainy, cobbled streets barefoot at night, tossing her long hair and laughing her cackling laugh, romancing and being romanced under the street lamps.

I was going to be her. I knew that fantasy life was out there, just beyond my fingertips. It was *waiting* for me. *In my bones, I knew. . .*

And this is exactly how we want our reader to feel about our story.

We want to give them characters within a hair's breadth of their fondest dreams of themselves — mistake-addled, misguided, and tormented maybe, but also intriguing, heart-breaking, witty, and, at long last, profound — who live in the one place they miss most in all their lives — the summer they were nineteen and lived in a shack on the beach, the winter after their divorce when they learned to night ski in the silent forests of Vermont, the evening that they suddenly realized in a blinding epiphany what black holes are and why you don't want to be an ant crawling around the rim of one.

We want to give our reader, as well, the fantasies that they've had of living places they've never lived, of having adventures that they'll never have.

We want to take them wholly and completely into these characters' worlds: into the minutiae of telling moments, the details branded on the retina in an instant of passion, the tactile experience of being alive — being alive — just being alive.

We want to reach into their dreams and pull something out that's still tied to them by the heart-strings. We hold it up and turn it under the light:

"It's beautiful. It's devastating. It'll eat you up and spit you out, make mush of your brains and liquid of your soul. It'll be around the globe three times before you even know what direction it's gone, and you'll spend forever chasing after it."

We show it to them. *"It's your life."*

Part 2

Revision

Chapter 26

Writing & Rewriting
with Franz Kafka
Do-It-Yourself editing

Franz Kafka lived and died an unknown. Although his stories are so vivid and philosophically brilliant that the adjective 'kafkaesque' has become a part of our language, Kafka himself labored in obscurity.

A German-speaking native of Prague, he grew up in the Jewish quarter of Prague's medieval Old Town at the turn of the twentieth century — an era that meant for Kafka less the rise of Jewish self-awareness or political unrest or even Modern fiction than the rise of *bureaucracy*.

He worked throughout his short life as an insurance company paper-pusher, resulting in his unfinished masterpiece, *The Castle*, with its dreamlike exploration of the constant fruitless motion of red tape, its nightmare quality of endless, struggling stasis. A novel of the most bizarre non-story, *The Castle* follows the adventures of Kakfa's hapless protagonist known only as K. from the moment he arrives mysteriously in a nameless village at the foot of a domineering castle — much as Prague, that most lovely of European medieval cities, lies across the Vltava River from Prague Castle — and begins his hopeless, utterly determined quest to gain entrance to "the Castle" for no particular reason.

Many years ago, I visited Prague. It was the winter that Czechoslovakia split into the separate countries of the Czech Republic and Slovakia, and I was so utterly innocent of political events that I was surprised to learn from a fellow tourist on the train leaving the city that my Czechoslovakian money would be worthless within 24 hours.

It was *cold*. I slid down Petrin Hill on ice through the trees, crossed the *art nouveau* Čech Bridge over the Vltava River, and walked the cobblestone streets of Old Town in a euphoric, shivering haze. I climbed the historic clock tower on Prague's medieval Old Town Square (with its magnificent astronomical clock) and photographed a 360-degree panorama of the city — all of those mysterious, winding little streets, all of those huddled, misshapen, tiled rooftops, the magnificent bulk of the castle like a dragon on the horizon.

A dream landscape.

And there's no question that Kafka wrote about it as a dream. *The Castle* begins pointlessly, proceeds through innumerable meaningless obstacles whose importance can be determined solely through the seriousness with which the characters take them, culminates in no actual progress whatsoever, and accomplishes, in the end, nothing.

Kafka had no visible plan, no structural goals, no inevitable Climax in mind (although we can extrapolate what that Climax could have been based entirely upon the needs of his poor protagonist, so abundantly clear and powerful).

However, it's almost impossible not to feel ourselves, as we read, in Kafka's place, hunched over his papers evenings and weekends outside his dull work hours, recording with feverish intensity his protagonist's unbearably tangible world. It's the same feeling behind Mervyn Peake's *Gormenghast* trilogy — that of a genius of observation working at the height of their power to get down in excruciating detail an alternative universe as real as our own. There's the very strong impression that obsession with the meticulous is what kept this writer *alive*.

Although Kafka's novel is twisted to serve a philosophical function far beyond that of storytelling — a darkly-comic illumination of bureaucracy as a lifestyle — it is this white-hot passion for noting the moment-by-moment experience of living that makes his fiction sing. And even more vitally, among his papers after he died were discovered not just the manuscript of *The Castle,* but numerous variations on the manuscript: an alternate beginning, a continuation beyond the ending, countless fragments, excised scenes and paragraphs and phrases, rewritings and reworkings of events, characters, and developments. Some of the excised episodes go on for thousands of words.

The same story told over and over again, in every permutation and detail its author could possibly imagine.

This is the nature of fiction, writers, this multiplicity of storytelling. Truly, our first draft is barely a fleeting glimpse of the story we really mean to tell. It is only after we've waded in over our heads and rooted ourselves in an unshakable perspective upon our characters' experiences that we can begin the real work of recreating those experiences for our reader.

Kafka died of tuberculosis at the age of 41, barely published (his masterpieces unrecognized and unknown), a man who'd spent his life agonizing over whether or not to marry a woman he wasn't certain he wanted to marry (who wasn't certain she wanted to marry him), his amazing intelligence wasted on bureaucratic paperwork, finally at long last in love, the day after the father of his young beloved refused him permission to marry her.

We all seek in fiction some euphoric release from the drudgery and heartbreak of daily life. We open ourselves to our imaginations, writing and rewriting and rewriting yet again, inserting and removing scenes, paragraphs, episodes, and lines. And it is through this repetitive, painstaking process — over and over — that we find ourselves immersed in our unique, detailed, and yet utterly *real* fictional landscapes.

There is no avoiding boredom and agony, but there is this temporary, ephemeral escape.

We are all Kafkas at this work.

Chapter 27

Vision & Revision

The story you need to tell

We have come *so far*.

Remember way, way back in the early days, when we talked about the difference between character arc and narrative arc? Remember how we talked about who we are—solitary, individual human beings having ourselves some needs, forming ourselves some opinions, following our agendas wherever they happen to lead us, as we wander around out here on the surface of this planet our whole lives through? Remember being a noun? Remember having verbs?

Let's walk back through our story together now with all of this teeming beneath the surface of everything we've written, and we'll re-envision the original vision that first lead us to these iridescent shores.

Rethinking Motivation for Character Arc

Cause-&-effect. Needs. Choices.

The things that make us human.

We've created a protagonist with two or more intensely powerful, intensely conflicting needs. Those needs have forced this protagonist to behave and speak in quite specific ways. And the ways in which they behave and speak have created for them a variety of situations that, once they were in them, they desperately wanted out of, situations that they couldn't get out of without making things immeasurably worse.

We've put this protagonist into a room or garden or culvert or on a street or island or mountain or under a thundercloud or tent or blanket with some other characters, who also have their own needs.

We've thrown in a stick of dynamite and leaped out of the way to see what would happen.

And it was *brilliant.*

We've kept this up for a good, long time, until this protagonist's conflicting needs collided in a life-changing shower of fireworks and we forced them to choose.

And eventually, footsore and weary-worn but with a gleam of well-earned satisfaction in our eyes, we've fetched up here alongside everyone else in Revisionland. We're a bit surprised to see the others looking *quite* so footsore and weary-worn. But we're gentle souls and would never dream of mentioning this. Not out loud, anyway.

Now we've taken a big, full, satisfying rest after all that hard work, and we're ready to get back into our story, to begin the second phase: revision.

So the first thing we're going to do is pull out a notebook and ask ourselves, "How well do I know this protagonist?"

And we're going to dig for the answer — to this and to a few other pertinent questions.

What is our protagonist's primary overwhelming need? I know that we wrote this down way back in the beginning and stuck it up on post-it notes over our desk (*you didn't?*), but I want to ignore that at this point, and we'll apply ourselves solely to the protagonist in the Climax that we so recently and brilliantly wrote. We'll pretend that Climax is a short story (flash fiction even), and we've come to it cold without knowing that any of the rest of this story exists. We'll put on our thinking caps to analyze what we get out of reading this Climax as though for the very first time.

What's the *fire* in this strange new protagonist's belly, the death-defying drive that makes them forge straight into this Climax and fight there tooth-&-nail for everything that they love and believe in? What makes this protagonist *go*?

We'll write the answer at the top of a fresh page of a notebook.

We'll draw a box around it. Spend some time inking in the lines of the box, making them thick and dark and curved just a tiny bit into the corners. Doodle in three-dimensional sides for the box. Add shadows. And dents. And cracks. And travel stickers. Add a cat sitting at a distance with one of those inscrutable cat expressions, not saying or even thinking anything, just looking at it. That's the witness.

Got it?

Good.

Now, what deep inside this protagonist is pitted *against* them in that Climax? Not external forces — internal. What do they love and believe that's irreconcilable with their first need? What's the equal-but-opposite fire in their belly in this Climactic scene that's *fighting back*?

Remember to focus only upon the climax scene of the Climax.

We'll write it down on the middle of the page below the box we just drew. Decorate it with its own little box, its own light and shadows, its own dents and cracks, its own evidence of having traveled a long and painfully difficult road. If the first cat is looking too directly at the first box, we'll give this one a cat of its own. Otherwise, one cat will suffice.

Got it?

Good.

We'll doodle some lightning bolts between the two boxes.

Now we'll ask ourselves, "Exactly how could these two needs have gotten this protagonist into this dreadful calamity?"

We'll take copious notes on this, fleshing it out as fully as possible. We won't re-tell the story. We'll forget we ever even *knew* the story. We're not looking for surface issues, we're diving beneath the wave, re-envisioning the story from a completely different perspective. This is essential in order to know that the story we've told is, in fact, the story we've meant to tell.

We'll ask ourselves, in all honesty, "What do you suppose *happened* here?"

Then we'll ask ourselves, "*And how could these needs have led somewhere else?*"

We'll write about this for awhile.

We'll draw circles and brackets around especially important points as they come up in our notes or as we notice them afterward, using arrows and asterisks, scribble little comments to in the margins about things we forgot to mention. We'll fill up pages. Keep our hands moving. (When we scratch our cheeks, we'll try not to draw on our own faces.)

We'll always be wondering, "What do those two needs imply about this protagonist? How could my character have responded to their problems differently, given their fundamental, driving forces?"

We'll write sideways on the pages if we feel like it. Write at an angle or in loops or upside-down. Write in a fake accent, if it helps. Nobody's ever going to see this stuff. (By the time we send it to someone like me, it'll be all cleaned up and back in its public disguise again.)

Then we'll ask ourselves, "What would have been the perfect compromise to this Climax, the best possible way for a protagonist with these particular needs to convince themself that they weren't going to have to choose between those needs after all?"

It doesn't need to be a scene or even an event. Just an idea, a possibility—some way for them to wriggle out of their nightmare right before it happens.

We'll deliberately avoid thinking about the original solution to their dilemma. If we can't avoid it, we'll think about its opposite. Pose the question as if for the first time ever.

We'll take notes.

And we'll keep in mind that a Faux Resolution is a negative Climax—where the hook of a Conflict or Climax is jarring, the hook of a Faux Resolution is soothing; where the conflicts of a Conflict or Climax are increasingly full of conflict, separated by momentary lapses only to catch the breath, the conflicts of a Faux Resolution are increasingly resolved solutions separated by momentary lapses into tension, one at least of which pokes the reader out of their comfort zone; and where the faux resolution of a Conflict or Climax is a clear, kind, writer-to-reader respite, the anti-faux resolution of a Faux Resolution is a real *bear*. This makes the climax of a Faux Resolution a truly *fake* resolution.

We'll create a diagram for the relationship between the Climax as we have newly perceived it and the Faux Resolution we've just illuminated, a flowchart or family tree sort of thing, tracking our protagonist with their burning internal fires from the Climax backward into the effects that caused it, all of the myriad possibilities branching off in all directions.

Think about how many second or third or fourth cousins we must have who have never even dreamed of our existence. There are simply *dozens* of distant cousins to our protagonist's choices populating the parallel universes of the story inside our imagination.

We must ask ourselves what they are.

We'll continue to back up all the way through this story in this manner, working backward from the Faux Resolution through Development, addressing each Conflict as it comes up.

We'll always keep in mind as we do so: what does this protagonist need? and what else do they need? and how does the mutual incompatibility of those two needs keep banging them against themself, striking sparks?

And what if *something else* happened instead?

We'll uncover the hidden aspects of our protagonist's internal conflict. and record them in great, whacking, glorious detail.

Eventually we'll arrive at the Hook and write long and copiously about that. And finally — sprawling all over the pages of one full notebook or more — there will be a whole multitude of deep, intricate roots to this Climax, as developed backward through the Faux Resolution and Conflicts and Hook and as defined through the lens of our protagonist's internal conflict.

Take a long breath and admire it. You had no idea a story contained such *depth*, did you?

Then we'll go through it all slowly and thoughtfully, doodling circles or boxes or pyramids or stars (we can use different colors, if we like colors) around only those most special, magical roots at each, separate layer, the ideas with the freshest, most amazing potential.

"She remembers the abyss between her parents." "They're forced to collude against their will." "It becomes clear that they've made a terrible mistake." "He begins to fight back against himself, but in a funny way." "She first intuits that it's not going to work."

It doesn't matter how many there are. All we care about right now is that they're different, surprising, *magical*. And it doesn't matter where they might lie in relation to the scenes we've already written. Some might be spot on, and some might be a million miles away. It's okay. We're not outlining something we've already outlined before—we're searching for those hidden potentialities that vibrate with the greatest possible tension and significance.

We'll know them. They'll make our fingertips tingle when we pass our hands over them.

We'll copy them onto a fresh sheet of paper under their headings: Hook, Conflict #1, Conflict #2, Conflict #3, Faux Resolution, Climax. The most special, magical roots of character. We'll dink around until we know they're right.

We'll make sure, as we group them under their general headings, that they increase in tension from Conflict #1 to Conflict #3, from beginning of the story to the end. Then within each general heading, we'll number them in order of increasing tension.

Now we'll take out *another* fresh sheet of paper (you didn't know revision took so much fresh paper, did you?) and draw a sweeping curve, skewed toward the far end, and letter in extremely small letters each of those special, magical roots in chronological order according to their numbers and general headings, beginning at the Hook and finishing at the Climax.

There.

Our protagonist's real character arc.

Reorganizing Events for Narrative Arc

This is retro-design. And once we have our protagonist's fresh character arc all laid out before us, we can use it to determine the real story, the real series of scenes buried inside our first draft.

We have a character arc tracing the path of a series of essential elements of character development, leading the protagonist from the moment in which life first conspires to force them to change, all the way through that change, to the point of tossing the reader unexpectedly off the rainbow at the end of that protagonist's change.

Which point I like to consider the *ex*-change.

We've explored and solidified the character development of the story, both reaffirming those choices that gave us our first draft and discovering the new and deliciously unexpected aspects that our first draft is meant to discover. And now we can see it—the beauty of the geometry.

So we're examining our Climax and how it serves the purposes of our protagonist's character arc. They've reached some nightmare moment in which they can't possibly meet *both* of their fundamental, driving needs. Is this really the event that they were headed toward all along? Did something extraordinary occur along the way that sent them somewhere else—someplace far more earthshaking, more illuminating of their nightmare? Someplace that makes their choice between needs even *more* agonizing?

It should be right there in our notes.

We'll hunt it down, purse our lips over it, and put the end of our pen thoughtfully to our nose.

Is this it? The *real* premise?

We'll think about it for a long time. We'll search our notes for alternatives, scribble our latest, most exciting flashes of intuition, tap the end of our nose as we think. (Stick out our tongue as far as we can to prove no one's watching.)

We'll take as long as we need for this part. Hours, days, weeks, months. Truly. . .what's it all about?

Eventually we'll know — the *real* event that crowns this story.

Got it?

Good.

We'll take a fresh notebook and write at the top of a fresh page in our best calligraphy, "Once upon a time. . ." and fill in our real premise, the event that we've come so far to create. It's fine if we've already created it. It's fine if we haven't. We'll keep it in one sentence, just as we've done before when we discussed premise and Climax.

Once upon a time. . .

Our best calligraphy.

If we screw up the calligraphy, we'll tear off the page, wad it up, throw it over our shoulder, and write our premise again on the next page. (Try not to do this more than once, though, because some poor tree did have to *grow* that page.)

Take a good look at it.

Isn't it *lovely*?

Now we'll read back through the elements of our protagonist's character arc that appear under the Climax. Add to this list the alternatives to our premise that we've just discovered. Shuffle them around until they're in increasing order of tension. Think about some perfect little faux resolution event to this Climax — an instant in which our protagonist believes that they've just slipped in under the wire. Put this where it belongs. It's okay if right now there's more than one choice.

We don't need to add these to our clean sheets with our best calligraphy. Just have them jotted down in our notes and clearly identified for later.

Then we'll read back through the elements of our protagonist's character arc that appear in our notes under the Faux Resolution. They're in chronological order, yes? And within the context of the Faux Resolution, we can tell which element carries the most punch, the one that this Faux Resolution is all about, yes? This is the climax to the Faux Resolution — *yes?* We'll play around with them until we're certain that this is the best Faux Resolution for this particular Climax.

We'll think up new ones. Let our intuition explode like fireworks.

Now we'll imagine (or track down) an event in which this momentous element would be best illuminated.

Maybe we've already written it. Maybe we haven't.

We'll write it — again in our best calligraphy — a few lines below our premise on the same page. One sentence. Some event to reassure our protagonist in their most vulnerable hour that they will not after all be facing what, in fact, we know they will.

It should be a negative version of the premise directly above.

Beautiful.

We'll continue now to back up through our protagonist's character arc identifying the most devastating change under each of the three main Conflicts. We'll picture for each one an event in this Conflict that would best illustrate the trauma that creates this change. Maybe this scene is already on paper. Maybe it's not. Maybe it's somewhere in our notes, maybe it's in our journal, maybe it's been set aside in our imagination, or maybe it's simply never *occurred* to us before now.

We'll write a one-line description of each of these three scenes (one for the climax of each Conflict) with utmost elegance below the other, spaced every few lines down the page below the Faux Resolution. Just a scene, an event, a moment in all eternity to illuminate the corresponding step in the character arc, a moment after which our protagonist will never be the same again.

"*She remembers the abyss appearing between her parents* — they were making hand-cranked ice cream." "*They're forced to collude against their will* — they reach a point on the glacier where they can't go forward and they can't go back." "*It becomes clear that they've made a terrible mistake* — she admits to him that the giraffe was a bad idea." "*He begins to fight back against himself, but in a funny way* — he develops an aversion to his own hair." "*She intuits that it's not going to work* — she breaks her own heart over the costume."

If we simply can't decide between more than one, we'll write both.

Again, we'll take a really long time over this. Days. Weeks. *Months.* Although it involves such minimal actual writing, this phase is a *huge* amount of the creation of a story. And it takes a profound inner connection to our guts, to our subconscious understanding of this protagonist and this particular change in their life — to this story. That kind of profound connection takes a long time to grow from seed and even longer to foster to full maturity.

Eventually, after we've worked our way backward through all three Conflicts, we'll arrive at the bottom of the page, and there we'll sit, staring at those final elements of the character arc that appear under the Hook on this long skewed curve across our character arc's pristine page.

These are the most fundamental aspects of our protagonist's personality. We may or may not find them familiar. Whatever they are, it is the combination of them that makes our story absolutely necessary to write. We'll find the one element in there under the Hook that causes the greatest curiosity in the reader. Ask ourselves whether or not this element is something new that's just now ready to surface from our subconscious. We'll allow to swim into in our mind some vision of some event that would be simply the most thrilling, most illuminating event with which to open such a heart-wrenching narrative.

"The avalanche first separates them. Or she races the train until she's hit. Or he runs down the street until he finds the unlocked door. Or the stranger bangs at the window."

We'll take several long, luxurious breaths to steady our hand.

And we'll write a brief description of this scene below all of the others.

Our best calligraphy.

We'll sit back then with a sigh and contemplate this page. Appreciate it. Luxuriate in it. Think about framing it and hanging it on the wall over our desk. Ask ourselves whether or not we'd need to re-paper the wall in order to bring it out to greatest effect.

We'll read this list through, bottom to top, in a gentle, sonorous voice, running one finger tenderly up the page past each element as we read, until our finger comes softly to rest at the very top. The end.

We'll lay our palm flat on the page when we're done. Feel how this series of events encapsulates the change in our protagonist's life.

These are the essential elements of our story's narrative arc.

Re-ignoring Theme through Tao

Remember when we talked about the Taoism of theme? And I neglected to say exactly what's so Tao about forgetting about it?

This, my friends, is *Tao*.

The mystics claim that the less we know about Tao the better we are at it, which means that, since all I know is this one little epiphany, I'm practically an *adept*.

It's an epiphany that will take us everywhere.

The first real novel I ever completed was about love. *Awww.* That one got me through eight years of higher education.

The next novel I completed was about death. *Ooooh!* That one got me through the last sorrowful years before my grandfather eventually faded away.

I was working on this second novel in the early 1990s at the same time that my closest writing friend was trying to break into Regency Romances, and she asked me one day to help her identify her 'themes' according to the rules of the Regency people. Her themes were, not surprisingly, mostly centered upon love.

"I try not think about theme too much," I told her. I'd explained about approaching Resolution mystically, like the Red King, as though it weren't there. "I explore what I want to explore. I've written one novel about love and another about death. The only thing left for me now is *taxes*."

Virtually everything we can discuss about writing fiction is craft: character, plot, structure and development, techniques and details and holistic understanding.

And yet the purpose of fiction, when all is said and done, is art: flinging the reader into an epiphany at the core of the universe of themself, a flash of insight that makes their own world and experience of life greater and more meaningful *because* it is their own.

Only the light that we shine on the iridescent underbelly of our story — in the final analysis — turns out to be the illumination of our themes.

Chapter 28

Reshuffling Your Deck

Revision

Now, if you're anything like me (and every serious writer I've *ever* known), at this point you're just about ready to settle for those two pages of arc for your entire story and go on with your life.

All that *work*. All that *time*.

We're not getting any younger.

However, if you're still anything like me (and every serious writer I've ever known in my *entire* life), at some point in the future you're going to pause in the middle of whatever you're doing and wonder, *But how would it have turned out?*

When nobody's looking, we'll be back in front of those two pages of arc with a pen in hand, and we'll be hearing voices coming toward us out of the distance, through the paper. The voices of our characters.

And we'll begin our revision.

Brainstorming

The first thing that we'll need to do is review exactly what our story is. We'll pull out our two beautiful pages of paper with the character arc and narrative arc all spelled out for us.

We'll read them through cold to see if we can raise goosebumps on our arms. If we can, good. We're ready. If we can't, we're in luck. We've got notes.

We'll go through our notes — all of those notes that we took in the revelation of the real character arc and narrative arc, as well as the notes that we took throughout the writing of the first draft — and explore exactly what we discovered when we wrote them. It's very possible that we didn't notice the core of our story when we were in the heat of writing about it. Even if we did, this is the time to make sure that we knew what we were talking about.

Then we'll do some number-crunching on our first draft — all of those scenes we've written, developing our stylistic voice — to determine how many words we tend to average per scene, and we'll make notes to ourselves beside every step of each element in our new narrative arc on whether we'll use one or two or three scenes for each step.

We'll make some comments to ourselves about what goes into those scenes and how they cause their own chronology, how they build on each other, each leading to the next step.

We'll develop a symbol to mark which scenes have already been written (and where in our manuscript they are right now).

Then we'll spend some time writing fresh notes on individual scenes or sequences of scenes.

Overall Organization

Now we'll set up the organization of our new draft. We'll take a bunch of paper or open a fresh, untouched document on our computer, and we'll sketch out this new organization that we've designed. Leave the notes we just assembled separate. They're not the new draft.

280

This is.

I like to break my new draft up into separate documents for separate chapters. Or else I break it up into the six basic elements of plot structure with a narrative arc of chapters within each element. Sometimes I even create a document for each scene in a chapter, all the documents in one folder.

No matter what, I never write a full draft of my manuscript in one document. I need to bring the document down to a manageable size. Otherwise, it gets too large and becomes a *total* nightmare to navigate. There's time to put everything into a single clean document in the very end, when it's in its final polished draft.

Once we have the documents, we can insert a line describing each element and each chapter, in order—even each scene, if we've got it. So we know what goes where.

Lots of blank, empty, innocent space in between the labels.

Scene-by-Scene Arc

Now we'll take our first draft and cut it up scene-by-scene, dropping each scene where it belongs in the fresh draft. This can take a really long time and become *really confusing*. So we'll keep the notes that we assembled handy as we move back and forth between our first draft and our fresh draft. Double-check a lot. If we scramble the organization at this point, we'll wind up writing a whole other story from the one we intend.

We'll keep a list at our elbow to keep us oriented toward the Pole Star of our Climax.

We'll flag scenes yet to be written in something that leaps out at us—like fire engine red.

Intuition

Now we get to the weird part.

We're going to take off our jacket or overshirt, roll up our sleeves, remove our shoes, and climb on our desk or table. Move breakables out of the way.

We'll very carefully climb into the first document.

Sit down in it.

Gaze around.

Get used to being there.

We'll move slowly and with great sensitivity on our hands and knees from the hook of this chapter or episode, through the development, to the faux resolution and climax, feeling as we go for irregularities.

We'll move back and forth. Search for holes in logic, cracks in character, inessentials. Eliminate scenes and feel the result. We'll move things around if we like. Use our antennae. We're building tension toward a faux resolution and, ultimately, life-altering climax.

When we can close our eyes and move through this document from hook to climax without looking, and it all makes beautiful, crazy sense, we'll pat ourselves on the back.

Then we'll climb out of that document, shake the kinks out, and move on to the next document.

We'll progress this way through all our documents. It will take a very long time, but when we reach the point of beautiful, crazy sense in each one it will be like bathing in warm, fragrant oil.

We'll use our most obscure muscles. Set our nerves alight.

We'll feel our heart when we've finished them all.

Does it feel good?

We're probably ready.

Fun

We're going to choose a scene somewhere in the early middle of our story and sit down to write. We can use fresh paper or a new document if we like. We can cut-&-paste this scene into place later. Whatever we do, we won't pressure ourselves.

This part is a bit like going into labor. Prodromal labor is misery and produces absolutely nothing, so don't go there. We'll relax, kick back, pat our stomach.

Breathe.

When we begin to visualize our characters in some particular scene (or anywhere — maybe we accidentally chose a different scene to start with), we'll go ahead and start recording them in words. Long, luxurious, way over-the-top detailed words. First the hook of the scene, aimed at the first conflict. Then the next, and the next. Maybe unexpected conflicts, maybe ones we've planned, but always moving toward the climax we've decided is *exactly right*. . .and after awhile the contractions will begin. (And they'll be a whole lot more fun and exciting than *real* contractions, I can guarantee.)

We'll sink in up to our eyeballs. Feel it through our whole body. Feel the shiver of excitement.

We're writing again!

Scene after scene after scene, we're back in the saddle. We thought we'd never get here again, and yet *here we are*.

Don't worry if it takes a few scenes to fully make the transition out of the planning part of the brain and into the writing part — this is why we're starting in the middle of our story instead of the beginning. We can come back and work this scene over later, after we're in the groove. We're saving the beginning scenes for when we've got the wind up and are moving like greased lightning again, that magnificent soaring feeling of being a *writer*.

Scene after scene after scene.

Writing.

Do this for a really. . .long. . .time.

Staying in Motion

Do it.

Resting When Necessary

Do this, too. We'll get up and go downstairs at the end of each day of work. Hug our shnookums. Sit on the back porch listening to the frogs in the sunset. Rub our bare feet in the dirt. Scrub our scalp.

Think about how lucky we are to be alive.

We'll wake up the next morning thinking about that next scene we're going to write that day.

Rewriting Out of Chronology

We can go ahead and leap around in the manuscript. If we get the urge to write for a long time, we can always blast through a whole series of scenes that have yet to be written. If we're feeling a bit skittish and unfocused, we can fill in the gaps between scenes that we've already written or migrated over from our first draft.

We'll try not to go back to the beginning and write a fresh Hook until we've gotten most of Conflict #1 and maybe Conflict #2 finished—even the Faux Resolution. Conflict #3 is second only to the Hook in importance, and the Hook is second only to the Climax.

We'll write our most powerful scenes when we feel really on *fire*. We want our skills to be at their most scintillating when we write those.

Taking Notes

And as we write, we always take lots of notes. We'll keep a notebook open by our side and pause to jot down significant bits at the ends of scenes. We'll pause in the middle of scenes if we think we'll forget by the end, but we'll do our best not to interrupt the flow. We're in the writing part of the brain.

Think of new scenes. New ideas! Our brains are frothing cauldrons of creativity! Write those new scenes.

Write.

A Word of Warning about Resolution

But whatever we do, *we won't write our Resolution.*

I don't care whether or not we wrote one for our first draft Sometimes we have to write one to get it out of our system. But after that. . .let it lie.

Focusing on our Resolution now will diffuse our energy and congest the flow of the narrative. We're not going to save these characters from their doom right now. We're going to abandon them to their fate, and we're going to make this the worst possible fate that we have in us.

We're going to make their nightmare so damn gorgeous that even *they* can't think about anything else.

Remember the Tao of theme.

Chapter 29

Spiraling Up the Helix

Multiple drafts

And will this draft be the final draft?

I mean, really—how many drafts could it *possibly* take?

This is the hollow, diabolical chorus of laughter from every serious writer who ever has come before us on this planet, living or dead. That burst of laughter's not fading away, either. It's getting louder and more cacophonic, a swelling orchestra of demented shouts and mocking hee-hawing and shrieks, until it degenerates into the deafening noise of Original Chaos, exactly how the universe sounded just before the Big Bang.

I'm sorry. I don't make them do this. They just launch into it every time someone asks that question.

The answer, of course, is: *far more drafts than we can ever imagine.*

But for your convenience and out of the sheer kindness of my heart, I'm going to narrow that number down to five. Five *complete* drafts.

First Draft

The first draft is for the writer. *Zippety doo-dah!* We're having *some* kind of a good time!

We can pants if it's absolutely necessary. I pantsed five novels before I got wise, and now I plot mine out ahead of time. But I still write that first draft just for me.

Some of the lines that come out of me as though by osmosis — *oh,* this is the reason I do this work.

Second Draft

The middle drafts are for the characters. They have a story. We may or may not know what that story is. But it's our job to find out and then tell it.

So we work our way through our protagonist's real character arc, and we use this to develop their real narrative arc. We design a new draft with all of the scenes that we're keeping and the scenes we're discarding and the scenes we have yet to write.

And we write this second draft, making a point of cleaning up our grammar and spelling and punctuation as we do so, because if we don't we're going to have one *heck* of a time reading it objectively later to determine whether or not it's beginning to sound plausible. Remember that our goal with each successive draft is to be progressing from amateur to professional. If we refuse to improve, we're just spinning our wheels.

We finish this second draft, by which time we're probably truly and heartily finished with the whole thing.

It must be done, *mustn't* it? It's just like when your baby first learns to communicate with gestures, before they learn to speak. That fundamental act of communication is the big hurdle, isn't it? Isn't the rest of it — all the learning to talk and study and take college exams and everything — kind of anti-climactic once they've gotten the gist of it?

We know that any small, trivial errors we might have left in this draft will be practically invisible in the glare of genius with which the rest is so thoroughly infused.

So we put it in a drawer to go cold. And we go away for awhile.

Third Draft

This is a baffling draft. This is where we pull that manuscript out of the drawer some months (or years) later and read it through.

It's not *almost done*. Good grief.

It's barely *started*.

I can't teach you how to keep this from happening, but I can promise that the longer we let it go cold, the less painful this moment is.

If we let it go cold for a really long time — six months, people, a year — we'll have forgotten by then how certain we were when we put it away in that drawer that it was simply the *living end*. We'll have developed other babies that we've been working on in the meantime. We'll be, frankly, rather taken aback by how good it is when we come across lines, paragraphs, whole scenes that we've forgotten we wrote.

We're writers! This is so thrilling to read! *In spite* of how little we knew about the craft way, way back in the Dark Ages when we wrote it.

Hey, there's some real gold in here. This might be salvageable!

So we do another round with character arc and narrative arc, looking specifically for holes in the logic and great, galumphing windows onto whole vistas that we were blind to before.

We heave a rather impatient sigh and Copy Edit it with a red pen, perhaps hoping to shame our writerly selves out of the habit of confusing 'your' and 'you're' and jumping tenses as though we're playing leapfrog.

We create a whole new batch of fresh, untouched documents into which we migrate the scenes that we want to keep (more than last time — *yippee*!) and outline the ones that we're chomping at the bit to write.

And again, we *write*.

Scene after scene after scene. Sinking into this fictional world that we left behind so long ago. Looking around at it with unexpected lucidity, with a sensitivity to telling detail and significant action and witty dialog that we never had for this story in its early incarnations.

And we fall in love all over again. We have those great scenes that we wrote without knowing we were writing them so well to spur us on. We're developing our skills — we're *writers*.

Then, with much greater equanimity than last time, we'll put it away again.

We have other babies calling out to us.

Nth Draft

This draft is like the open-walls phase of building a house, when we've got a house framed up and we've got a lot of electric wires and plumbing and insulation and unidentifiable stuff that we don't even know what it is. All we know is that all of that stuff has to go into our walls before we can seal them up permanently.

This draft takes for-freaking-*ever*.

And it breaks our heart while it does it.

This is the Draft of Despair.

The last time we took this manuscript out of cold storage, we were both shocked and pleased, expecting both much more and much less than what we found.

But this draft doesn't seem to have changed *at all*.

Why hasn't anything happened to it? Wasn't there some kind of alchemy that was supposed to alter its basic molecular structure while we weren't looking? Weren't there things that we were supposed to have forgotten, things we weren't supposed to have seen before?

Some of our improvements have worked, yes, but some of them must be restored to the way they were in the first place. Even then this story is completely predictable.

These characters are *weak*!

There's a lot of crying during the first part of this draft. This is the draft that drives even the most professional writers to drink.

Later we pull ourselves together (possibly out from under our beds) and do some reading up on craft in our favorite books on writing. We ask a writer friend to show us their working manuscript—"Not for critiquing. I'll just give you a general thumbs-up." So they do, and we do, and we don't tell them that they've given us a fresh lease on life when we see *nobody's* doing it the way we know in our heart of hearts it truly ought to be done.

We take a lot of notes based upon the reading we're doing, then we go into this draft and ruthlessly toss all the stuff we've been saving from draft to draft that we sort of knew shouldn't be there. We repair past improvements that didn't work.

We spend some time staring at the chaotic shambles of what was once upon a time so vivid and meaningful and true.

And then we go get an opinion from an independent editor.

Final Draft

The final draft is for the reader.

And I am sorry. I truly wish that I could tell you we can do this draft without professional help. But with the industry in the condition it's in, the increasingly-rigid guidelines for publication and growing dependence upon famous names, the mushrooming number of aspiring writers competing with us for those dwindling precious spots on agents' and publishers' calendars, the cramming of bookstore shelves as POD brings back into eternal print all of the lost treasures of literature and a whole industry blooms around trading on the well-known names of the dead, plus the intense flood of self-publishing, plus now the option of ebooks — it's either professional help or a *really, really long apprenticeship.*

Say, thirty years.

I strongly recommend taking advantage of the guidance of an independent editor.

When we finally do take it we're on our way, learning what we need to do with this story and how to do it in the way we've always dreamed. We're being encouraged and challenged, compassionately supported and unsentimentally prodded, treated like a professional writer by this editor we've chosen who works with other writers to make beautiful and true their unfinished or even failed manuscripts *all the time.*

We're writers.

Writers who love their stories.

So we learn to accept the specific elements of this particular story. (Originally we wanted it to have *everything,* but now we know that there are some things that will have to go in our next book, the one already popping and fizzing in the back of our brain.)

We're prepared to use the skills we're developing to offer our reader the very best version of this one story that we can produce, knowing that it's no longer about falling into a great story by luck or winning the rich-&-famous lottery or stumbling inadvertently upon a genius talent that we always suspected in our soul but never had proof of before.

There's simply someone we will never meet out there in the world who doesn't know how to do this work and yet desperately needs help understanding their life. This one life they get. And we *do* know how to do this work. We've spent a long, dedicated time apprenticing ourselves to it, and now we're being mentored on a professional level.

This particular story can help that person. We can give that anonymous sufferer what they need — hope, validation, some greater awareness of the world, of paradoxical meaning — to make their life feel *real*.

And it turns out that nothing else matters, after all.

Chapter 30

Going Beyond the Beyond

The far side of Hell

I don't like horror movies — even squashed bugs freak me out — but I *love* the movie *Flatliners*. I love that concept of what's beyond the beyond.

You know how it is whenever we start a story, how we're flames alight, burning up everything around us, the very atoms of the air fuel for our creation? Our characters walk among mortals like creatures from a visionary universe. They live and breathe, crack wise, laugh, put a tender hands on our arm. They learn bad news, and our eyes fill. When their hearts break, we're sobbing as we type. Just sitting around the kitchen table with them all morning talking gossip as the sun crosses the window is as fulfilling as human contact can ever be. Everything that we never get from real life is here, in these manuscript pages, waiting for us to wake up every day and join them again.

Fiction is our way of creating tribe for ourselves.

Then we've gotten it all down, and we're transforming it from our own personal tribe into, well, literature.

The first part is about our needs. The rest is about everyone else's. Now we're creating a plot, an adventure for these characters, and we're using what we know about them to tell how they would act in any given situation, to show how they get themselves from one pickle into another, what facility they have for disaster.

We don't want to do dreadful things to them. But there is that reader out there. And the reader wants our characters to help them understand the turmoil of real life. So we do this part, too.

Then we go into revision. Because we've had to combine these agendas—ours, our characters', and the reader's—and naturally there are some glitches.

This takes innumerable passes. At first we're drunk on the reality. Then we're drunk on the power of fiction to *speak*. Then we're drunk on the sheer potential for transforming this world that has meant so much to us into something that could mean so much to a complete stranger, simply through the artifice of language and fictional tools.

It happens. It really does! We've all read books of a beauty to take the breath away.

And we too can be among those who walk with our feet among the stars.

Finally we wake up one morning and go to our desk and pick up the pages. . .and something snaps inside. We realize that we're never going to get those words to transform.

Never.

Our reach has exceeded our grasp.

By about *five light-years*.

So here we sit with our faces lying sideways on the desk, feeling the tears trickle ever-so-slowly down to the bridge of our nose, across it, and drop with the most delicate little irritating mosquito-touch from our nose to the desk under our cheek. Our neck hurts, but it doesn't matter.

Nothing will ever matter again.

This is the point, in *Flatliners,* at which we have medically anesthetized ourselves to the point of death and just beyond, and we discover — much to our surprise — that the beyond is Hell.

And yet it seemed like such a good idea at the time!

Now, I am not here to act as our medical-student cohorts pulling us back from the anesthesia. I am not our pals reeling us in, waking us from the nightmare, patting everyone jovially on the back, and helping us off the table.

"You're not really dead. That didn't really happen. *Psyche!*"

Those are not the words coming out of my mouth.

Because I know something about this. I know that when someone does this, *Hell follows us home.*

And then we are well and truly haunted. The glaring errors remain and get worse. The stumbling blocks trip us up more and more, throwing us headfirst into the muck and mire faster and more heartlessly every time we attempt that impossible task of transformation. Peer critiques, if we get them, become more random and less predictable.

No one can agree on what's going wrong!

We might stick with it because the hype about Becoming a Writer is so powerful and omnipresent out there, and besides now all our friends are Becoming Writers too. Or because we're stubborn cusses and don't know when we're beat. Or because we have a story that we desperately want to tell. Or simply because we've always looked up to our favorite authors, all our life, and dreamed with our heart in our throat of the day we would join their ranks.

But the secret pain is crippling. And it is countered only by the numbness of turning ourselves into donkeys plodding in joyless drudgery after that coveted carrot.

No.

I am here to do the opposite: to push us through — because on the other side of Hell is *craft*.

And we can't get there by backing out. We must dive forward into the agony — sitting there with our face lying sideways on the desk — and discover within it every reason that writing is an *inanely* bad idea.

Tackle a task we only know vaguely through the second-hand results of someone else's lifelong efforts?

Tackle it with the wild-eyed hope that, although it takes professional writers their entire lives to polish their skills, years to produce a single novel, and the nearly-unlimited assistance of publishing professionals they pretty much lucked into, it will take us a matter of months because, after all, didn't Faulkner write *As I Lay Dying* in six weeks?

Tackle it with the idea of supporting ourselves, even though the greats almost universally died penniless and unknown?

Tackle it with minimal training and experience, barely a smidgen of comprehension, a whole lot of optimism, and the encouragement of people who stand to gain financially by our ambitions?

Tackle it with nothing but our bare hands?

We will lie there and sob. Gnash our teeth. This is how we learn to be us.

And when we are done, we will know something about life that we didn't know before: we will know how to survive. We will have gone *beyond* the beyond into the ephemeral, multi-faceted, tactile alternate reality of endless potential we knew was there — we wanted so badly to believe in — all along.

And then we'll have something to write about.

Riding Out the Winter of Our Discontent

The writing life

Oh, what a summer it's been — nearly endless overcast and rain last spring until almost the Summer Solstice, and then suddenly one weekend of hot, baking, Augustine days. My son reported cheerfully that it was 90 degrees in the shade. I sat under my holey old umbrella in the weedy meadow and fanned myself with a paperback like Blanche duBois (dependent, in this case, upon the kindness of the brilliant mystery writer Ngaio Marsh).

This is the writing life.

We get into it for the glory of the page. It's exactly like the day summer arrives — there's something tangible in the air, something that makes us sit up and smell the wind, turn to the horizon and say to ourselves, "I'd forgotten. The reason I'm alive."

People come to us in our daydreams, and they want to tell us what's happened to them, where they've been, what they saw there, whom they met, what they said to each other.

They're intensely striking personalities. We take one look at them, and we're already a little in love. So we're willing to listen. We're even, as Anne Lamott says, willing to transcribe it all.

We're so enthralled that we can't imagine this story ever ending.

At the same time, the world is chock full to the eyeballs these days with the push to publish. We'd have to be more than oblivious not to have noticed — we'd have to be *dead*. So as soon as we meet these characters and agree to be their scribe, we feel the heavy gravitational pull of publication dragging at our neck.

The rains are back. They beat and beat and beat at our windows, streaming down the glass and obscuring our vision. They make mud of our yard so that every time we leave the house we worry about slipping and breaking our neck. They flatten the blossoms that were beginning to appear, tear them off the bushes and turn them to mush, bring up the weeds before we can get outside to pull them, rot our back steps, fill our gutters with wet leaves until water overflows deathly cold on our head and — if we're really out of luck — defaces our ceilings with ominous, creeping brown stains.

We struggle and struggle to fight off the unseasonable rains, but they're washing us away.

Then one day we wake up, and the power's out, so we can't go online to check our email or Twitter or read blog posts on writing or dither around lending credibility as a writer to and accepting it from people we don't know, puffing each other's egos with talk of wordcounts and writerly preoccupations, with self-marketing and PR and query letters, patting each other on the back for being writers.

We're stranded! There's nothing for us to do now. . .except write.

We gird our loins. We haul a dusty old typewriter out of the back of the closet and brush it off or, if we don't have one, pick up a pen. We don't keep notebooks in the house anymore, but we do have paper bags.

We look at the pen in one hand and the paper bag in the other.

This is *ridiculous.*

But we're writers. So we sit down at the kitchen table. We take a deep breath. And we begin to write.

To write and write and write. . .

And when we look up hours later, we're sitting in a hot, glorious, weedy meadow under a holey old umbrella. Children are shouting with laughter and spraying the hose in the distance. Bees hang from the edges of vivid orange poppies near our knees, and a silky, half-grown black cat steps fastidiously through the grass in our direction. The smell of earth rises between our feet, the smell of dry-rot rises from the huge stump in which our umbrella stands, the smell of grass seed ripening rises into the white, white sun.

Ngaio Marsh's brilliant Chief Detective-Inspector Alleyn leans over and explains drily, in the most charming patter possible, exactly what hangs in the balance — and then asks inexplicably if we like party metaphors.

The world is brilliant with detail and charisma and utterly mysterious significance.

We're alive!

Alive.

This is how it feels to *be alive.*

Index

Index

Index

Index

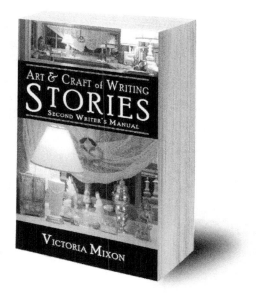

Please take a quick moment to review!

victoriamixon.com/stories

THANK YOU!

Mendocino, California

Art & Craft of Writing

Sign up to get your
free books on writing!

artandcraftofwriting.com/freebooks

"Buy it. I recommend it."
— Preditors & Editors

artandcraftofwriting.com

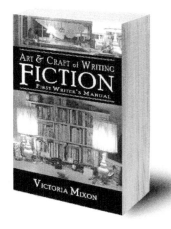

About the Author

Mixon has been a professional writer and editor for over thirty years. She is the author of the Art & Craft of Writing series, including *Art & Craft of Writing Fiction: 1st Writer's Manual* and *Art & Craft of Writing Stories: 2nd Writer's Manual*. She is listed in the Who's Who of America and has been covered for her expertise in fiction by the *Huffington Post*. She teaches fiction through *Writer's Digest* and the San Francisco Writers Conference. Mixon is currently writing a forthcoming *noir* mystery series.

victoriamixon.com

@VictoriaMixon